AF594478

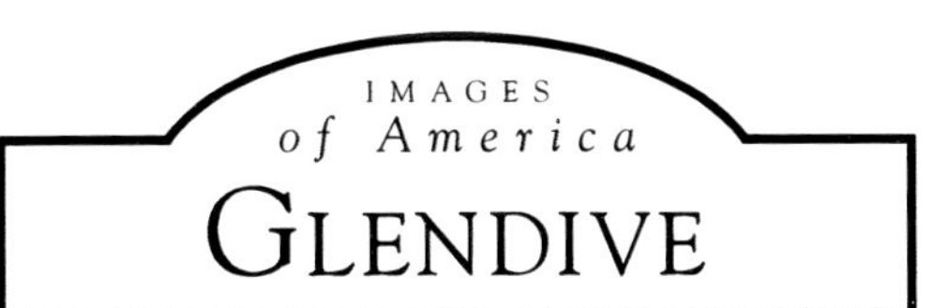
IMAGES
of America
GLENDIVE

ON THE COVER: The Northern Pacific Railroad Roundhouse in Glendive, Montana Territory, is pictured here with a steam locomotive in 1886. The Northern Pacific roundhouse at Glendive was completed in 1883. The original structure housed 11 stalls, and 11 more were added in 1890 to accommodate increased rail traffic through eastern Montana. (Haynes Foundation Photo Collection.)

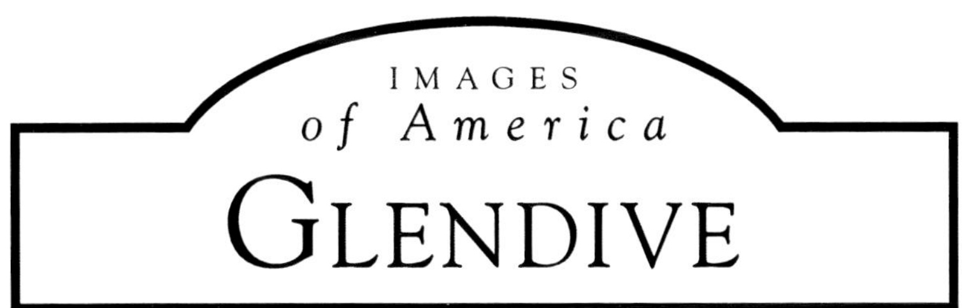

Dr. R. Michael Booker Jr.

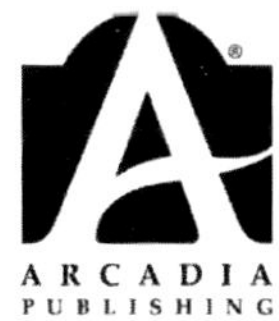

ISBN 978-1-4671-1519-3

Published by Arcadia Publishing
Charleston, South Carolina

Printed in the United States of America

Library of Congress Control Number: 2015954264

For all general information, please contact Arcadia Publishing:
Telephone 843-853-2070
Fax 843-853-0044
E-mail sales@arcadiapublishing.com
For customer service and orders:
Toll-Free 1-888-313-2665

Visit us on the Internet at www.arcadiapublishing.com

This book is dedicated to my wife, Jennifer, and my parents, Lt. Col. Mike and Renee Booker. I am forever in your debt for making my professional dreams come true.

Contents

Acknowledgments

So many individuals have helped with this project in so many ways that some must necessarily go unnamed, though they do not go unappreciated. My wife, Jennifer, has been a constant source of encouragement, confidence, love, and support. My son, Michael Booker III (Trey), has inspired me to work to make him proud and by his very existence reminds me of what is most important in life. My patrons and parents, Lt. Col. R. Michael and Renee Booker, have emotionally, morally, financially, and spiritually sustained me. For these things, I am forever grateful.

I owe an immense debt of gratitude to the staff at the Frontier Gateway Museum who generously shared their expertise and were gracious with their time and resources. Specifically, I would like to thank curator Fayette Miller and Trena Kuehn, who answered my questions with great patience and allowed me unfettered access to the museum's research library, archives, and photograph collections. Unless otherwise noted, all images appearing in the book were provided by the Frontier Gateway Museum.

I would also like to thank librarian Todd Knispel of the Jane Carey Memorial Library at Dawson Community College for his help in the process of writing this book.

Gratitude is also due to the cattle ranchers of Dawson County who offered pictures and valuable knowledge about the area. Their love for the land and western American culture is contagious and has surely helped me to produce a stronger book.

Finally, I want to thank my editor at Arcadia Publishing, Stacia Bannerman, for her patience and for keeping my nose firmly pressed to the grindstone.

Introduction

Glendive was established in 1881, when the Northern Pacific Railroad reached the Yellowstone River at Glendive Creek. Though the town was officially founded in 1881, the history of the area goes back much deeper.

Glendive is bordered on the southeast by the contiguous Makoshika Badlands, where fossilized remains of dinosaurs and prehistoric plants and sea life can be found in abundance. In 1896, J.R. Widmeyer poignantly described the area as a "natural amphitheater, surrounded on almost every side by picturesquely rugged hills."

Prior to the arrival of Europeans and Americans, the Lower Yellowstone River Valley served as a hunting ground for Crows, Lakotas, Blackfeet, Gros Ventres, and Assinniboines who hunted massive herds of bison, elk, deer, and antelope. American explorer William Clark camped on Indian land near Glendive in 1806 as the Corps of Discovery returned east from the Pacific. Americans began their conquest of tribal lands in eastern Montana following the discovery of gold in 1862 at Bannack in the southwestern portion of Montana Territory. It was during this period that an Army supply cantonment was located at Glendive, which would periodically be home to US military forces until the suppression of the local natives. Continued pressure on the tribal groups who lived along the major arteries to the Montana Territory goldfields prompted tribes like the Lakota and Northern Cheyenne to mount a sustained war on American interests in the region.

Following the defeat of George Armstrong Custer's 7th Cavalry Division at the Battle of Little Bighorn, the United States waged a ruthless campaign against natives on the eastern plains of Montana. The 22nd Infantry was stationed at Camp Canby on Glendive Creek during the Great Sioux War (1876–1877) under the command of Gen. Thomas Rosser. The infantry's primary responsibility was to escort wagon trains between the Glendive and Tongue River cantonments. It was also during this period that the great slaughter of bison by the Americans commenced. Glendive was a major player in the "Great Slaughter" because of its proximity to the remaining herds of bison on the northern plains. Glendive resident Henry Douglas shipped 250,000 bison robes to tanneries in the East in 1882 alone. The Great Sioux War, combined with the slaughter of the buffalo, forced the remaining Lakota and others living on unceded land in the eastern Montana Territory to acquiesce to the reservation system. This opened the door to the American concept of growth and progress. It was in this atmosphere of conflict and change that the town of Glendive was born.

Glendive's history is intimately connected with the railroad. Marion Place stated that Glendive was born "astraddle the tracks." When the first Northern Pacific steam locomotive roared into Glendive on July 5, 1881, it was a male-dominated town overwhelmingly comprised of saloons, dance halls, and brothels. By the end of the 19th century, the train had brought the civilizing influence of the East.

Northern Pacific stakeholders believed that in order to enhance their profitability in the northern plains, ranches and farms must be located along the route. Extravagant, colorful posters were printed for display east of the Mississippi and as far away as Europe to entice people to start anew in Montana Territory or the Dakotas. Immigrants from the eastern United States, Scandinavia, Germany, Russia, Ukraine, Ireland, England, Scotland, China, Japan, and beyond heeded the call of the Northern Pacific. However, it was the passage of the Enlarged Homestead Act by Congress in 1909 that prompted heavy migration into the region.

Glendive is nicknamed the "Gate City" because it is the first major town travelers encounter when they enter Montana from the east. Would-be railroad workers, dry farmers, ranchers, and the entrepreneurs that supported them were lured to the region in the early decades of the 20th century because of the boundless opportunities the land, river, and railroad offered. Glendive experienced its golden age from roughly 1890 to 1945. This was a time of immense growth and prosperity in the small frontier town. Because it was a major stop on the Northern Pacific passenger line, the downtown area of Glendive was usually buzzing with activity. Retail businesses, entertainments venues, saloons, and restaurants dotted the urban landscape. Stately civic buildings, like the old Dawson County Courthouse, filled Glendivians with a since of pride and accomplishment.

Following World War II, many of Glendive's unique buildings were demolished in the name of improvement and modernization. Although some of Glendive's historical treasures remain, most of the noteworthy buildings have either been destroyed or left derelict. The railroad remained a force in Glendive during the postwar era, but its influence was nowhere near what it had been during the first half of the 20th century. Ranching and farming continue to be a mainstay of Glendive economic and cultural life at the dawn of the 21st century and look to remain so well into the future. An additional industry gave renewed life to the area. Glendive is located on the southern periphery of the Bakken Shale Formation, the largest continuous crude oil accumulation in the United States. The Bakken Formation was discovered in 1953. Since that time, Glendive has several experienced "boom" and "bust" cycles related to extraction activity in the Bakken.

Today, Glendive continues to serve as a supply hub for ranchers, farmers, railroaders, and oil workers in the Bakken. It is also the home to boundless recreational and educational activities. The region's majestic badlands lure thousands of campers, hikers, disc golfers, hunters, paleontologists, and sightseers each year. Makoshika State Park and the Frontier Gateway Museum are both stops on the Montana Dinosaur Trail, and hunters from all over the world are still drawn to the remote region for its abundance of game. Glendive is known as the "paddlefish capital of the world," and as many as 3,000 fishermen descend on the region for the annual spring paddlefish harvest. Regardless of the season, visitors to Glendive will find a charming small Montana town, surrounded by spectacular scenery and populated by friendly locals.

One

The Arrival of the Northern Pacific and the Making of a Boomtown

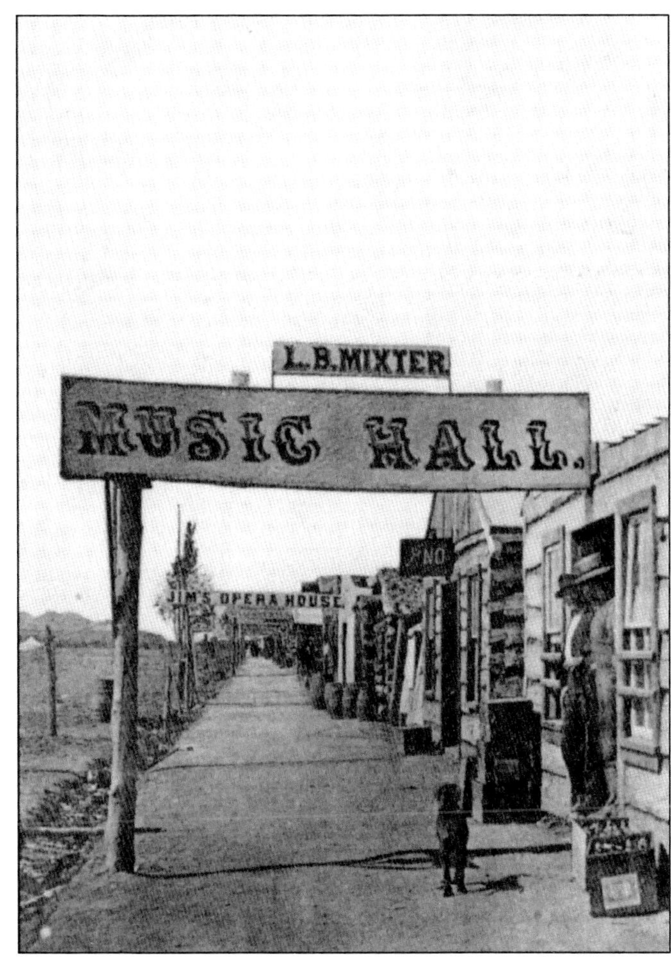

This is one of the earliest known photographs of Glendive. It features Glendive's main street at the time of the arrival of the Northern Pacific Railroad in 1881. Of the businesses here, 21 were saloons.

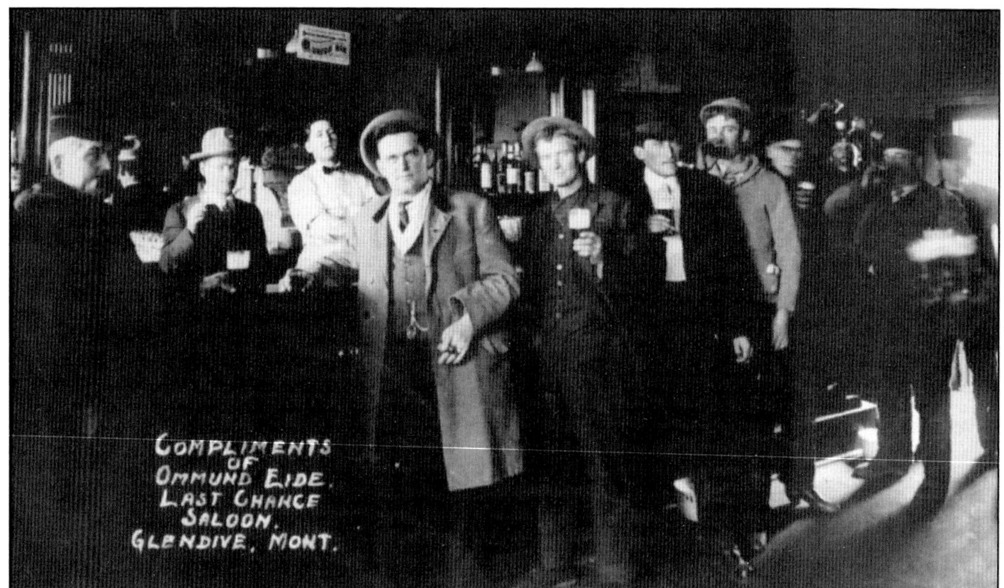

Drinking has long been a popular pastime in Glendive. This photograph offers a rare glimpse inside one of Glendive's early drinking establishments, Ommund Eide's Last Chance Saloon. Male patrons can be seen drinking stout and smoking cigars. Spittoons are situated at the base of the bar.

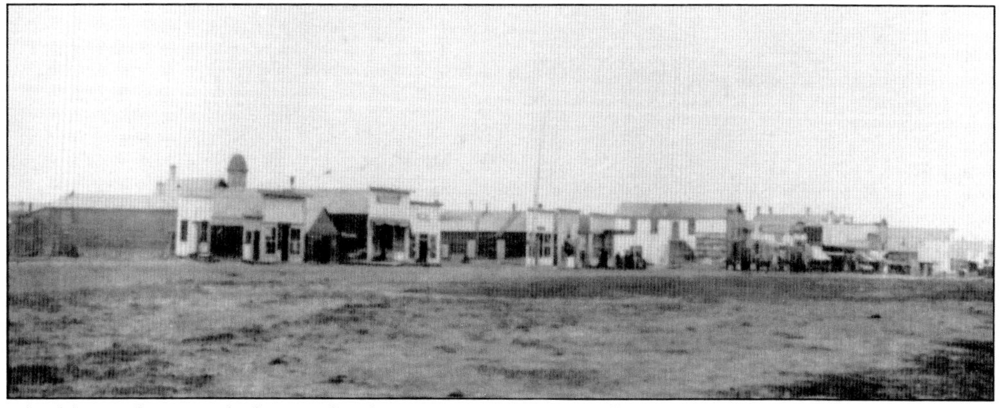

This blurry photograph shows Glendive's main street, Merrill Avenue, in 1883. Many of the earlier ramshackle buildings that were a hallmark of the settlement during the first years of the 1880s quickly gave way to more solidly built permanent structures by 1883. (Langdon Bell Collection.)

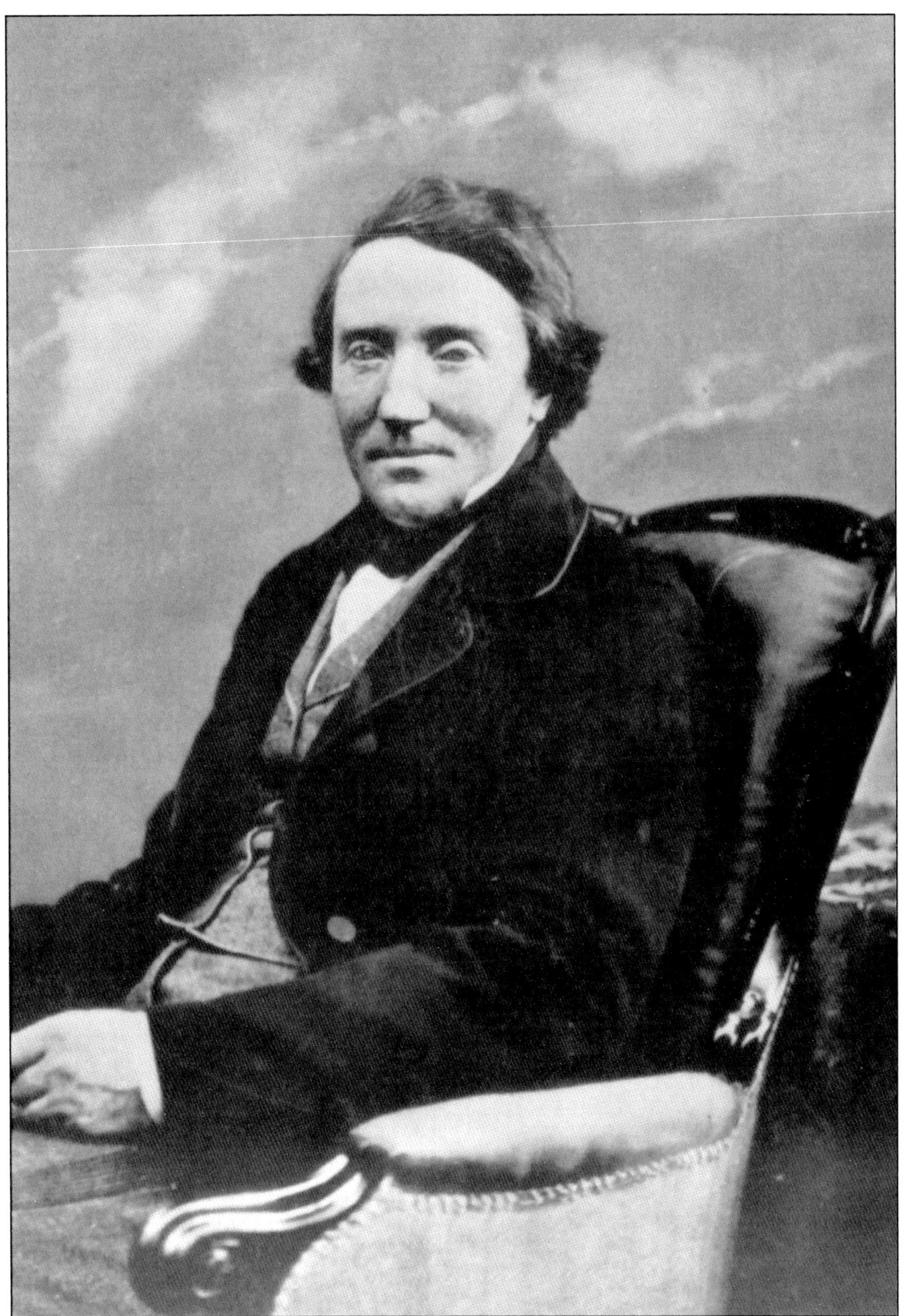

Glendive is the county seat of Dawson County, Montana. The namesake of the county is Maj. Andrew Dawson, manager of the Fort Benton Trading Post for the American Fur Company from 1856 to 1864. (Montana Historical Society.)

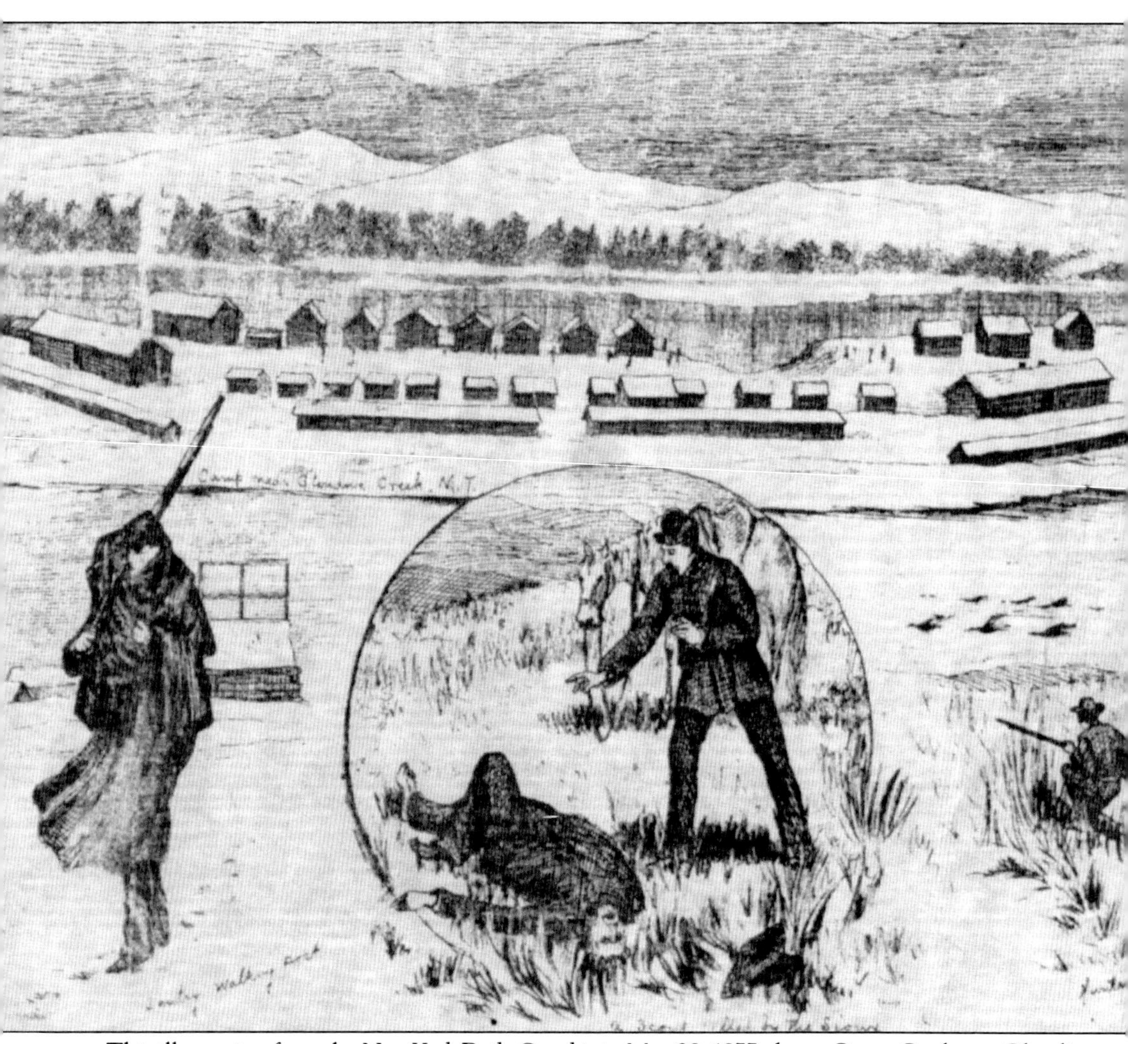

This illustration from the *New York Daily Graphic* in May 28, 1877, shows Camp Canby on Glendive Creek covered in snow in the winter of 1877. It also shows a man discovering a US scout killed by Lakota warriors. The Battalion of the 22nd Infantry was tasked with protecting Northern Pacific workers and travelers against Lakota Sioux and Northern Cheyenne forces in eastern Montana during the Great Sioux War.

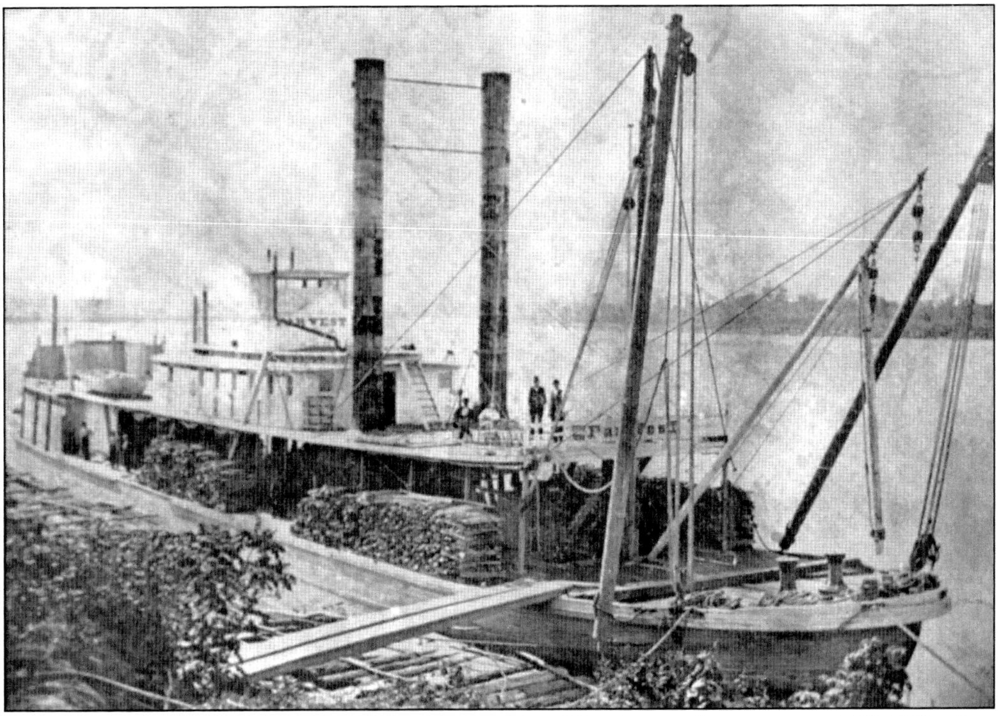

The steamship *Far West* is pictured here, anchored at Glendive in the summer of 1876. The ship was loaded with wounded soldiers from the US Army's 7th Cavalry on the way to the hospital at Fort Lincoln, located south of Bismarck in Dakota Territory, after the Battle of Little Bighorn. On June 25 and 26, 1876, a total of 263 soldiers, including Lt. Col. George Armstrong Custer, died fighting several thousand Lakota and Northern Cheyenne warriors.

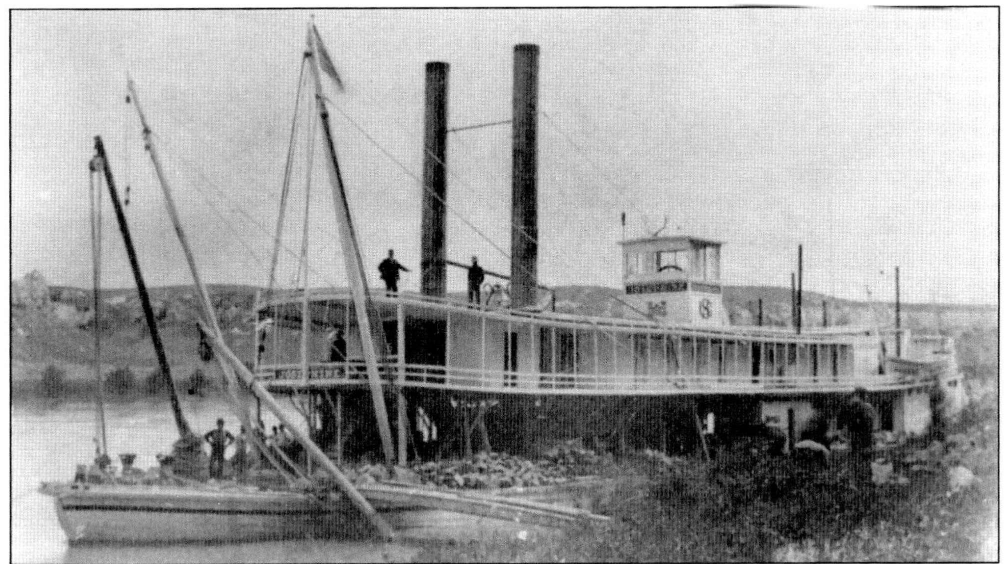

The steamship *Josephine* is pictured anchored in Glendive in the 1880s. The *Josephine* was a wood-hulled ship that was 183 feet long, 31 feet wide, and four feet deep. It was an asset during the Great Sioux War because it was one of only three steamships in the area that could navigate the fast portion of the Yellowstone River near Pompey's Pillar.

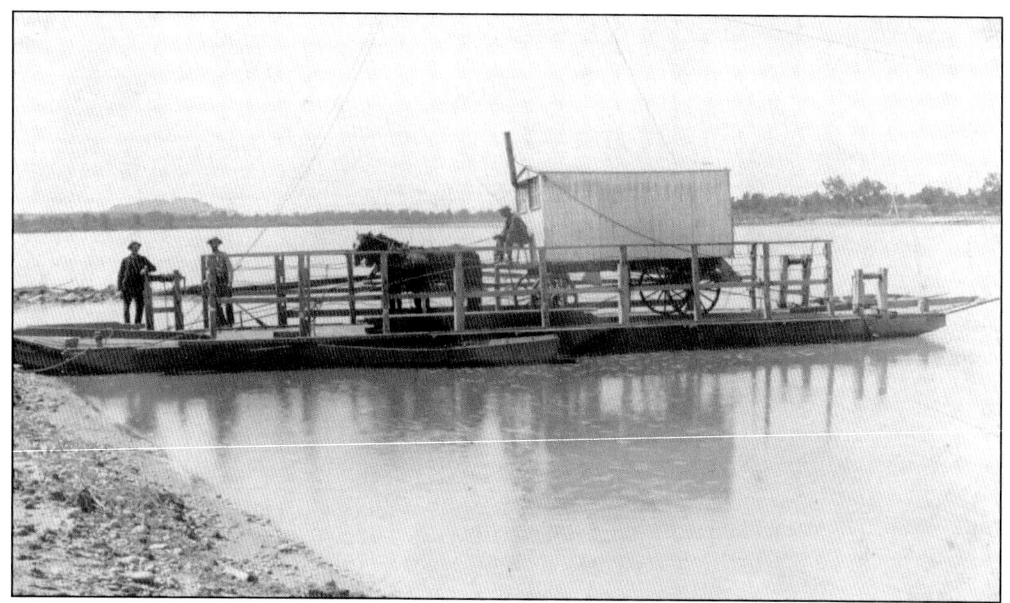

Prior to the construction of the first Yellowstone River Bridge, the only way to get across the river was by ferry. Frank Kinney was one of the earliest entrepreneurs to run a ferry service in Glendive. This photograph shows Frank Kinney's Ferry Service transporting Janis Sawyer's camp wagon across the Yellowstone River in 1882.

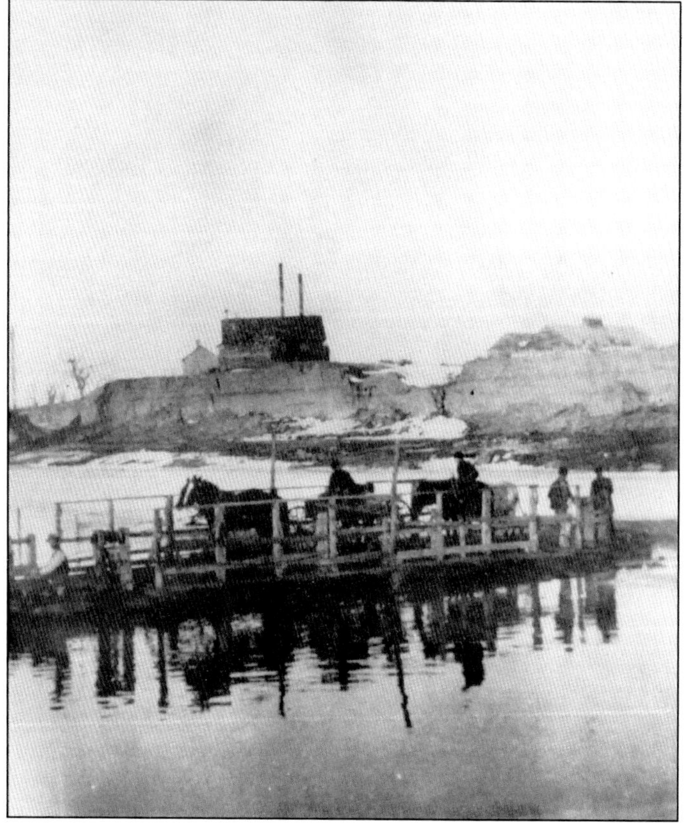

This photograph shows a horse-drawn wagon and three additional horses being transported across the Yellowstone River at Glendive in 1889. Less than a decade after its founding, Glendive was already showing signs of rapid modernization, evident in this photograph where Hughes Electric Power Plant sits above the ferry on the riverbank.

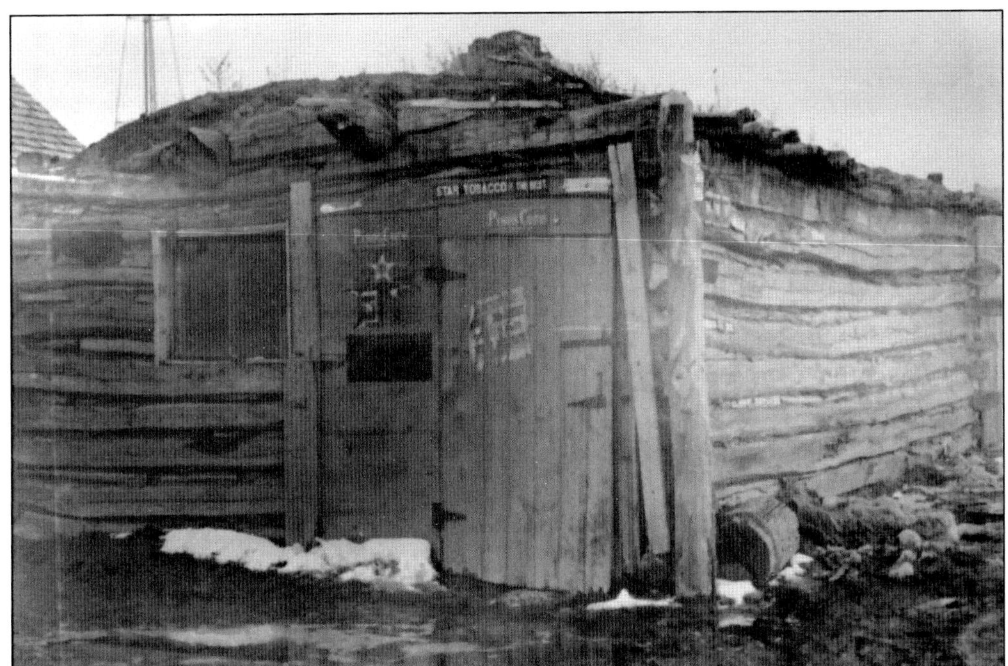

This early photograph shows Morris Cain's blacksmith shop in 1882. Cain's business was located at the intersection of Bell Street and Meade Avenue. Cain arrived in the Glendive area of Montana Territory in 1880 and opened the town's first blacksmith shop in 1881. (R.H. Foss Collection.)

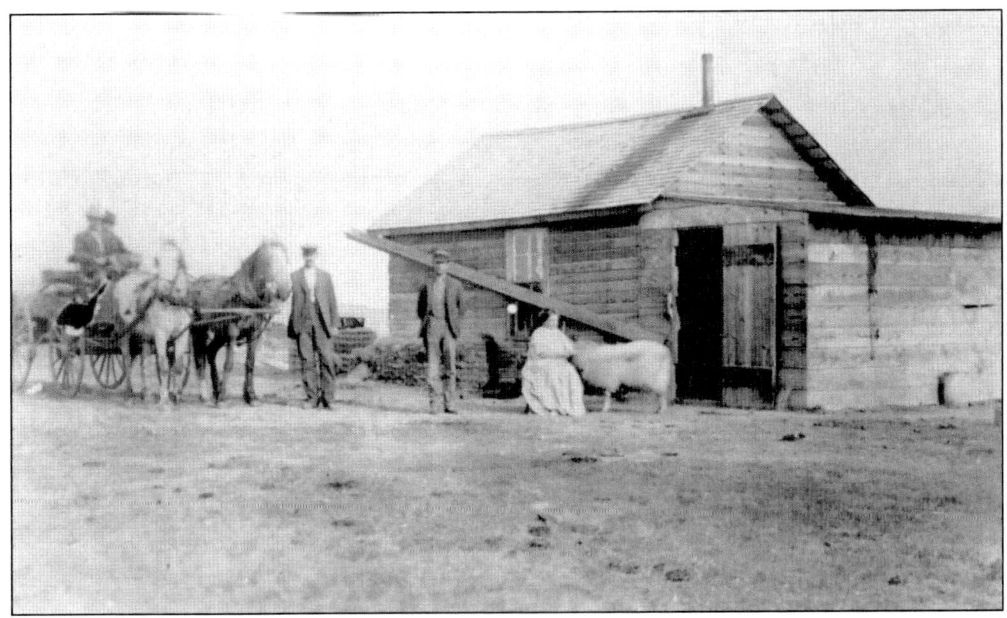

With the influx of people into the Glendive area in the early 1800s, regular and reliable postal service was essential. This simple wooden structure was the first US post office in Glendive, established during the early 1880s. (Skillestad Ranch Photo Collection.)

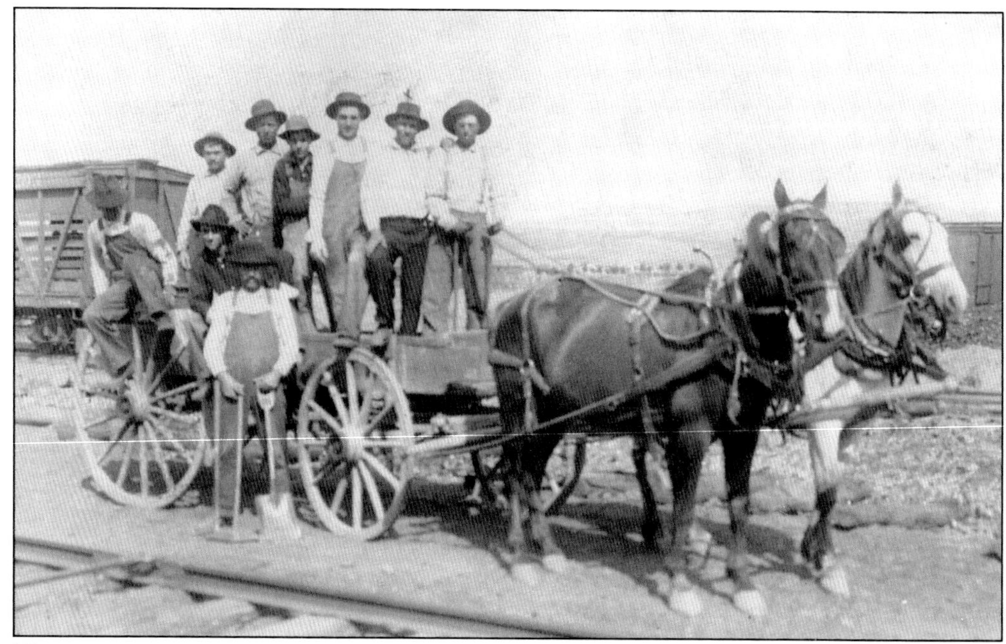

The primary reason entrepreneurs and job seekers came to the remote settlement of Glendive in the 1880s was the arrival of the Northern Pacific Railroad—and the opportunities that followed. The first Northern Pacific train arrived in Glendive in 1881. A Glendive-based Northern Pacific work crew pauses for a snapshot.

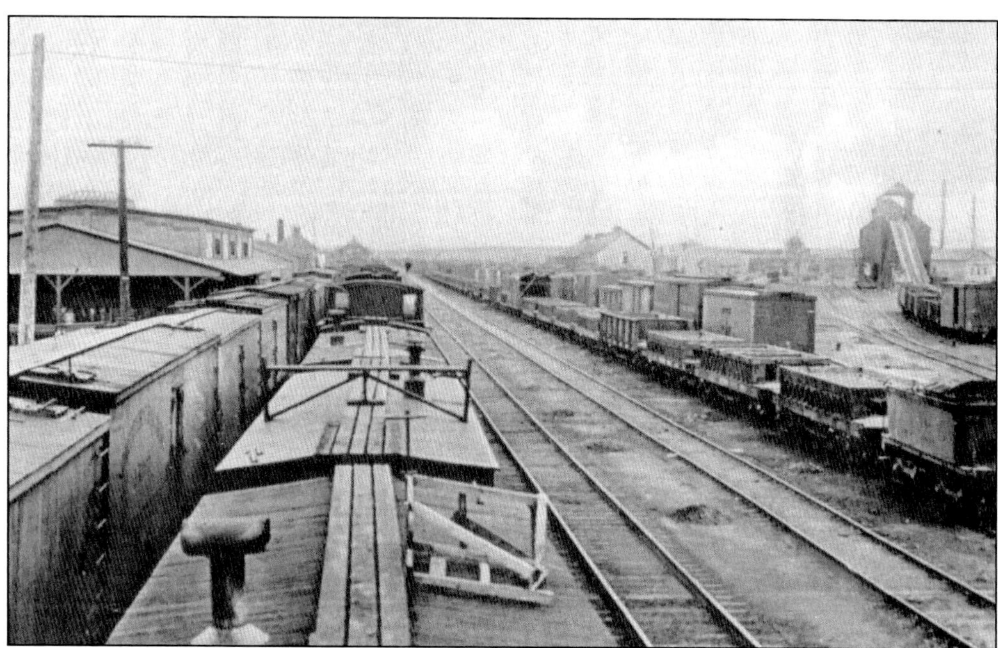

It did not take long for Glendive to become a bustling hub of railroad activity, as this photograph of the Northern Pacific rail yards at Glendive suggests.

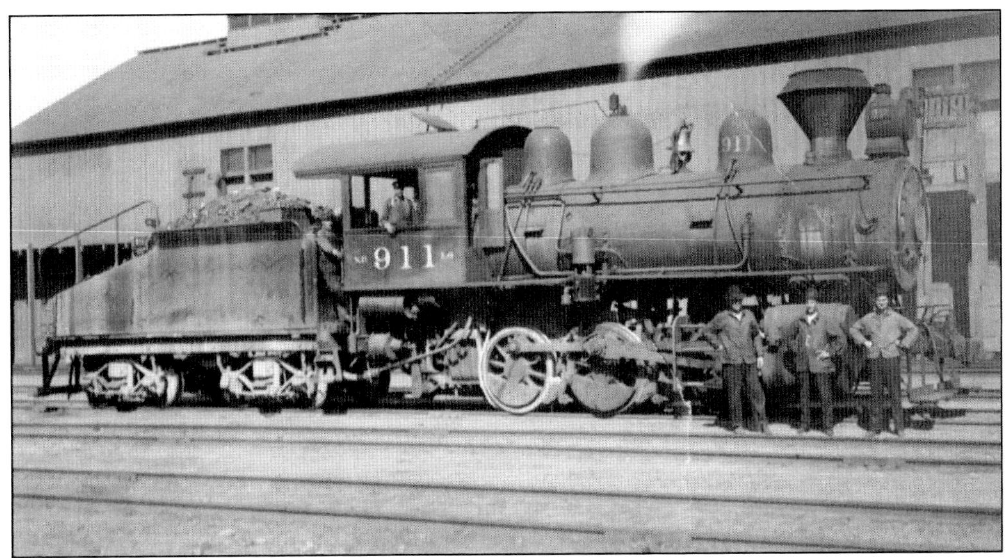

Pictured here are Northern Pacific employees with Engine 911 L-6 in Glendive around 1900. (Roy F. & Blanche Mildred Bruce Estate.)

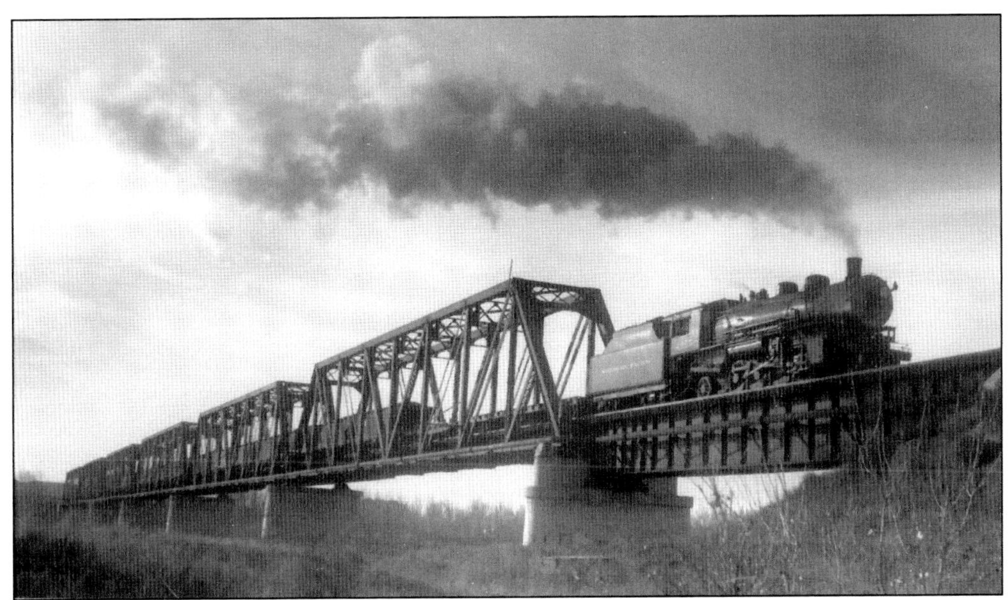

This photograph shows a Northern Pacific locomotive crossing the Missouri River Valley Railroad Bridge (today nicknamed the "Black Bridge") over the Yellowstone River in Glendive.

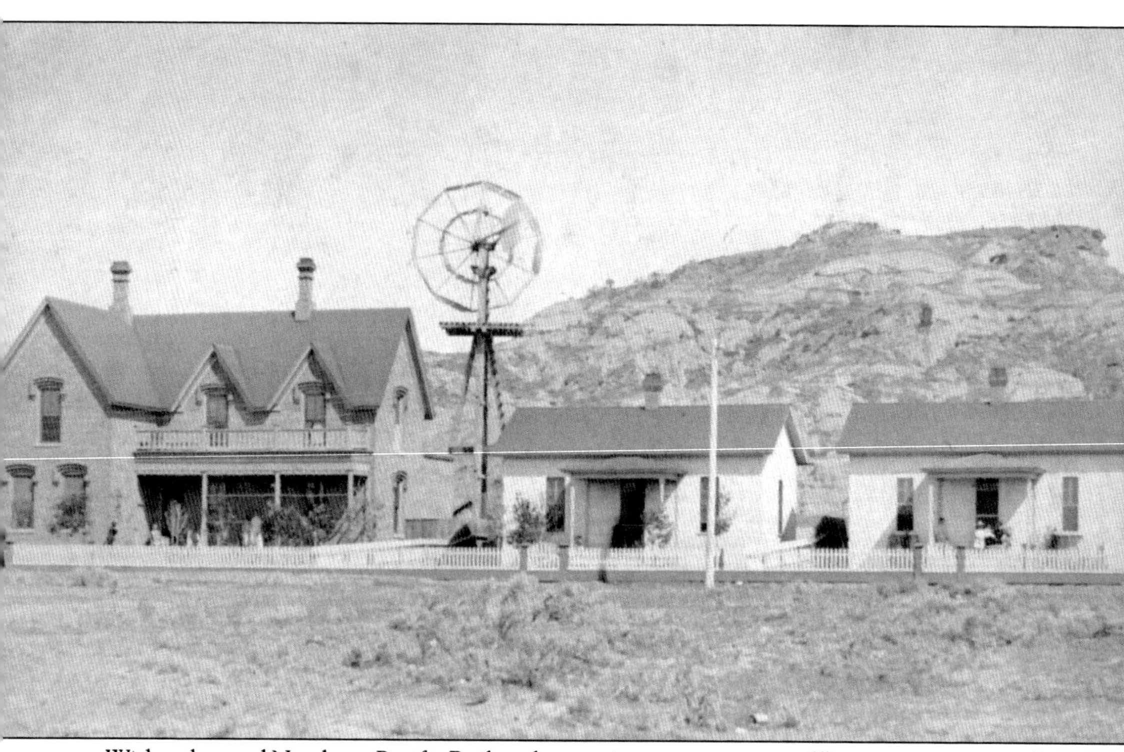

With enhanced Northern Pacific Railroad operations came a more affluent management class of worker to Glendive. Built in 1884, the Northern Pacific Railroad superintendent's home at 303 South Nowlan Avenue was an elegant home by Glendive standards.

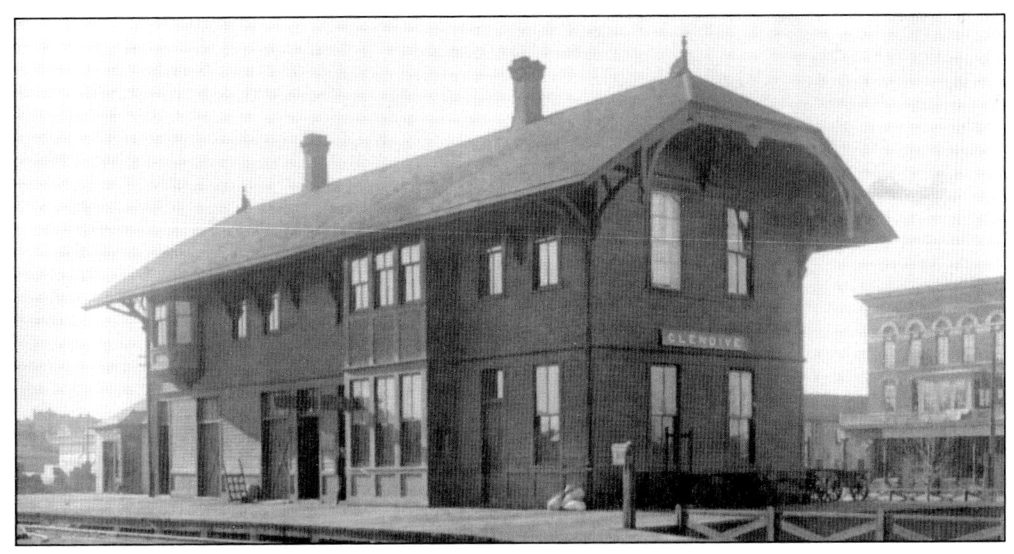

For around the first 40 years of Glendive's existence, the first building most travelers saw when they arrived in town was the wooden Northern Pacific Passenger Depot. The wooden depot was gutted by fire and replaced by a new brick structure in 1922.

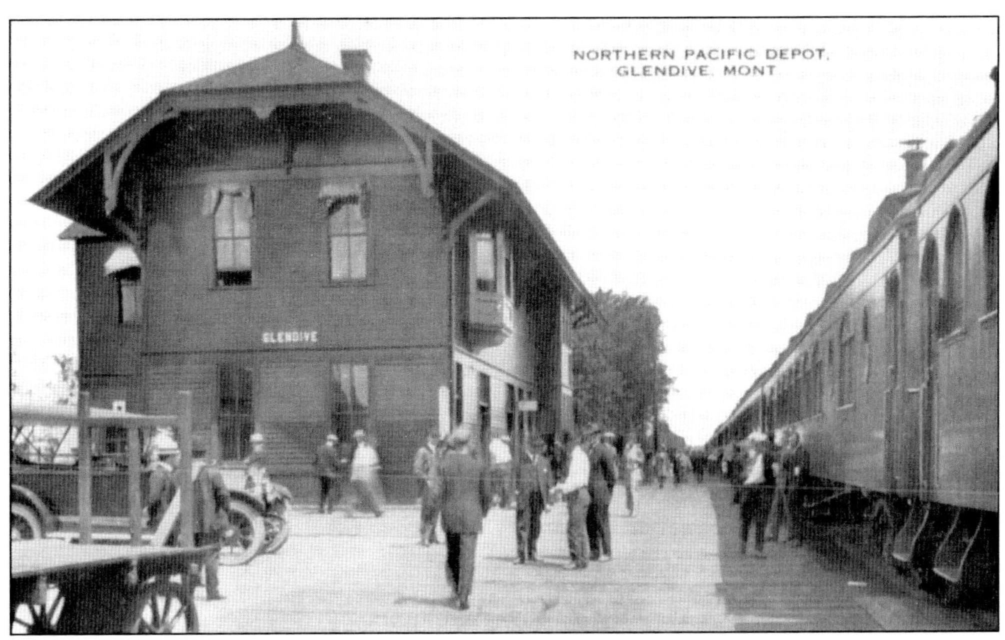

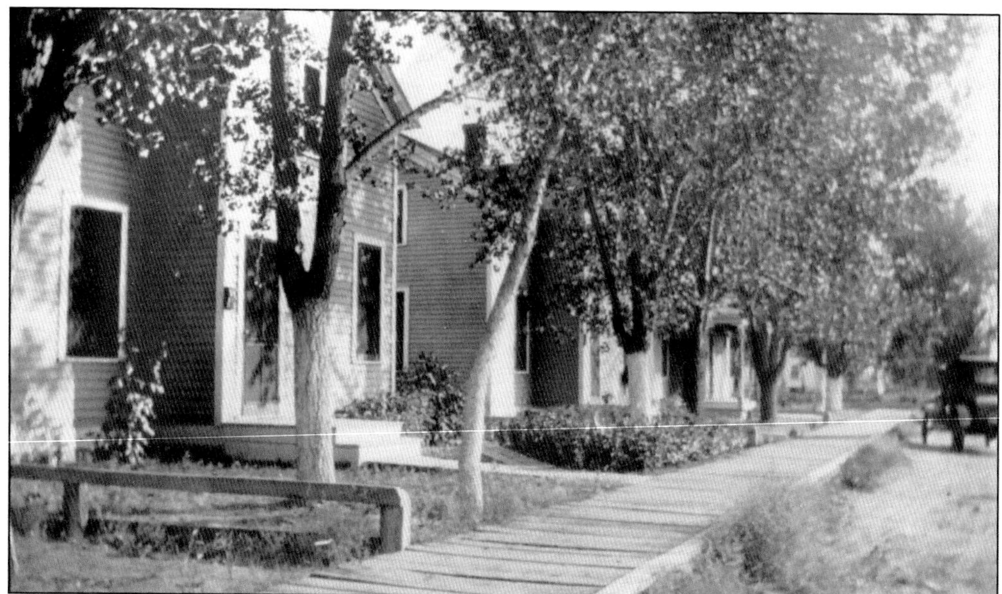

In the late 19th century, the Northern Pacific Railroad financed the construction of company housing for its workers in Glendive's Southside neighborhood. Located on East Valentine Street and North Sargent Avenue, each of the three-bedroom company homes shared the same architecture and interior design. Because the houses had no plumbing, each came with its own private outhouse.

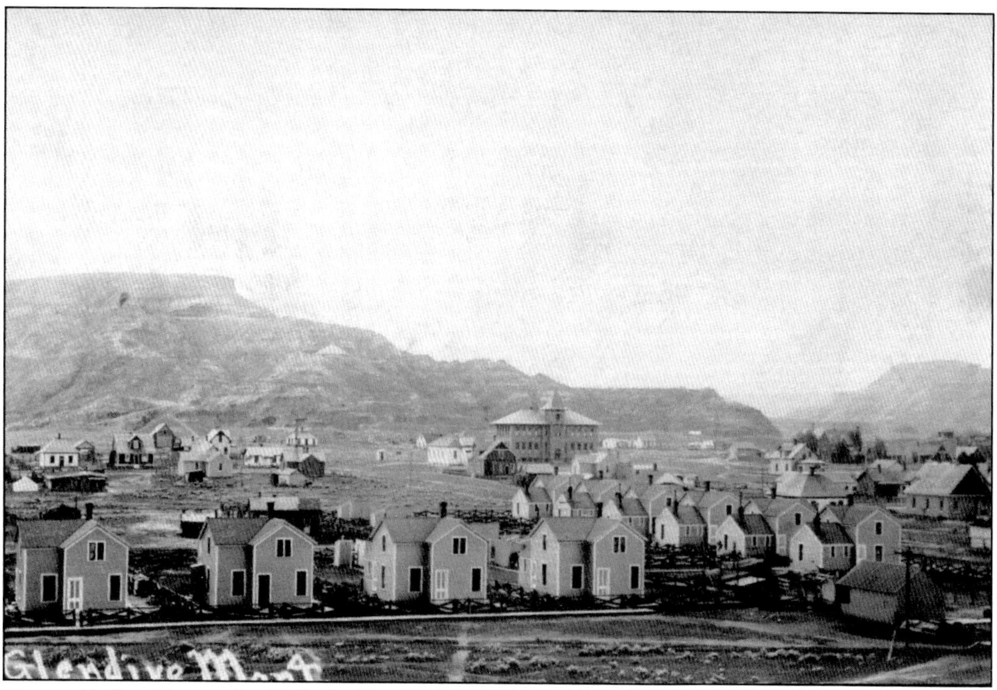

Situated below Hungry Joe Hill, the Southside was one of Glendive's first residential neighborhoods. Featured in the foreground are Northern Pacific employee row houses. In the background, the Lincoln School and other residential homes dot the landscape at the foot of the badlands. (Bob Petermann Ranch.)

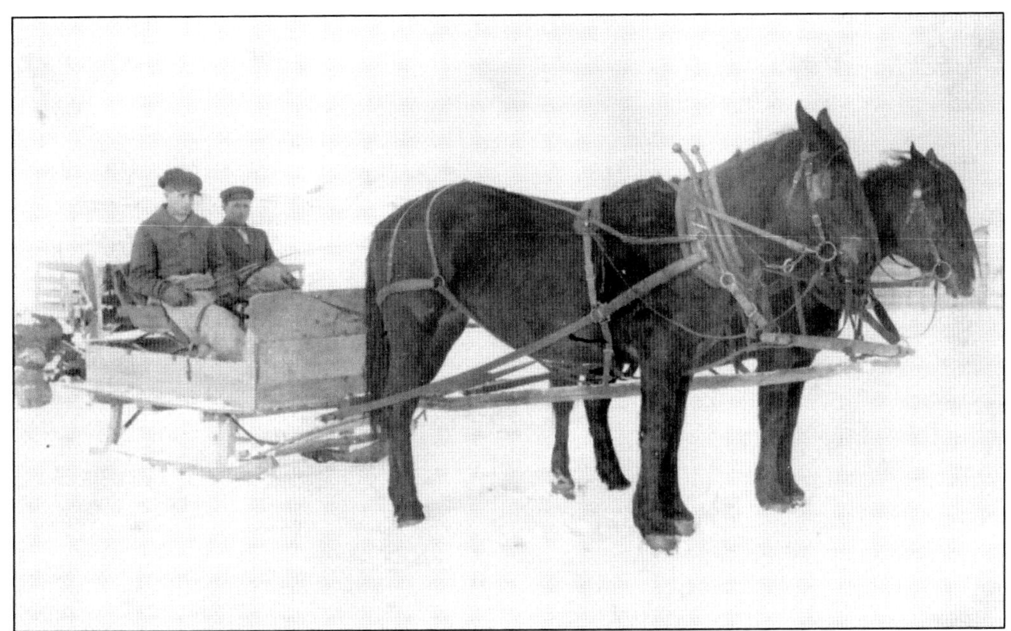

One of the things early migrants to Glendive found out was that winters on the northern plains are incredibly harsh. Heavy snowfall and long winters with temperatures reaching as low as negative 30 degrees Fahrenheit are common. In this c. 1890 photograph, two Glendivians travel by horse-drawn sleigh. (Goe Collection.)

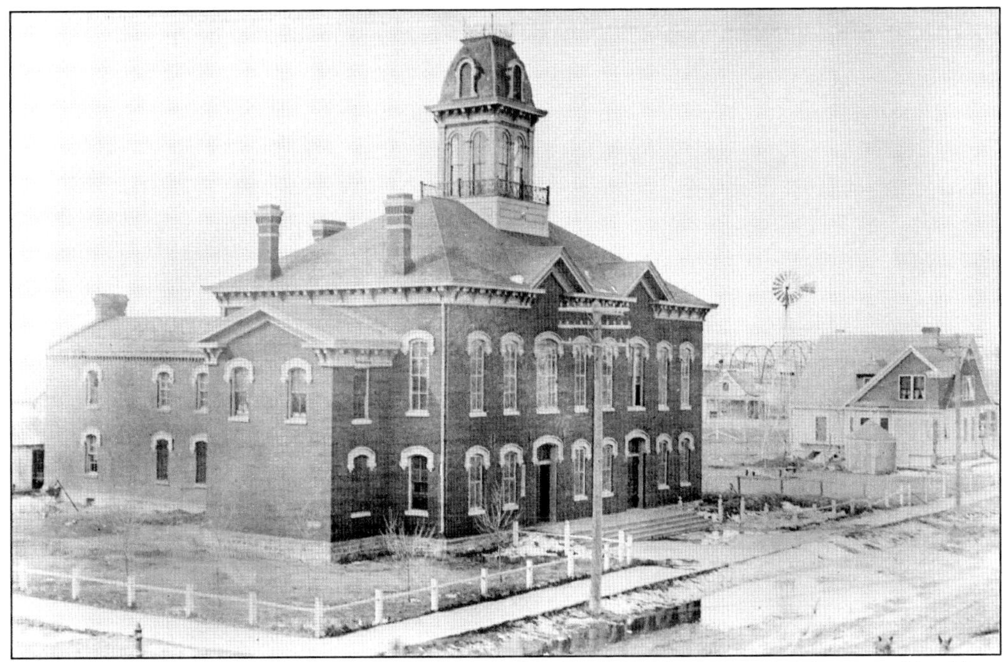

The first Dawson County Courthouse was completed in Glendive in 1889. This grand building dominated the urban landscape for decades.

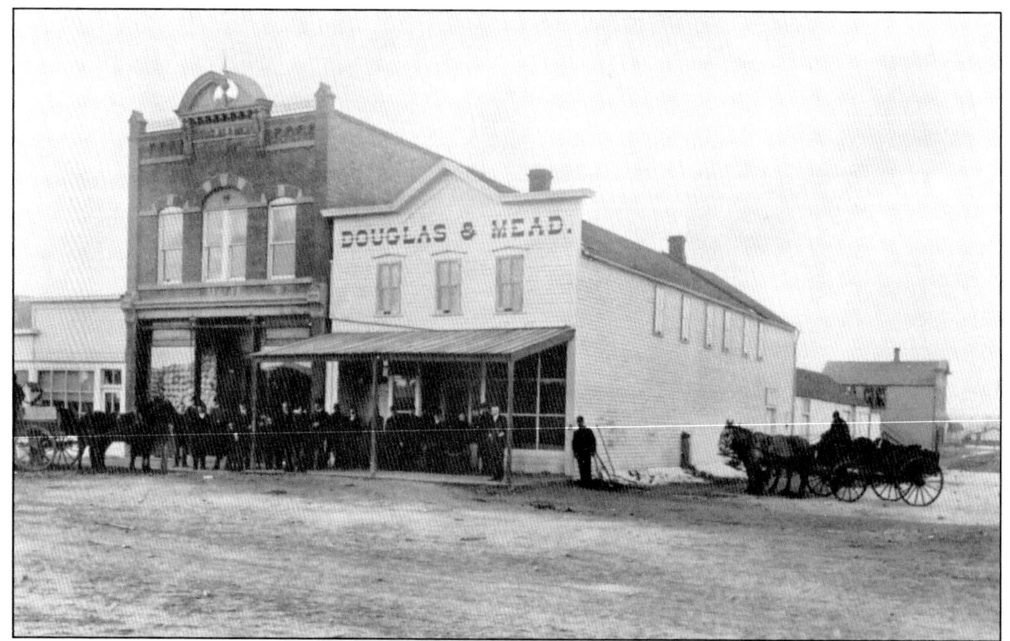

This photograph shows two incarnations of the Douglas and Mead Mercantile Store in 1886. Douglas and Mead opened their first general store in 1880, one year prior to the arrival of the Northern Pacific Railroad.

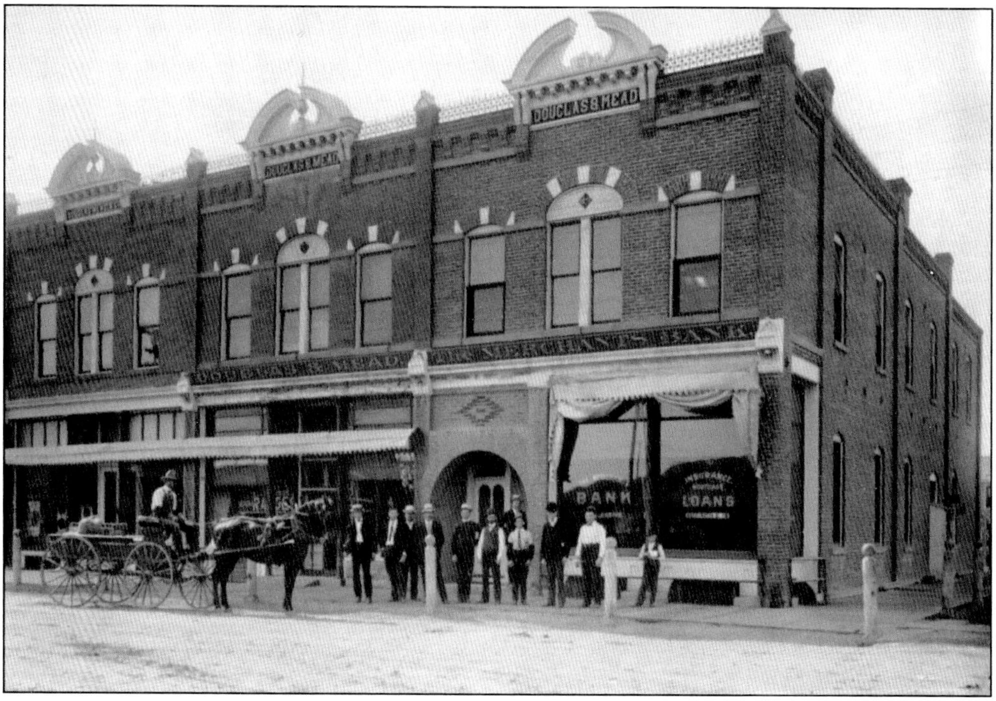

This image shows the Merchants Bank and Douglas and Mead Mercantile Store in the late 1890s. Hitching posts line the boardwalk around the building. Douglas and Mead was established in 1880, and the Merchants Bank followed in 1883. By the late 1890s, Glendive was beginning to resemble a modern Western town.

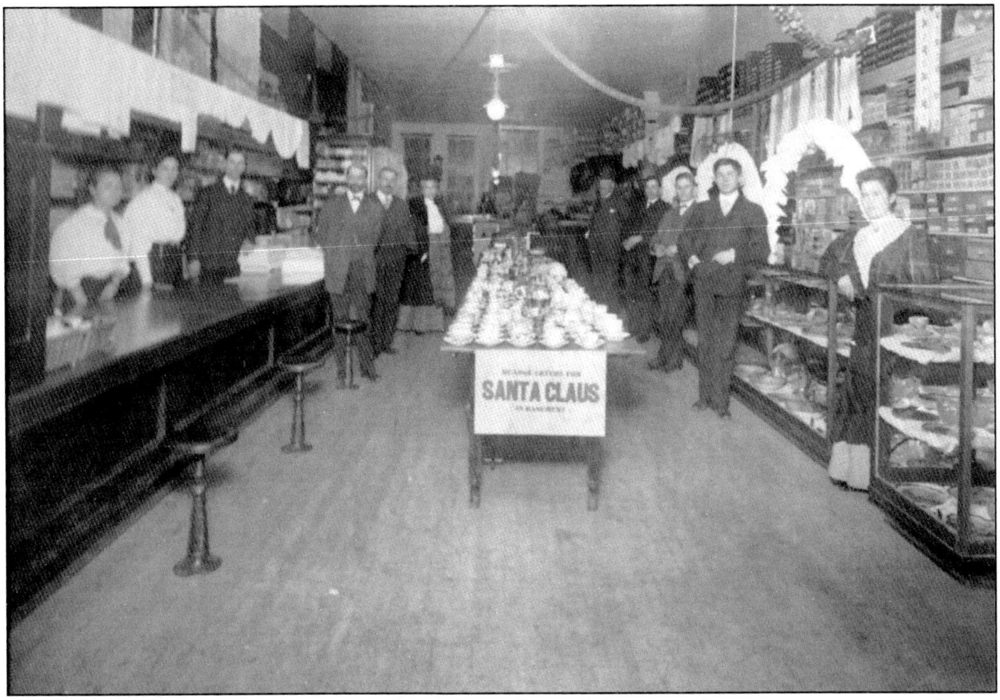

This rare photograph of the interior of Douglas and Mead shows employees posing together during the Christmas season, December 1913. The sign at the front of the store reads "Headquarters for Santa Claus in Basement."

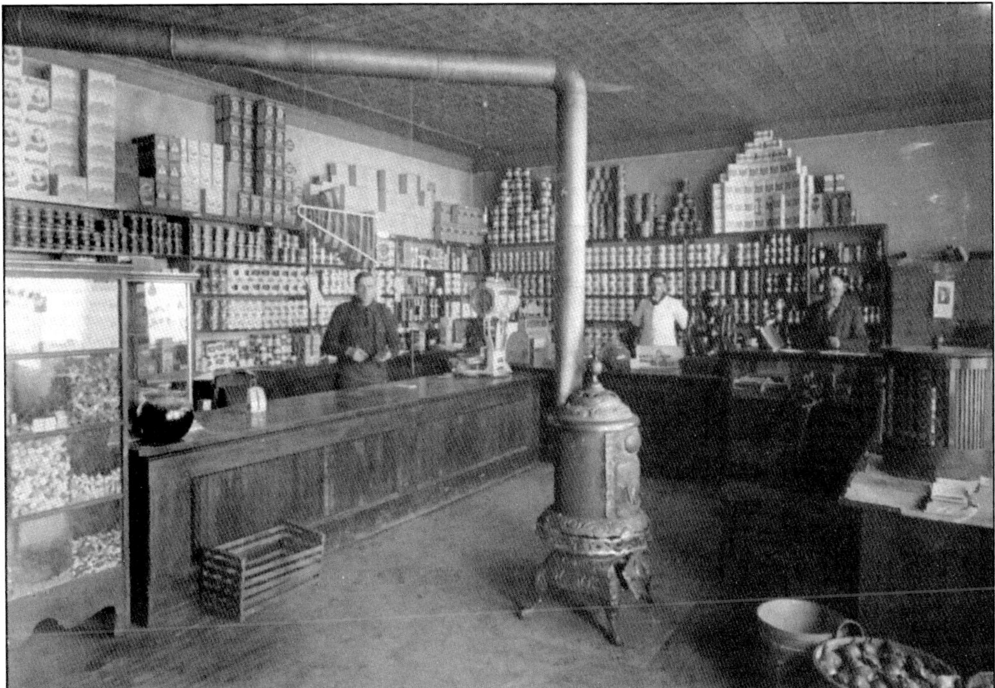

The interior of the Kolling Grocery Store in Glendive's Southside neighborhood is pictured during the 1890s.

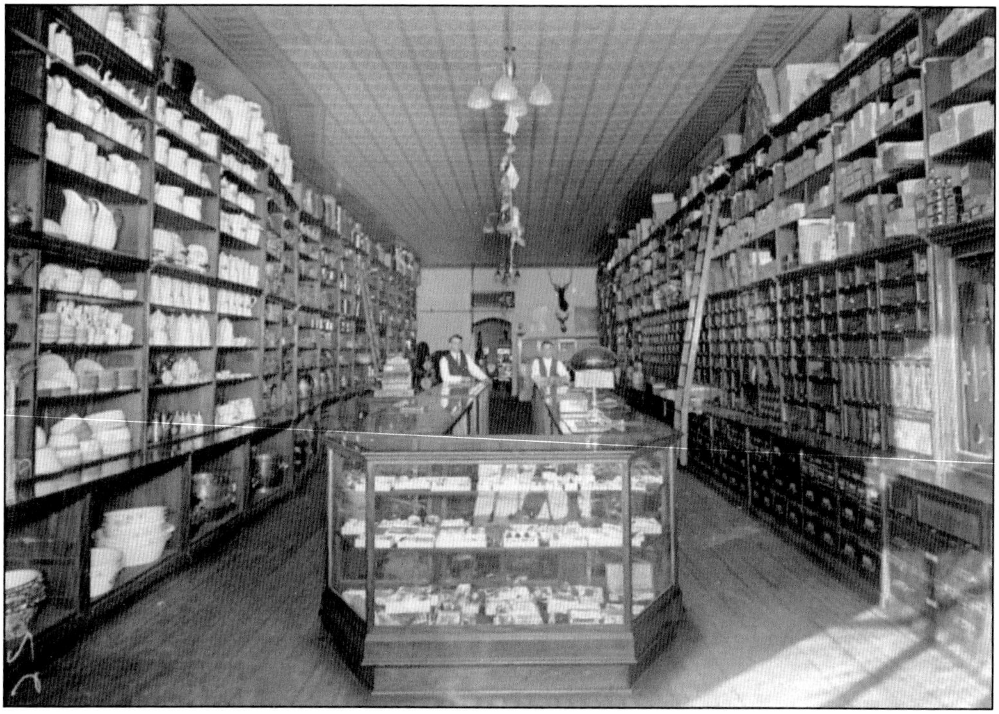

This rare photograph shows the interior of Lowe Hardware around 1900.

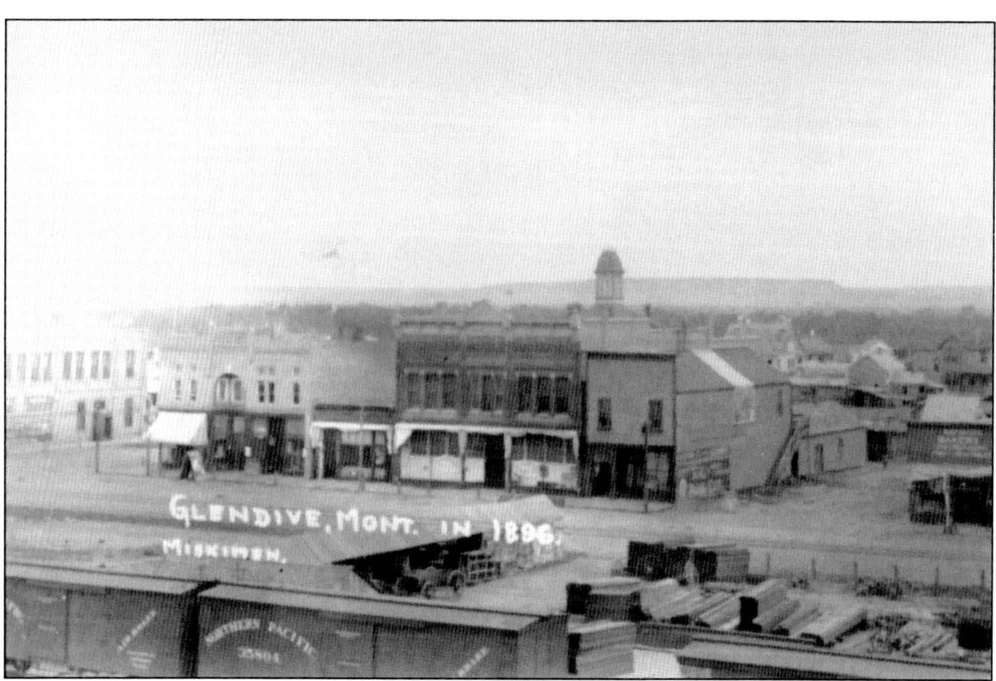

This photograph shows the remarkable development of Glendive from the vantage point of the Northern Pacific rail yards in 1896. (Langdon Bell Collection.)

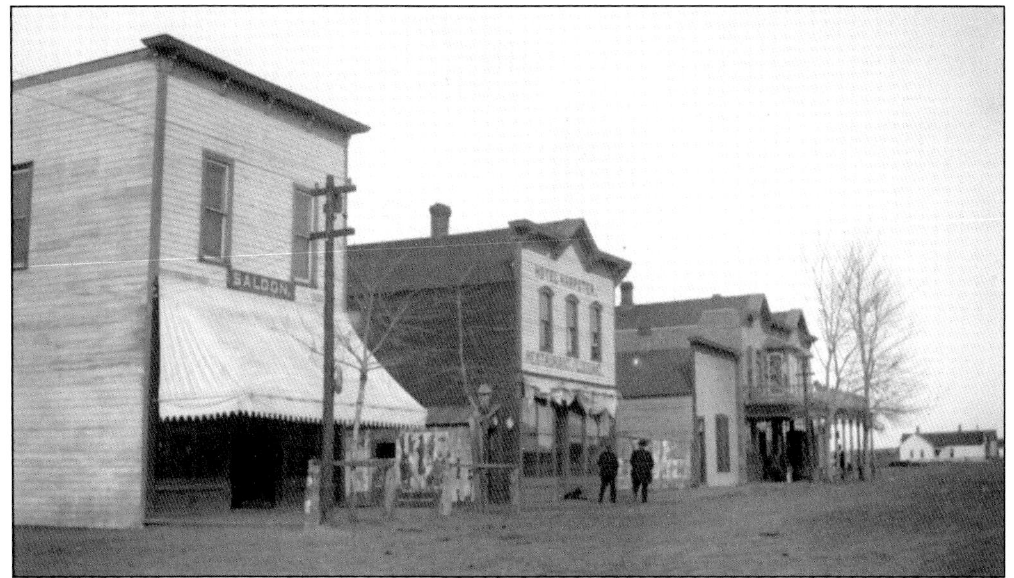

Here is a view of Merrill Avenue around 1895. This photograph shows a saloon, the Hotel Harpster, and the Yellowstone Hotel at the end of the block. The Harpster family owned a large cattle ranch outside of Glendive. In the 1880s and 1890s, when ranch hands were in town and needed a hotel room for the night, they were always asked where they worked. If they answered "Harpster" or "Flying O," no rooms were available, since cowboys from these two ranches had a reputation for being a bit rowdy. Thus, out of necessity, the Harpster Ranch built the Hotel Harpster.

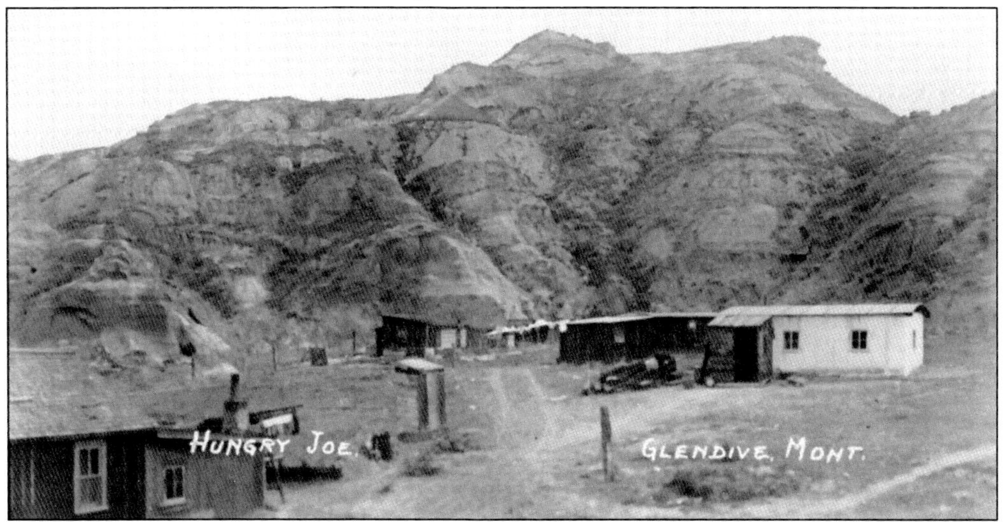

A man named Joe supposedly ran the Yellowstone Ferry for Douglas and Mead in the early 1880s. For ranchers, farmers, cowboys, and other travelers coming to Glendive from the west, the ferry was a vital link to town. It was well known that Joe did not like to miss meals. Every day at 11:00 a.m., he abandoned his post at the ferry and went home for lunch. In the early 1880s, there were few trees or houses on the south side of Glendive, so anyone waiting on the west bank of the Yellowstone could see him meandering slowly towards his cabin at the base of the hill. After he finished his meal, he leisurely made his way back to the ferry. Joe's predictable routine was supposedly repeated every day, and his nickname "Hungry Joe" stuck. This photograph shows Hungry Joe Hill with homes situated below in the late 1800s.

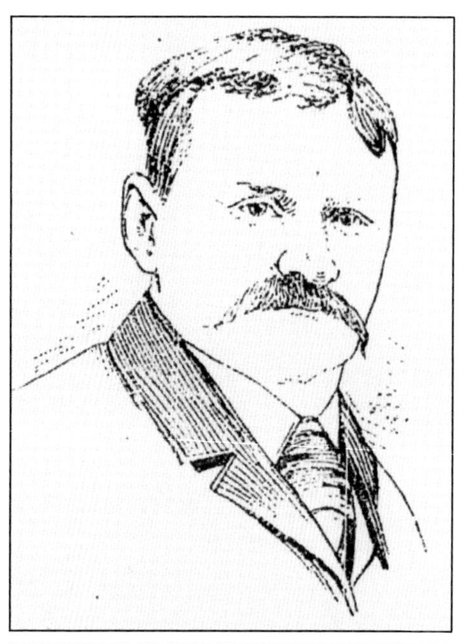

In 1898, Dominick Cavanaugh won a third term as Dawson County sheriff. On the morning of Christmas Eve 1898, Sheriff Cavanaugh's lifeless body was found outside of his Glendive home. Someone had bludgeoned him with a blunt object. Cavanaugh's political opponent in the previous election, Joe Hurst, was accused of murder and sentenced to hang despite the specious evidence of the prosecution. The trial garnered national attention.

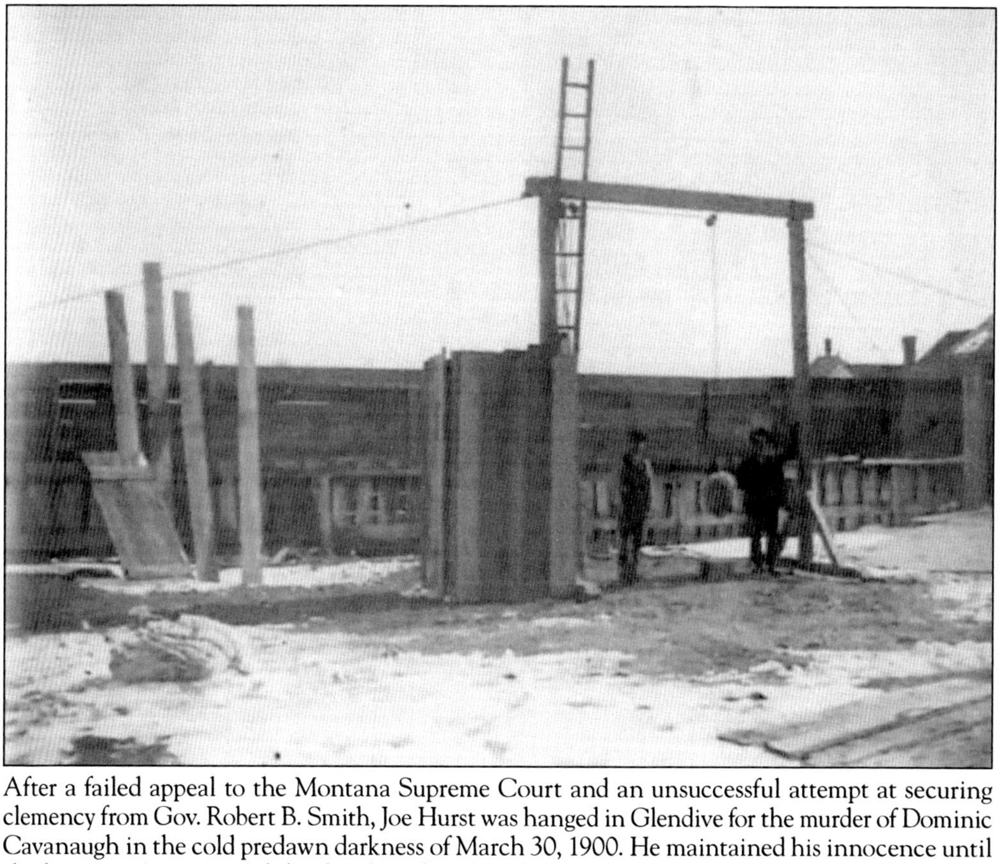

After a failed appeal to the Montana Supreme Court and an unsuccessful attempt at securing clemency from Gov. Robert B. Smith, Joe Hurst was hanged in Glendive for the murder of Dominic Cavanaugh in the cold predawn darkness of March 30, 1900. He maintained his innocence until the hangman's noose took his last breath. This photograph shows the gallows constructed for Hurst the day before the execution.

Two

Glendive's Golden Age

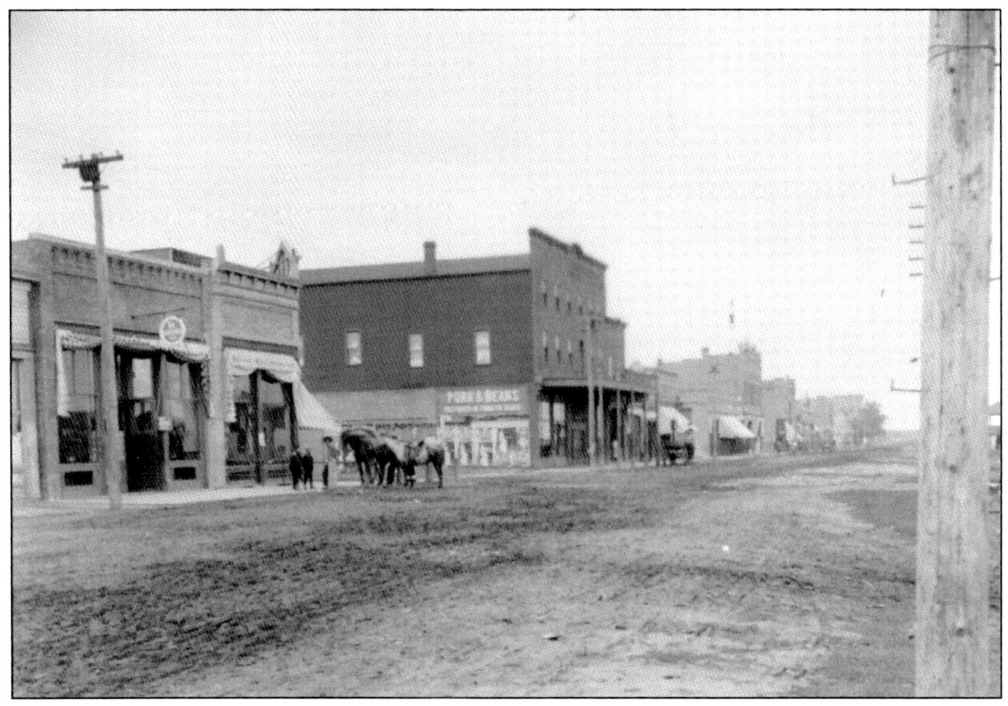

Glendive experienced a golden age of progress and productivity during the first three decades of the 20th century. The town was a hub for Northern Pacific activity, and the proximity of the railroad and the Yellowstone River lured hundreds of would-be farmers and ranchers to the local area. This photograph of the northern end of Merrill Avenue around 1900 shows the town's growth from its humble beginnings in 1881. From left to right are a Chinese American–owned laundry, the Montana Saloon, and J.J. Stipek's on the corner. (R.H. Foss Collection.)

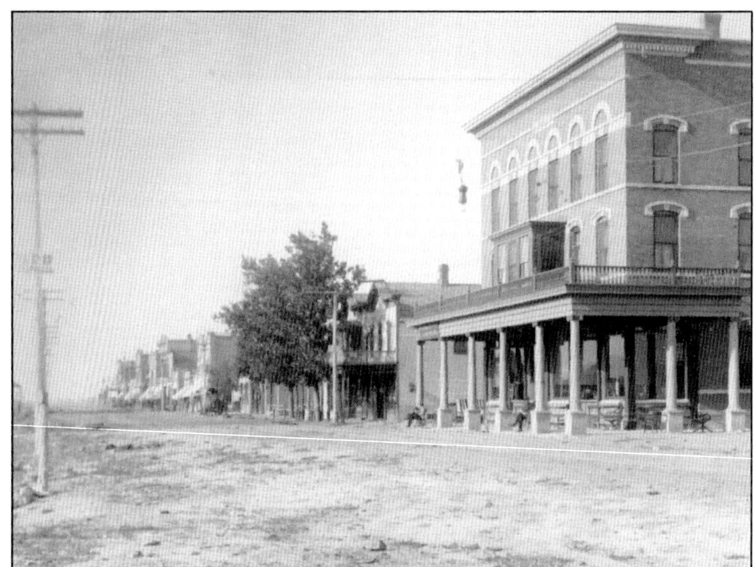

This photograph shows the recently completed Jordan Hotel and other businesses along the dusty streets of Merrill Avenue in 1901. William and Mary MacDonald Jordan purchased the Yellowstone Hotel in 1896 and built the Jordan Hotel in 1901.

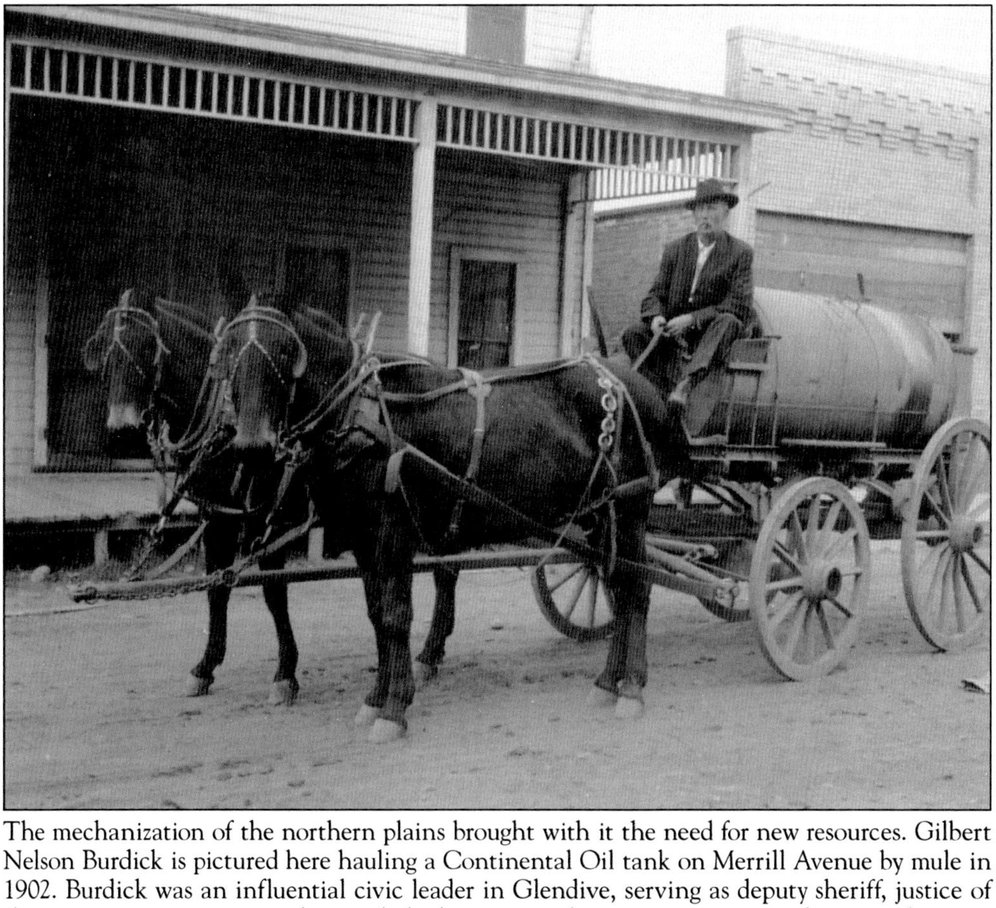

The mechanization of the northern plains brought with it the need for new resources. Gilbert Nelson Burdick is pictured here hauling a Continental Oil tank on Merrill Avenue by mule in 1902. Burdick was an influential civic leader in Glendive, serving as deputy sheriff, justice of the peace, county treasurer, deputy clerk, deputy recorder, city magistrate, and city weighmaster before his death in 1935.

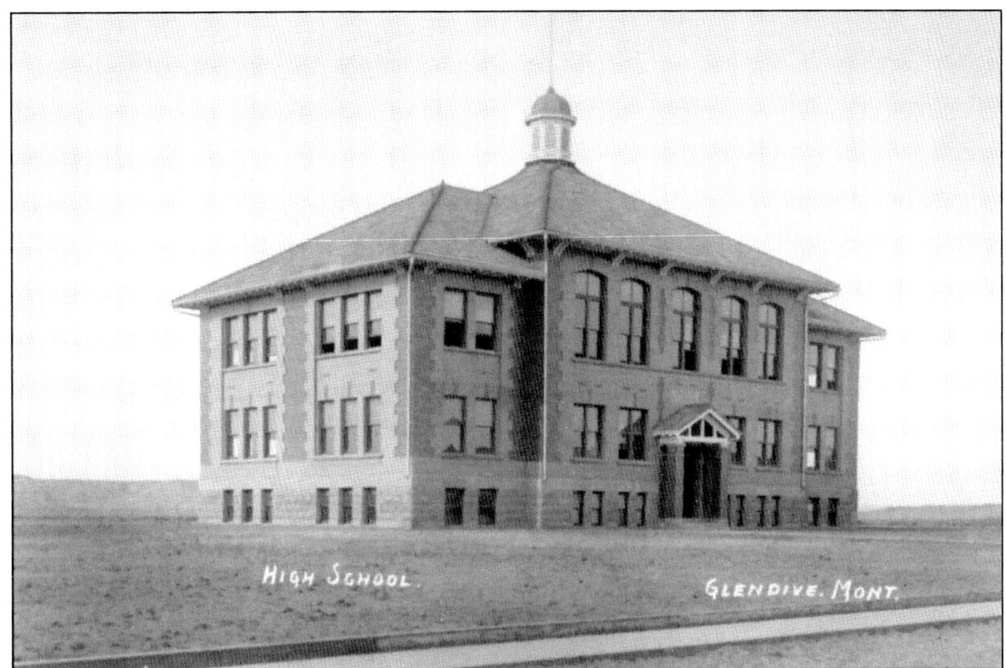

With more families moving into the Glendive region during the 1890s and first decade of the 20th century, there was a need for larger schools. This photograph was taken by L.A. Foster of the first Dawson County High School, which was constructed in 1909.

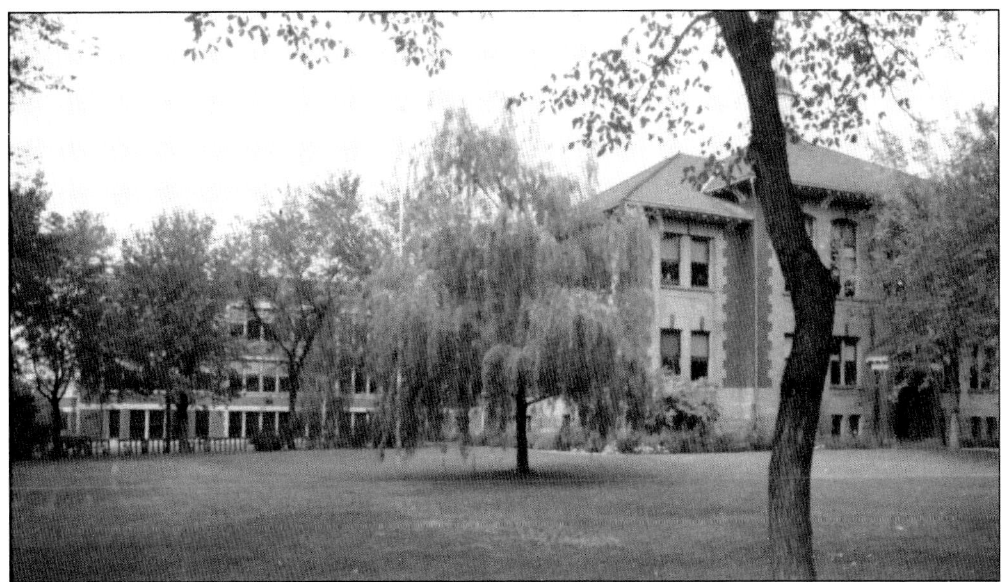

This photograph shows the second Dawson County High School, located on Kendrick Avenue. Built in the late 1920s, the facility was also home to Dawson County Junior College. Following a destructive fire in 1966, the building was razed.

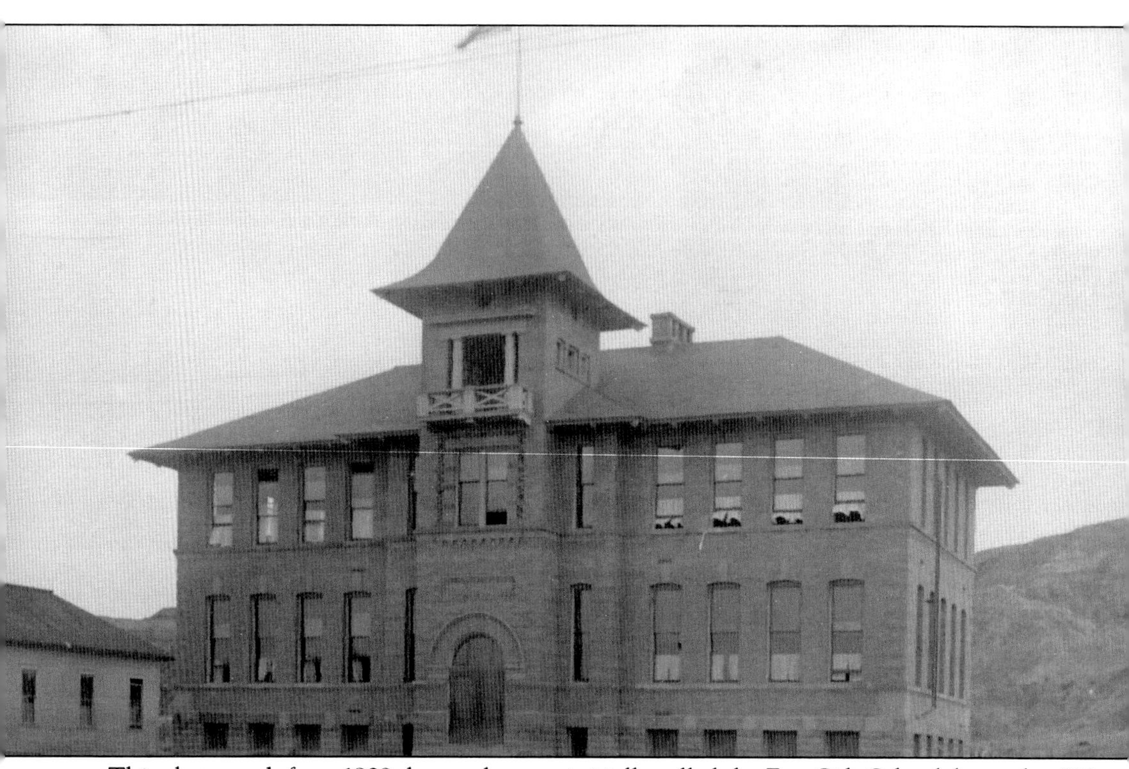

This photograph from 1909 shows what was initially called the East Side School, located at 313 South Nowlan Avenue. By 1913, it was renamed Lincoln Elementary School.

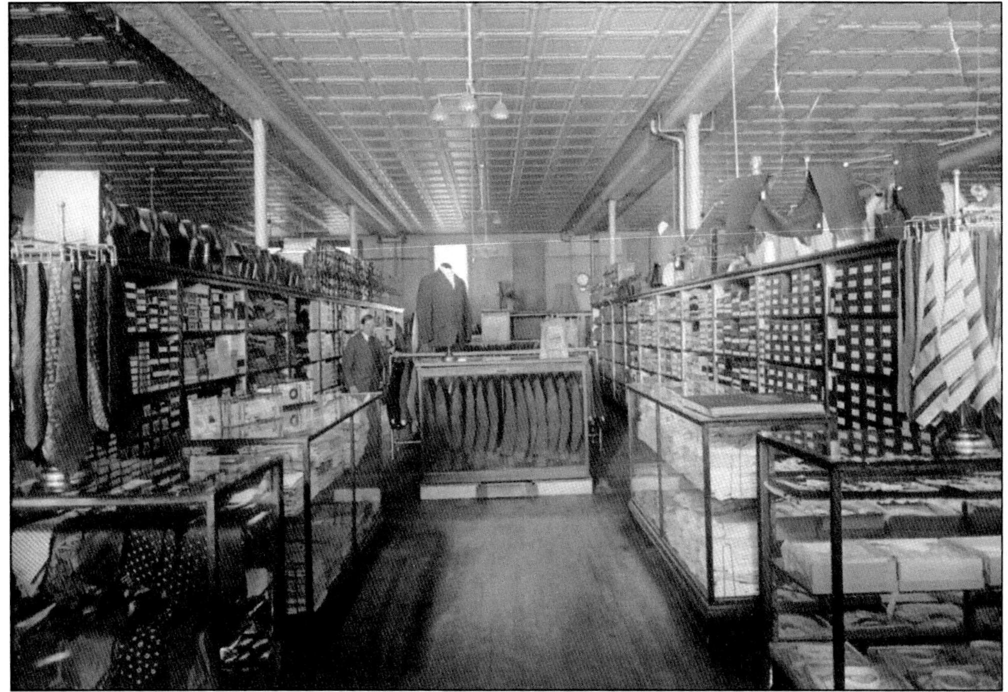

This photograph shows the interior of the Dion Mercantile Store around 1906. Built in 1905, Dion's sold clothing for both men and women, as well as fine china, crystal, and flatware.

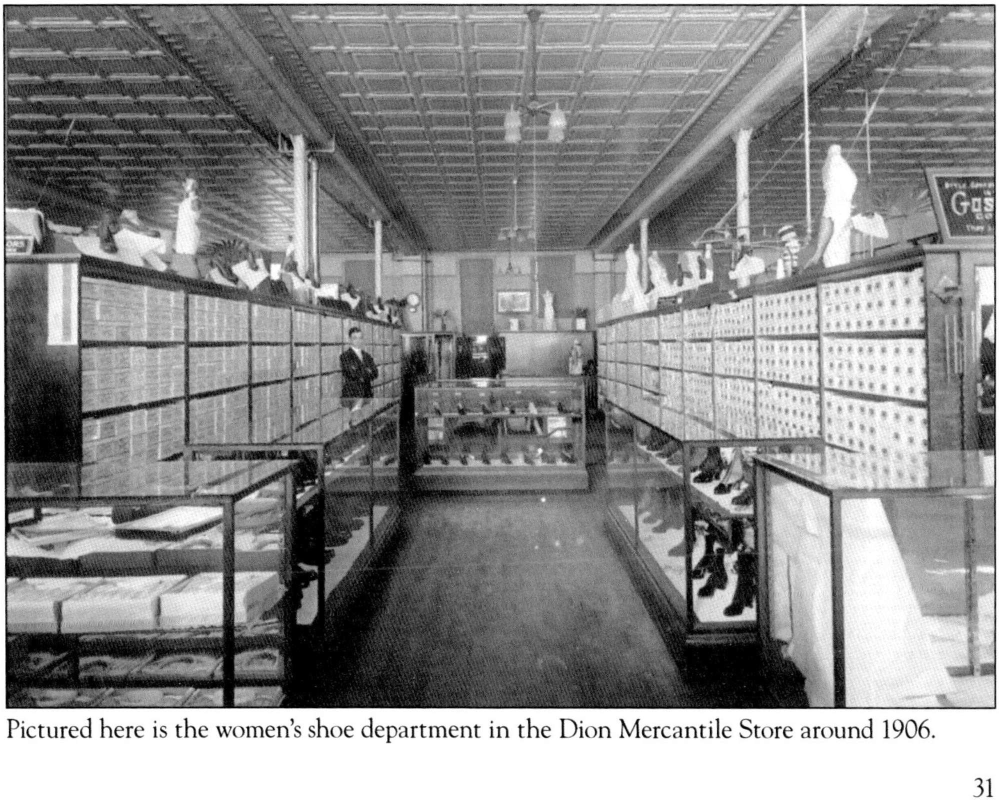

Pictured here is the women's shoe department in the Dion Mercantile Store around 1906.

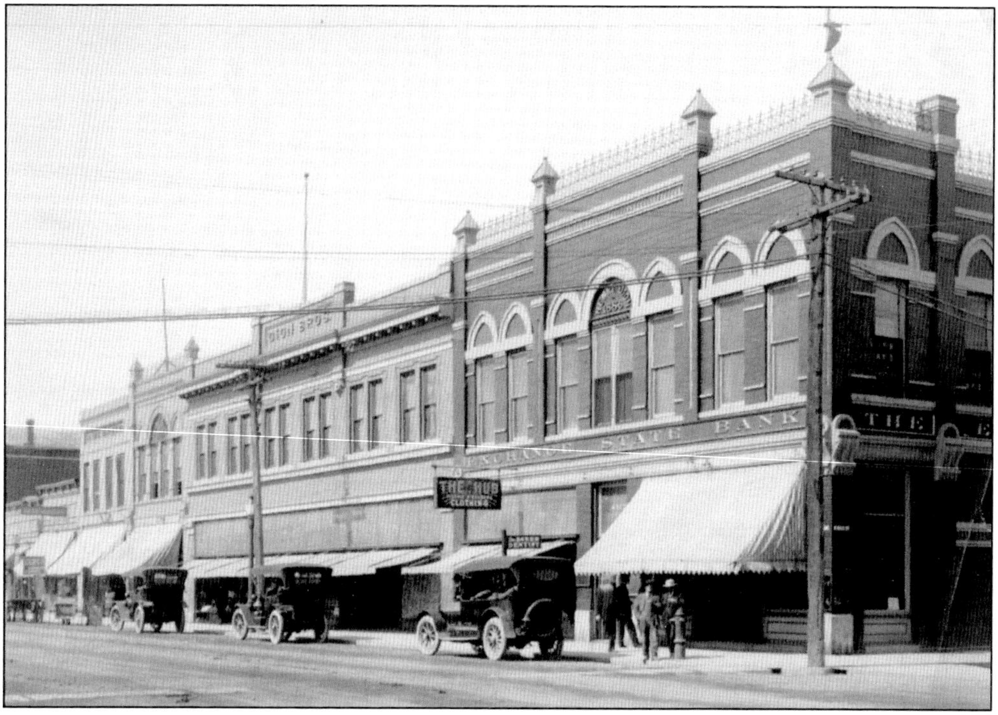

Outside of department stores and specialty clothiers, the large Henry Dion building was also home to the Exchange State Bank, pictured around 1915.

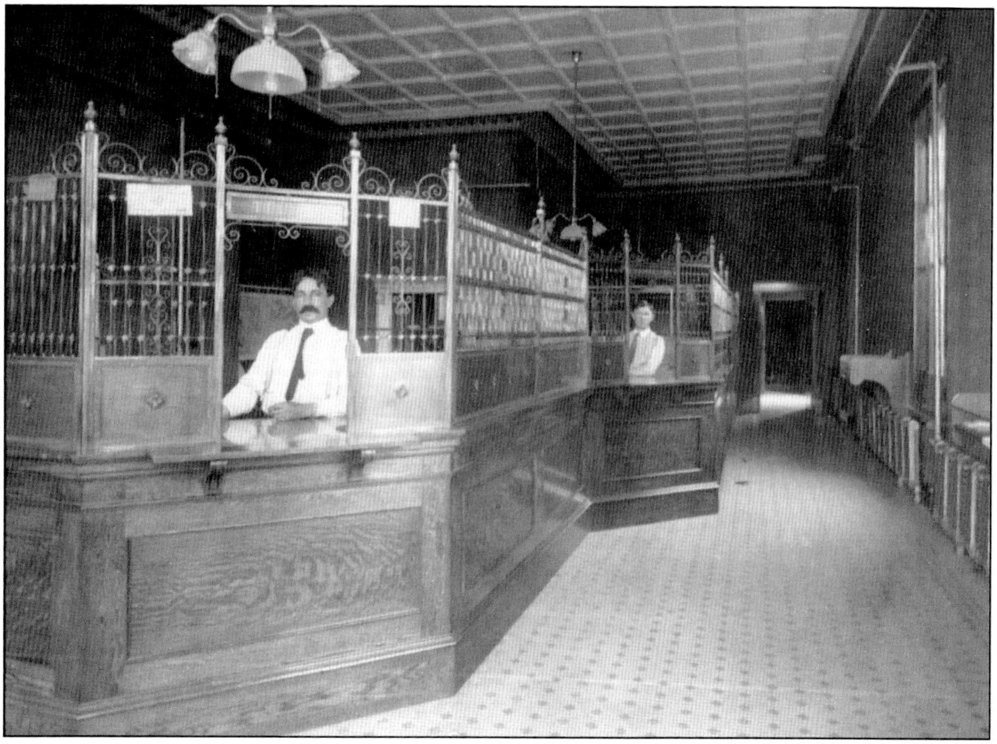

Two tellers pose at their windows inside the Exchange State Bank around 1915.

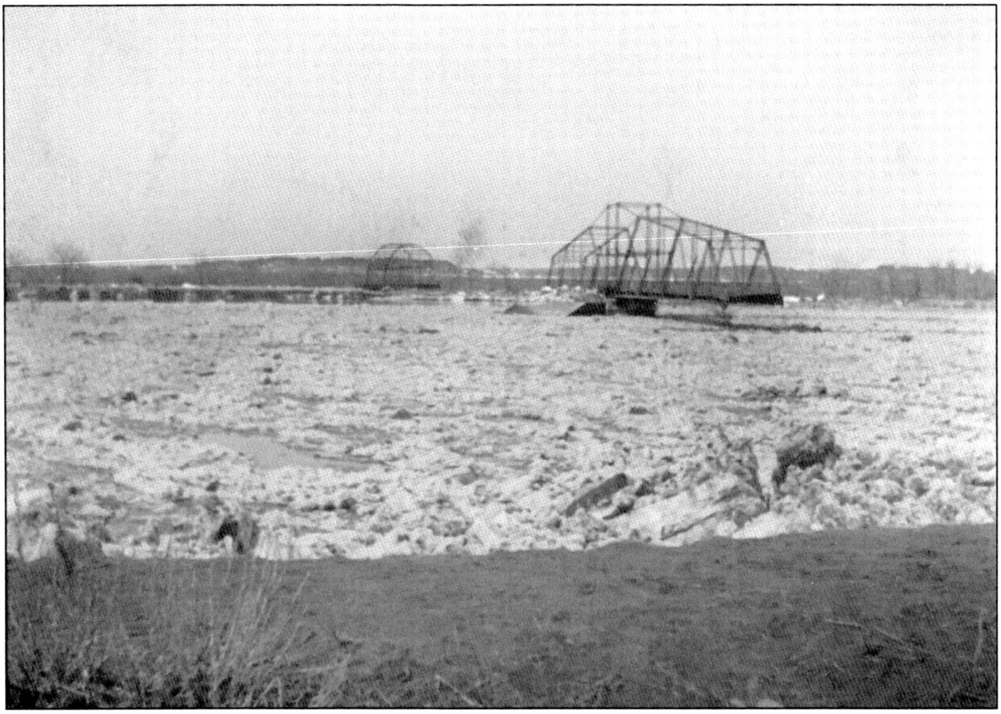

The Yellowstone River Bridge was built in the mid-1880s. The four-span bridge included a swing span because the Yellowstone River was still considered navigable. The bridge provided stockmen and farmers direct access to the railroad and made stage travel to points northwest much more reliable. This photograph shows the aftermath of the destruction of the Yellowstone River Bridge by ice jams when the river broke in the spring of 1899.

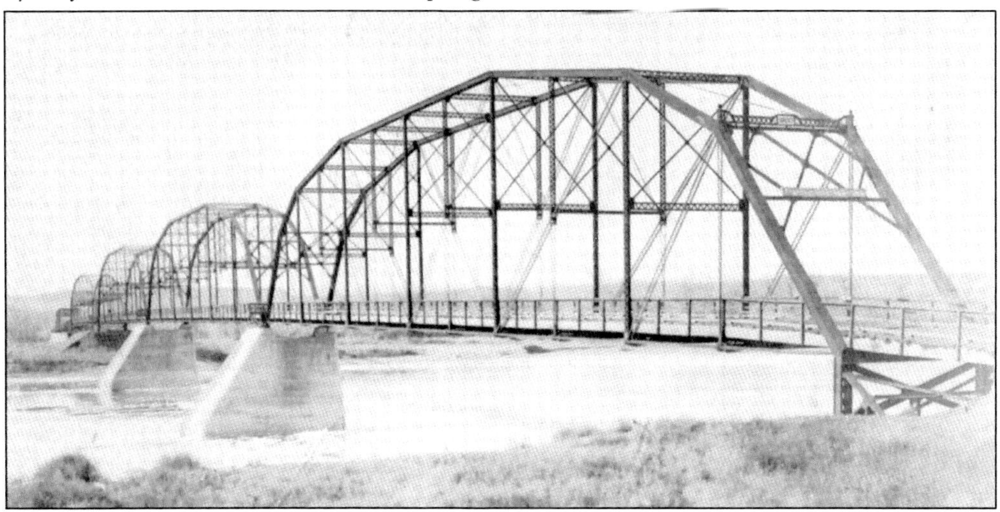

The second Yellowstone River Bridge was completed in 1900. The Army Corps of Engineers had by then determined the Yellowstone River no longer navigable, and the bridge was rebuilt using one original span plus three new ones. The second bridge stood until 1924, when newer technologies rendered the structure obsolete. It was replaced by the Bell Street Bridge, which was completed in 1926. During the first two decades of the 20th century, the Yellowstone River Bridge was known as the longest bridge in the northwestern United States (1,750 feet).

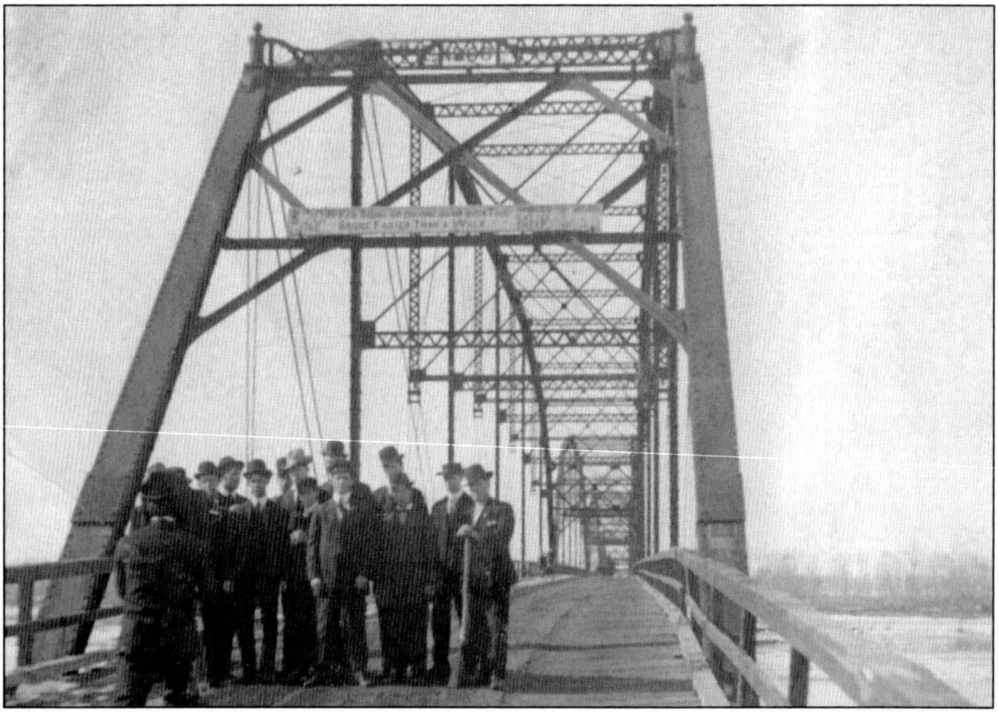

This photograph shows a group of local men posing on the second Yellowstone River Bridge around 1905. The sign above them reads "$20.00 fine for riding or driving on or over this bridge faster than a walk. Horses: 15 head; Cattle: 15 head; Sheep: 500 head."

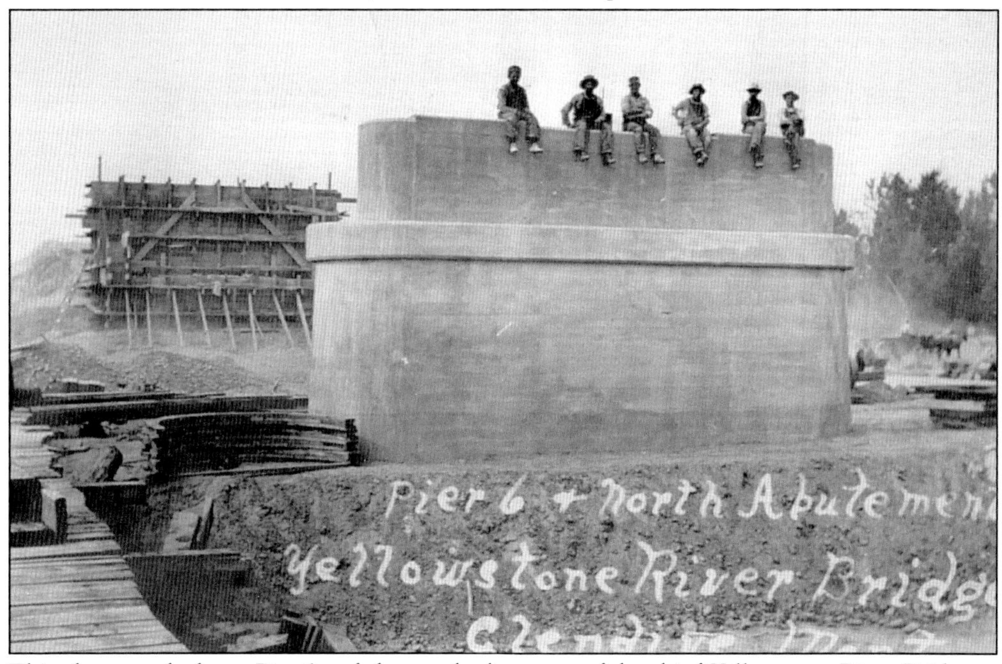

This photograph shows Pier 6 and the north abutment of the third Yellowstone River Bridge at Glendive under construction in 1923. The third Yellowstone River Bridge was renamed Bell Street Bridge when the Towne Street Bridge was built in the mid-1950s to distinguish the two.

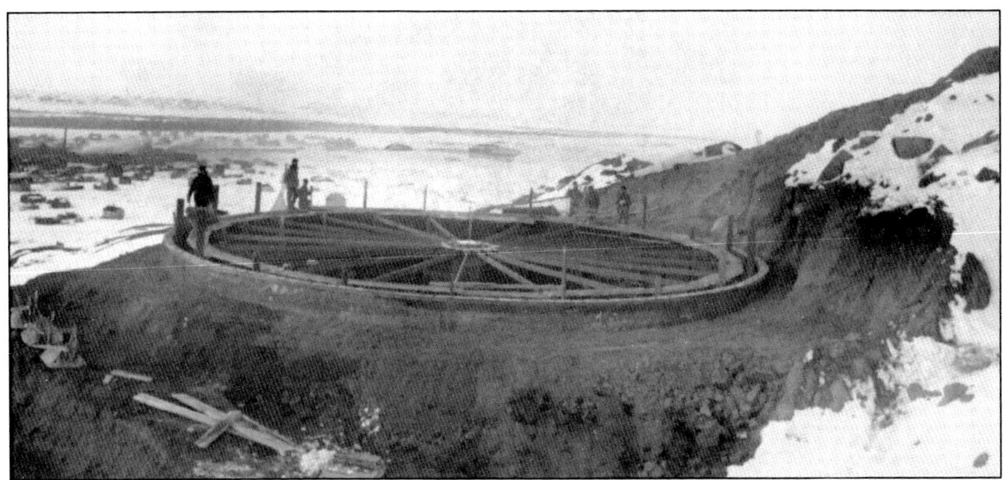

The water of the Yellowstone River, delivered in wooden barrels for 25¢ each, served Glendive's residents in the 19th century. Glendivians used red flags displayed on their homes to signal if they needed water. The red flags were often misinterpreted as a sign of quarantine by visitors. A $50,000 bond issue passed in 1905 for construction of a pump station, wooden water mains, and a reservoir. The early system was for water distribution only, and it was another decade before bonds financed $130,000 for a filtration plant. Pictured here is Glendive's first water tank, installed by the city in 1906. (G.G. Hoole).

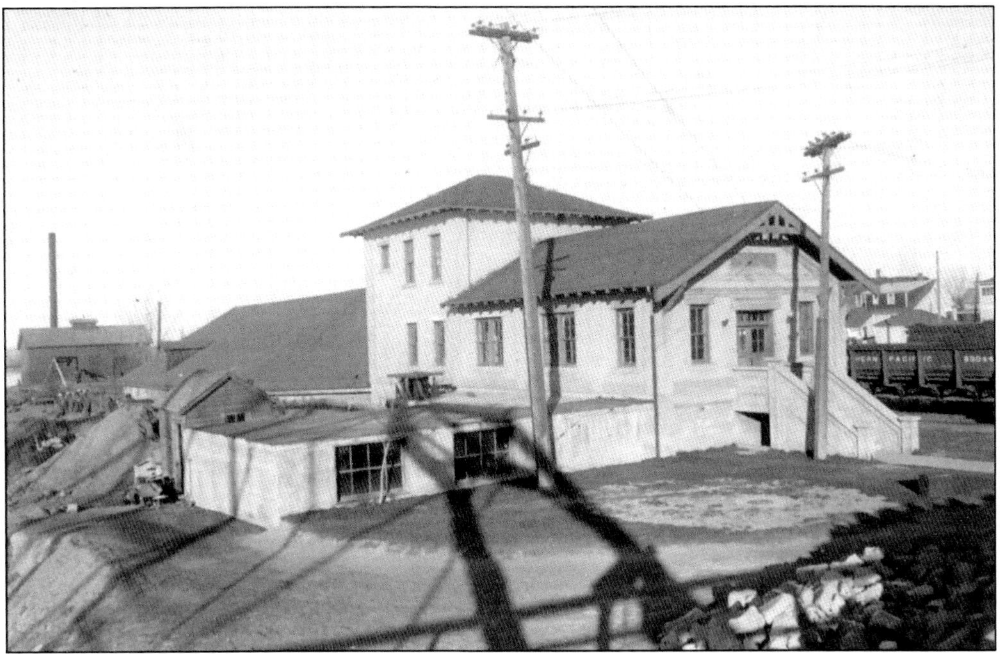

Glendive commissioned the Northwood Engineering Company of Florence, Massachusetts, to construct the one-story front section of the filtration plant, which was completed in 1917. A two-story brick addition following the original design was added at the rear in 1923, and the state's first water softening system, designed by city engineer C.W. Eyer, was installed in 1934. Expansion and modernization of the plant occurred in 1941 and 1960, but the original sections of the building remain in use. They represent the most controversial, expensive, and far-reaching project undertaken by Glendive's early citizens.

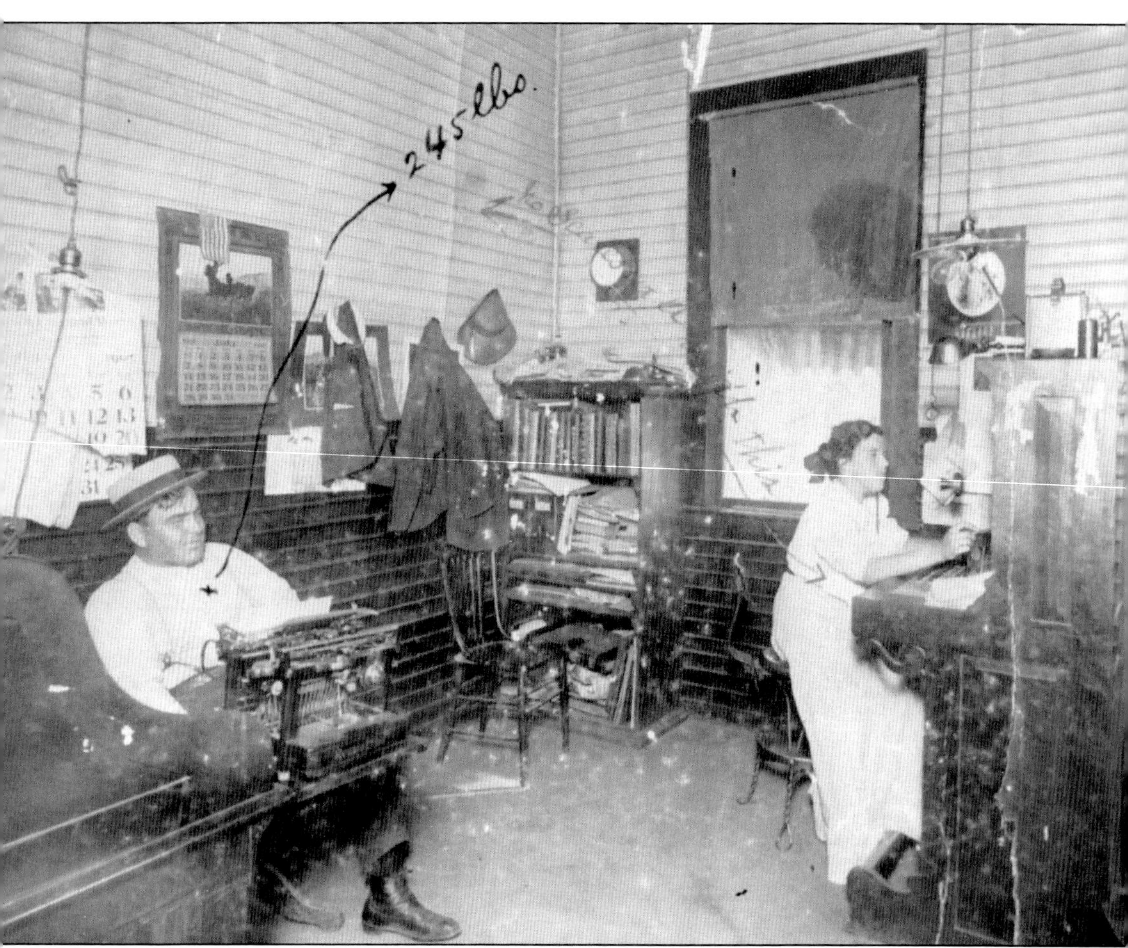

By 1902, Glendivians with means living in town had access to telephone service. In its first eight months, the Glendive Telephone Exchange serviced around 52 telephones. Pictured in 1907 are manager Frank C. Hughes and chief operator Martha Osborne of the Glendive Telephone Exchange.

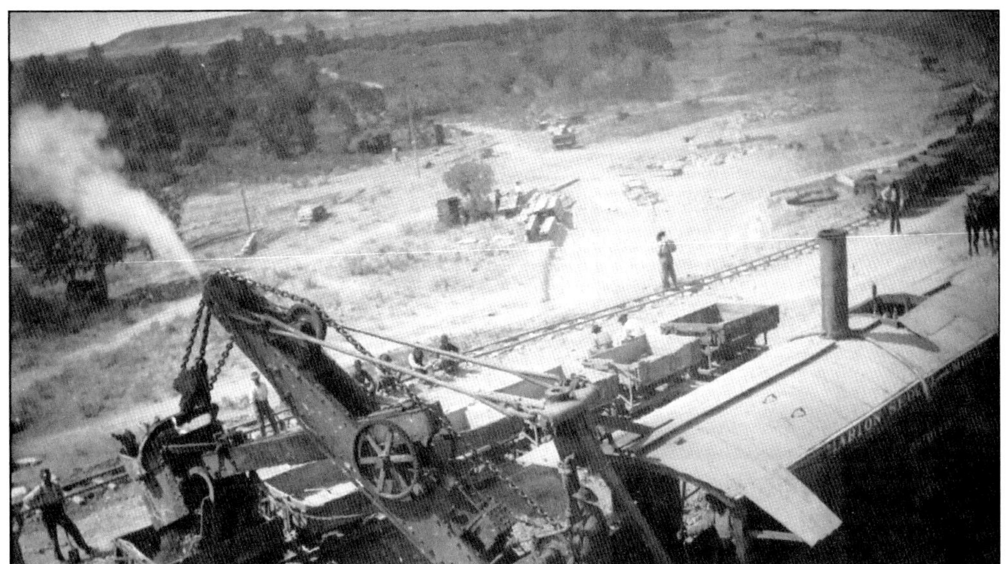

The Intake Diversion Dam is located approximately 70 miles upstream of the confluence of the Yellowstone and Missouri Rivers near Glendive. Secretary of the Interior Ethan Allen Hitchcock authorized the Lower Yellowstone Project on May 10, 1904. The Lower Yellowstone Project was designed to provide a dependable water supply sufficient to irrigate approximately 52,000 acres of land on the benches above the west bank of the river. This photograph shows the Freeman Crew using a steam shovel to move earth during the construction of the Intake Diversion Dam in 1907. (Grant Bates Collection.)

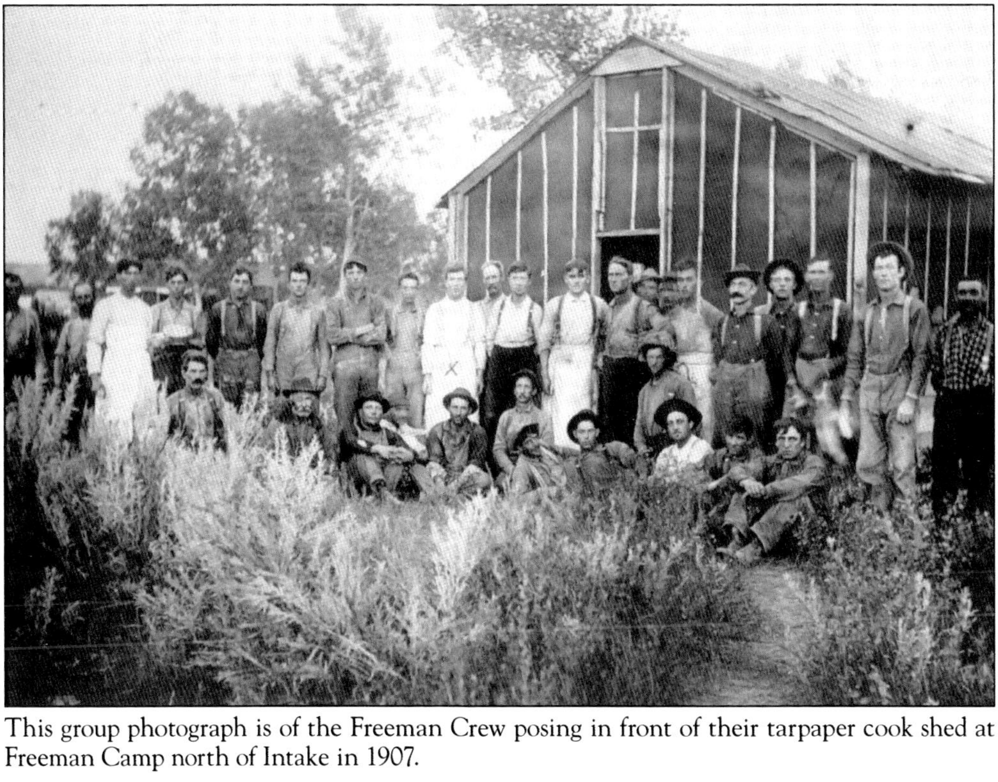

This group photograph is of the Freeman Crew posing in front of their tarpaper cook shed at Freeman Camp north of Intake in 1907.

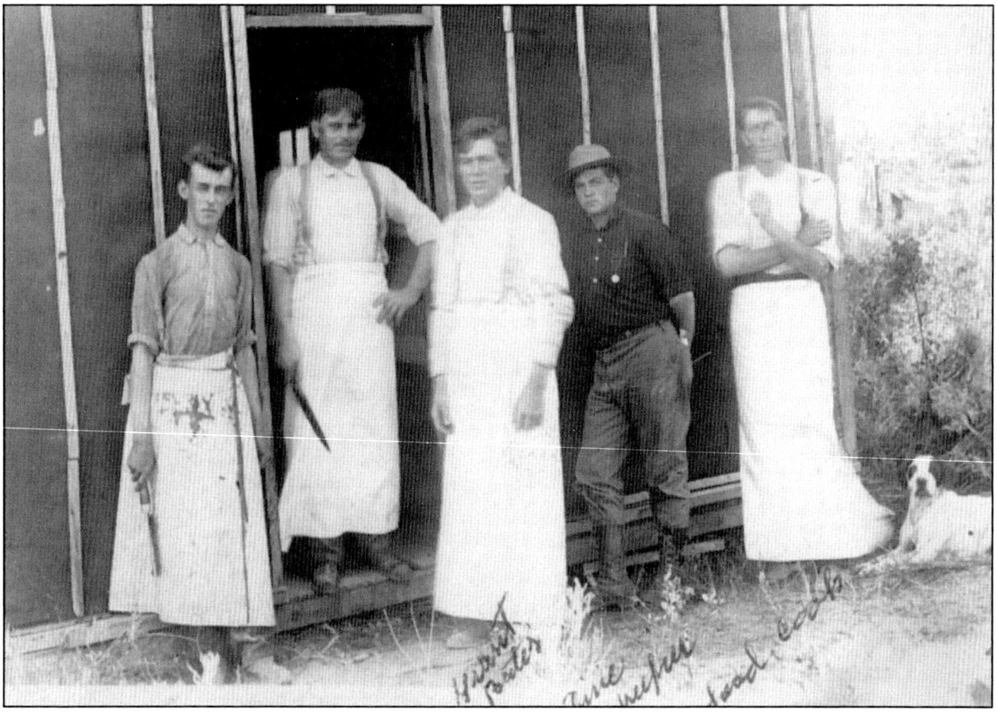

Three cooks and a timekeeper pose in front of their tarpaper cook shed at Freeman Camp north of Intake in 1907. (Grant Bates Collection.)

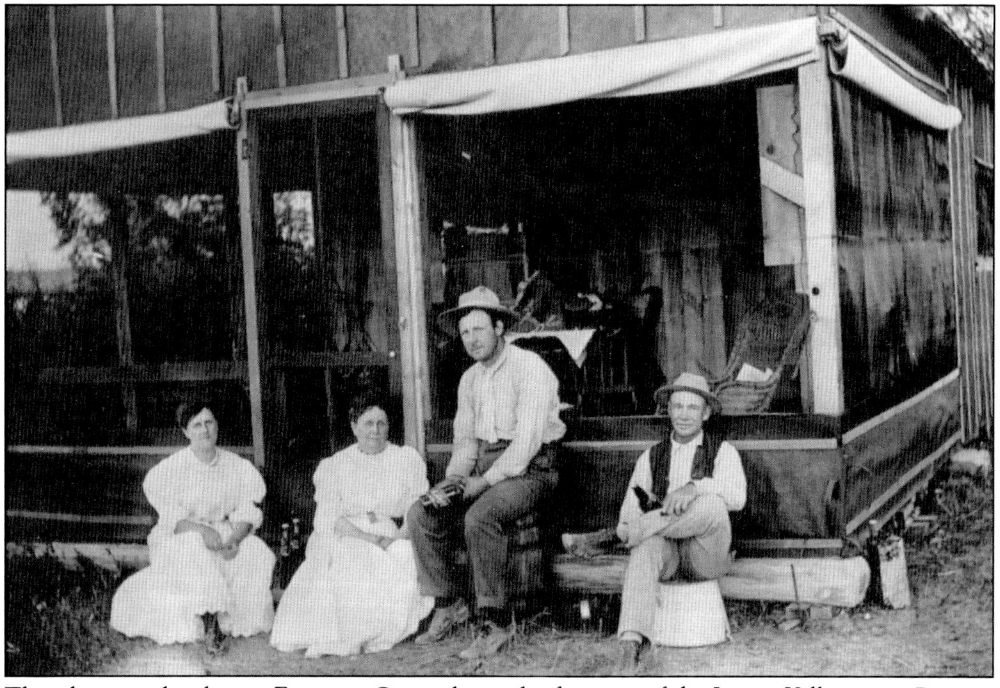

This photograph taken at Freeman Camp shows the foreman of the Lower Yellowstone Project, Willard Freeman (sitting on barrel), pictured with his wife and mother-in-law. Also pictured is John Corned. (Grant Bates Collection.)

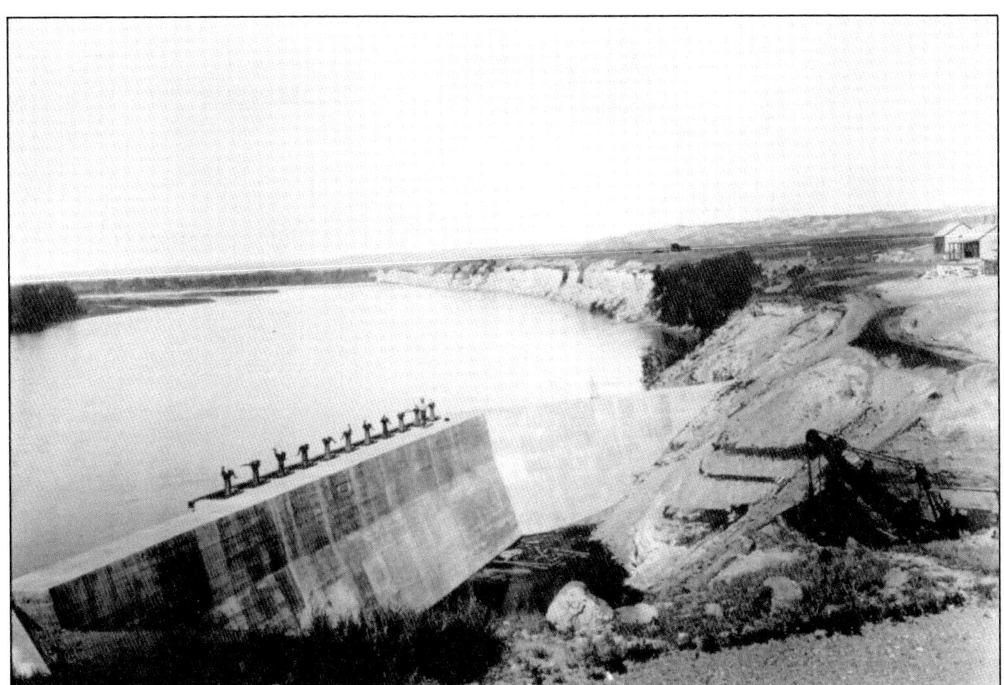

The dam at Intake is a 12-foot-high wood and stone structure that spans the Yellowstone River and diverts water into a primary canal for irrigation. It was an engineering marvel on the northern plains and a symbol of the modernization of the region. Here, workers from the Freeman Crew pose for a picture on the completed headgates of the Intake irrigation canal in 1907. (Lowe Collection.)

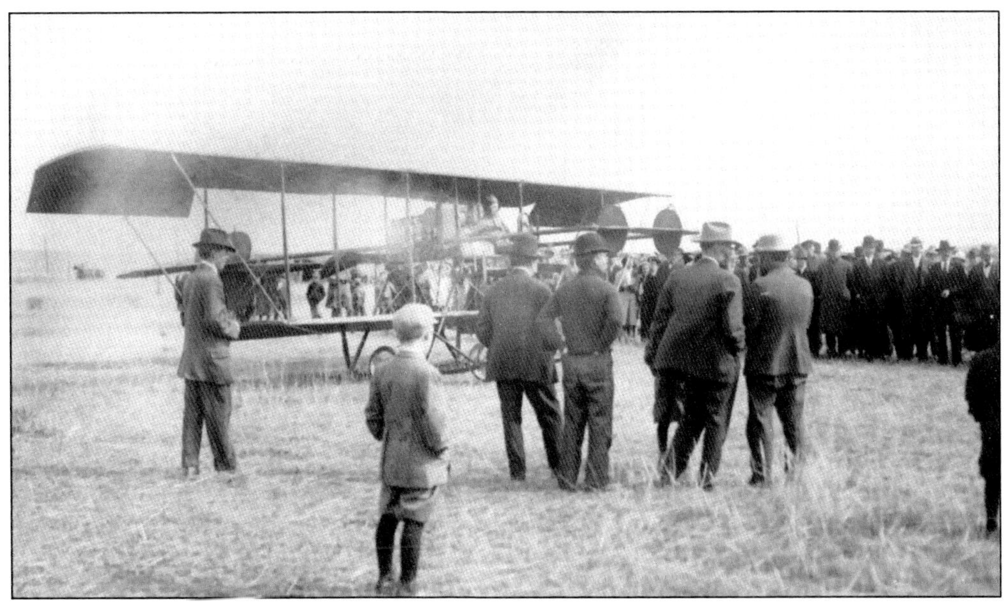

Locals gather to witness a demonstration of an early flying machine in Glendive around 1909. This photograph by L.A. Foster of an early airplane shows modernity not so subtly creeping into the frontier town of Glendive. The Northern Pacific and agriculturalists in the region soon adopted this new technology for multiple applications. (Mary Meissner Collection.)

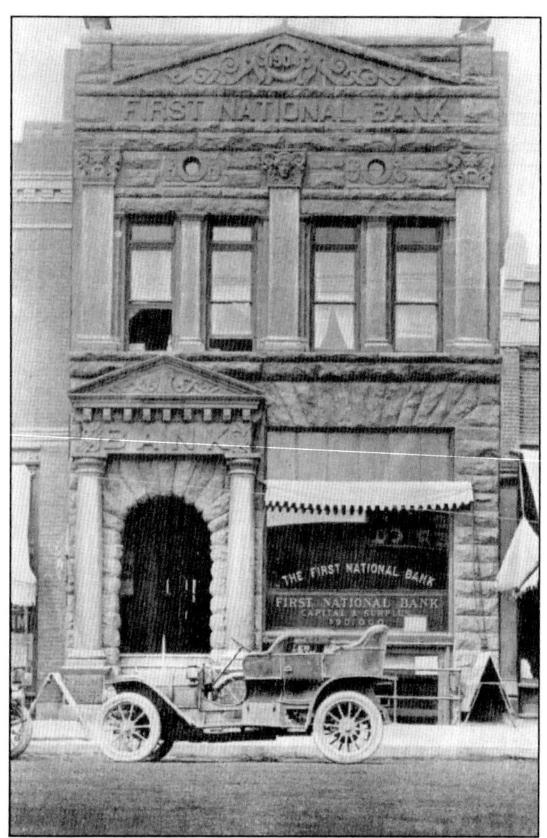

The First National Bank of Glendive in Montana printed $184,920 worth of national currency. This national bank opened in 1904 and stopped printing money in 1935, equaling a 32-year printing period—a fairly normal lifespan for a national bank. During its lifespan, the First National Bank of Glendive issued six different types and denominations of national currency: 1902 $10 Red Seal National Bank Note; 1902 $20 Red Seal National Bank Note; 1902 $10 Blue Seal National Bank Note; 1902 $20 Blue Seal National Bank Note; Series of 1929 Type1 $10 National Bank Note; and Series of 1929 Type1 $20 National Bank Note. The First National Bank of Glendive was located in Dawson County and assigned charter number 7101.

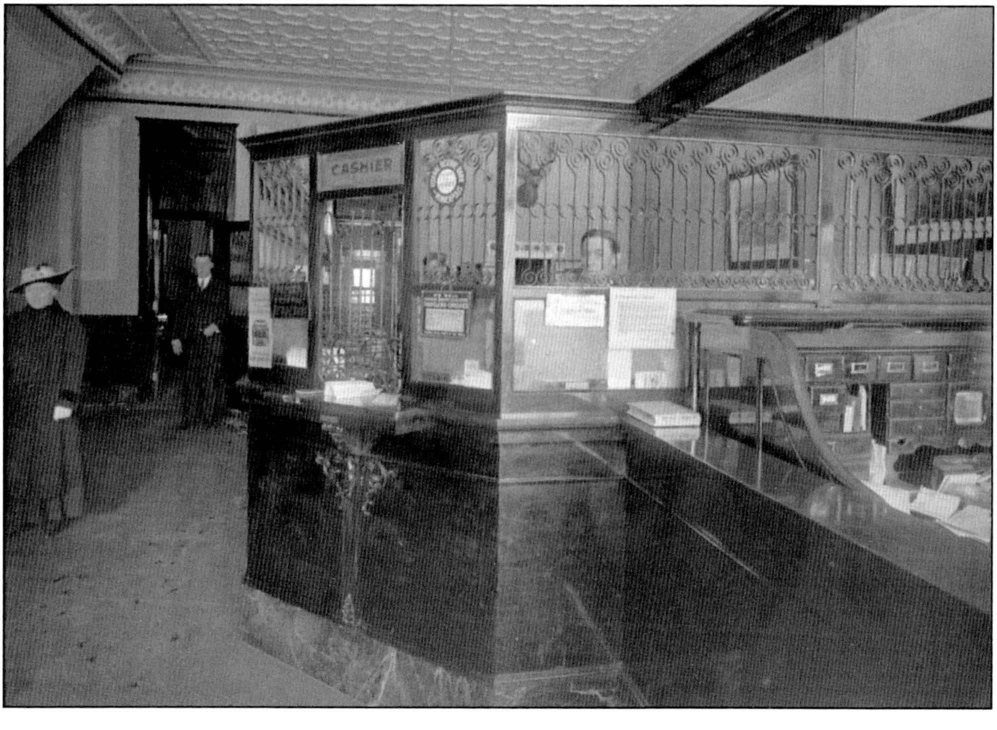

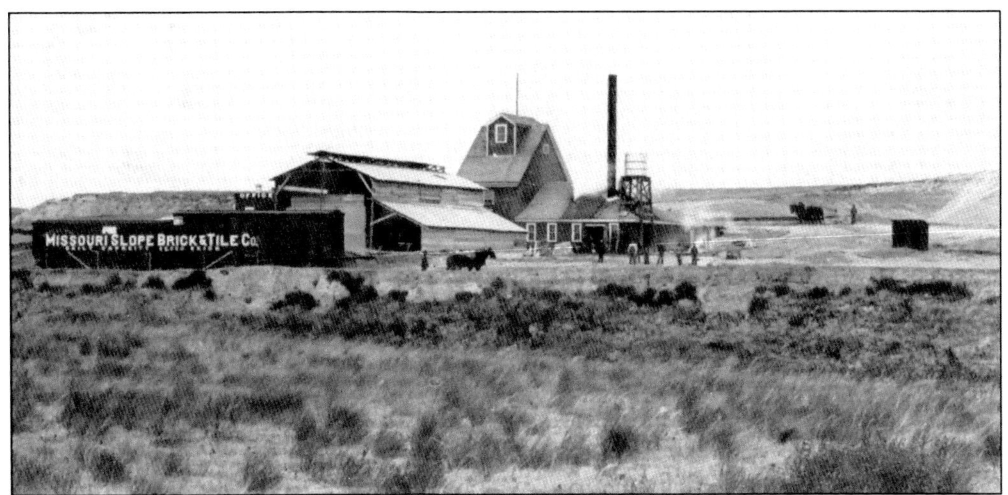

As Glendive continued to modernize, industrial businesses like the Missouri Slope Brick and Tile Company were created to meet an increased demand for building materials for the growing town. This photograph shows the company in 1908.

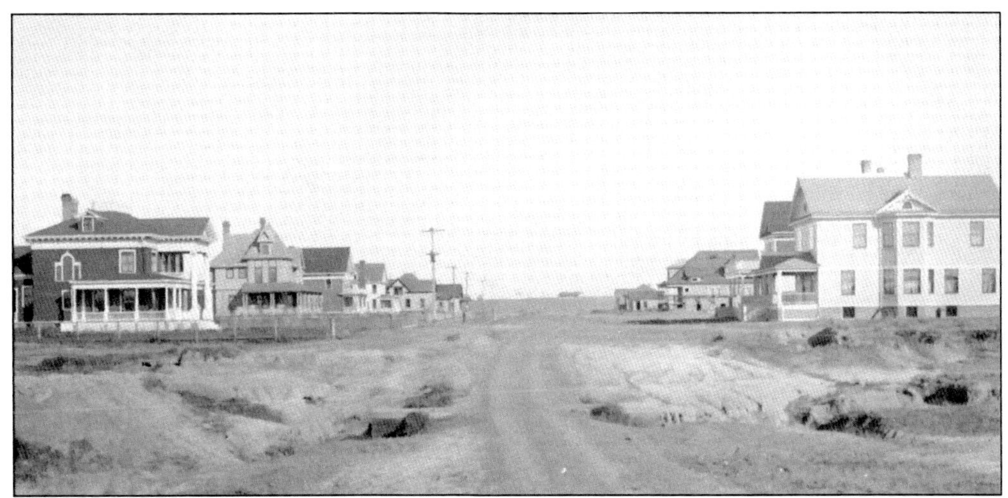

This photograph from 1909 shows middle-class residential homes lining Mead Avenue.

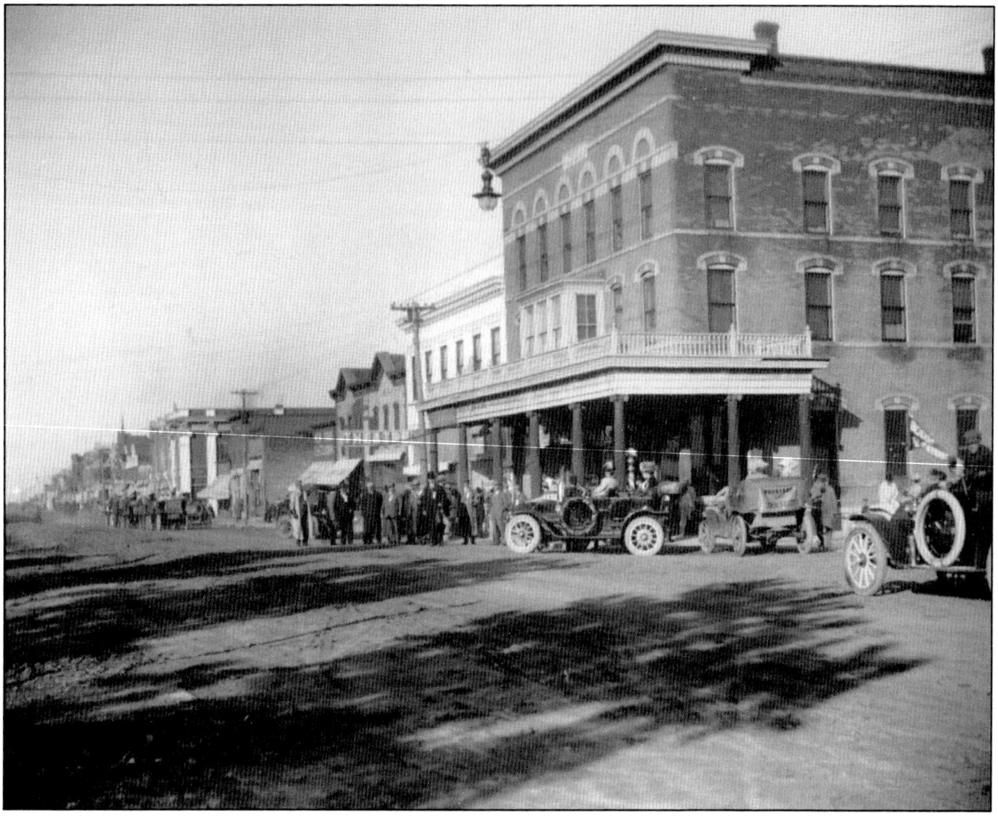

This photograph depicts the Glendive Booster Club going to a celebration in honor of the Lower Yellowstone Valley Irrigation Project water settlement on May 31, 1911.

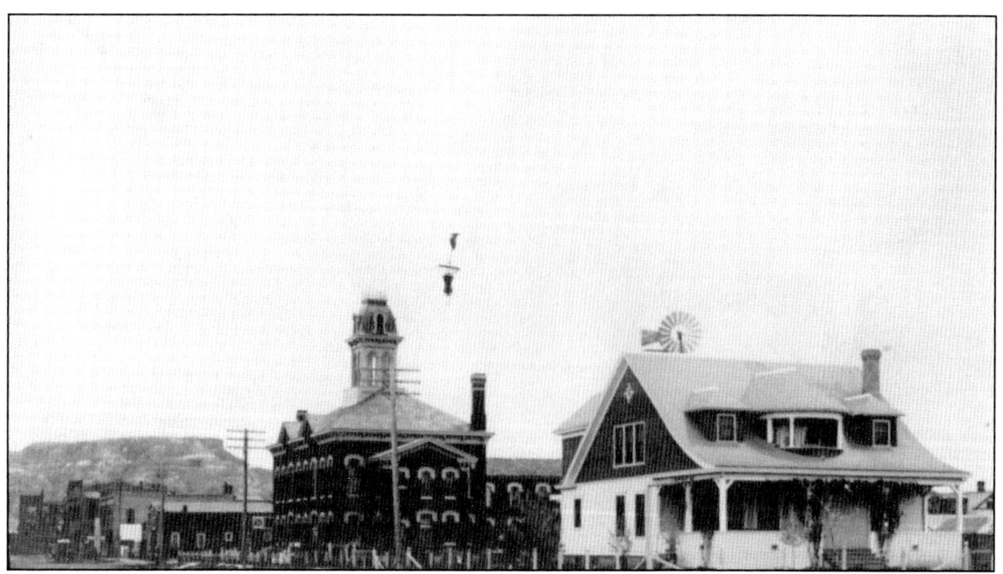

A view down Kendrick Avenue features the old courthouse in 1912.

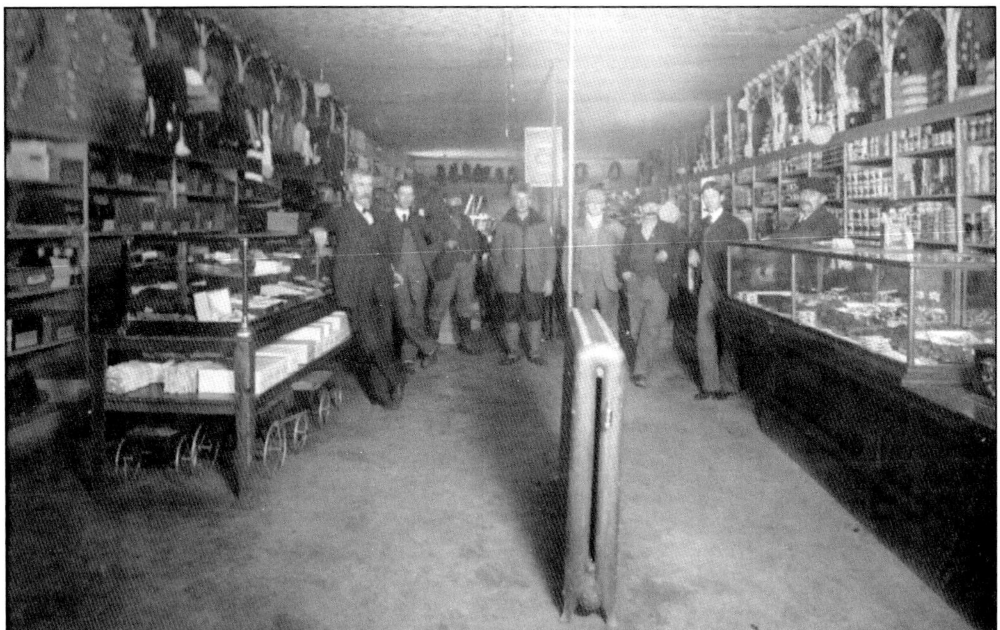

The interior of B.F. Dawson General Merchandise at 217 North Merrill Avenue is pictured in 1912. In addition to the general merchandise in the store, B.F. Dawson sold farm machinery and wagons.

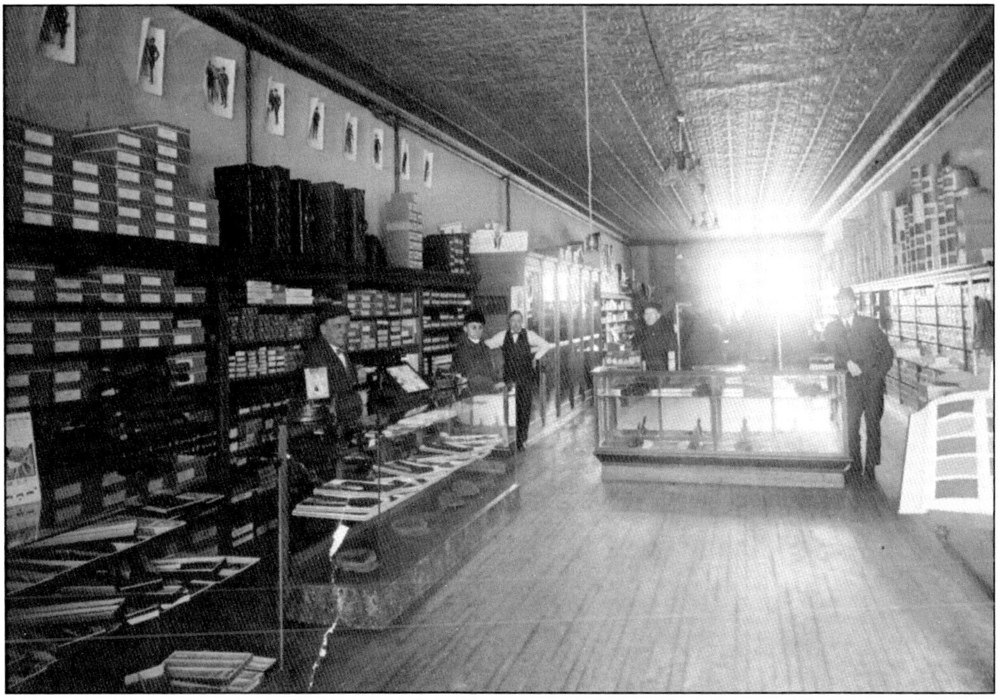

Owned by Einar Rivenes, the Toggery Men's Store was located at 204 South Merrill Avenue. This photograph shows the interior around 1912.

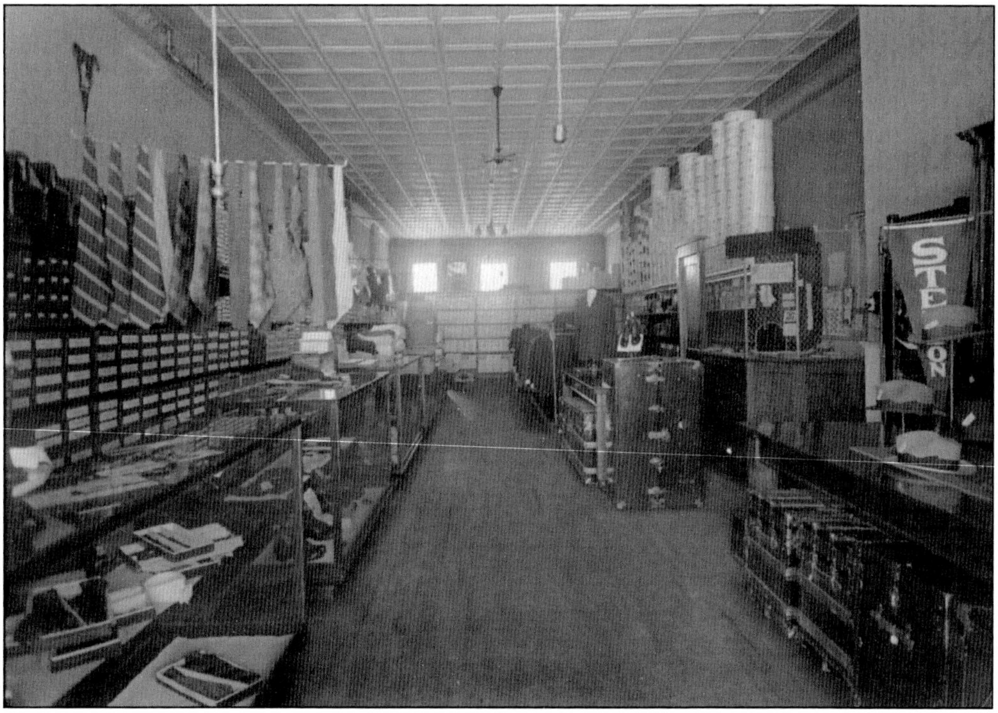

Here is a rare glimpse inside of the Hub, Tisdale & Andrews Clothing, in 1913. The Hub was a fine gentleman's clothier located at 201 South Merrill Avenue in the Henry Dion Building next to the Exchange State Bank.

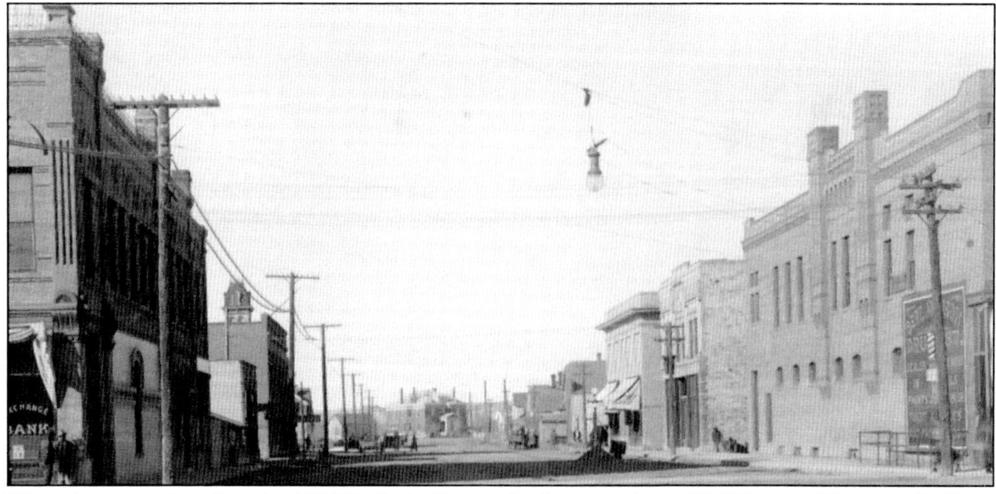

This photograph, taken in 1913 by L.A. Foster, looks west down Bell Street. The stately Krug Mansion is situated prominently at the end of the road.

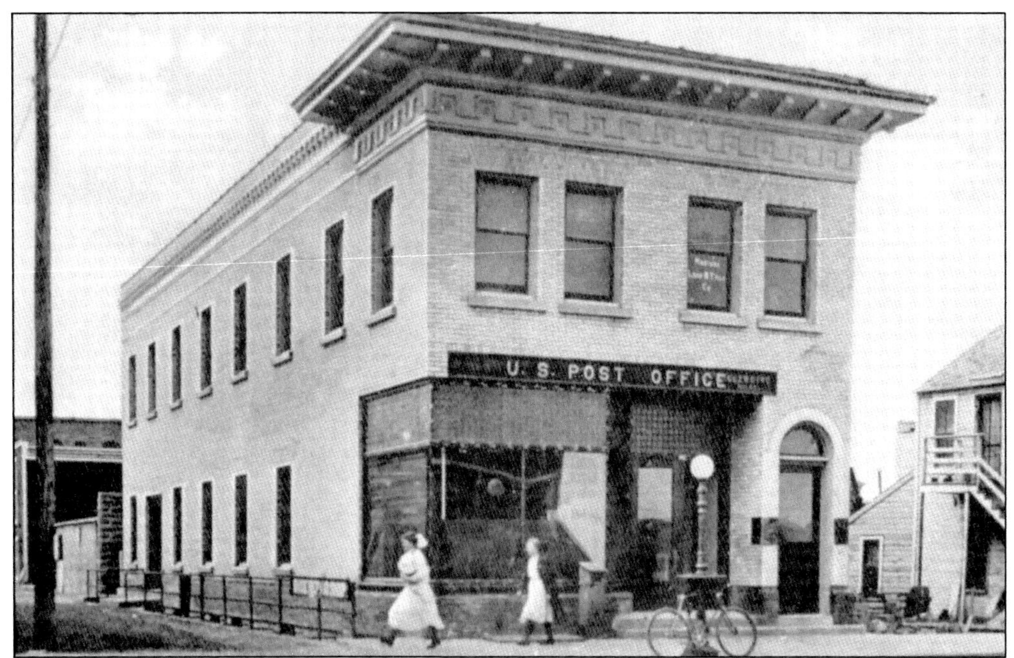

Glendive's first post office was a small wooden structure built in the early 1880s. By 1900, it became apparent that the original post office was inadequate for a town the size of Glendive. Constructed in 1913, the second post office in Glendive was a larger, more solidly built structure designed to handle a larger volume of mail. It was located at 113 West Towne Street.

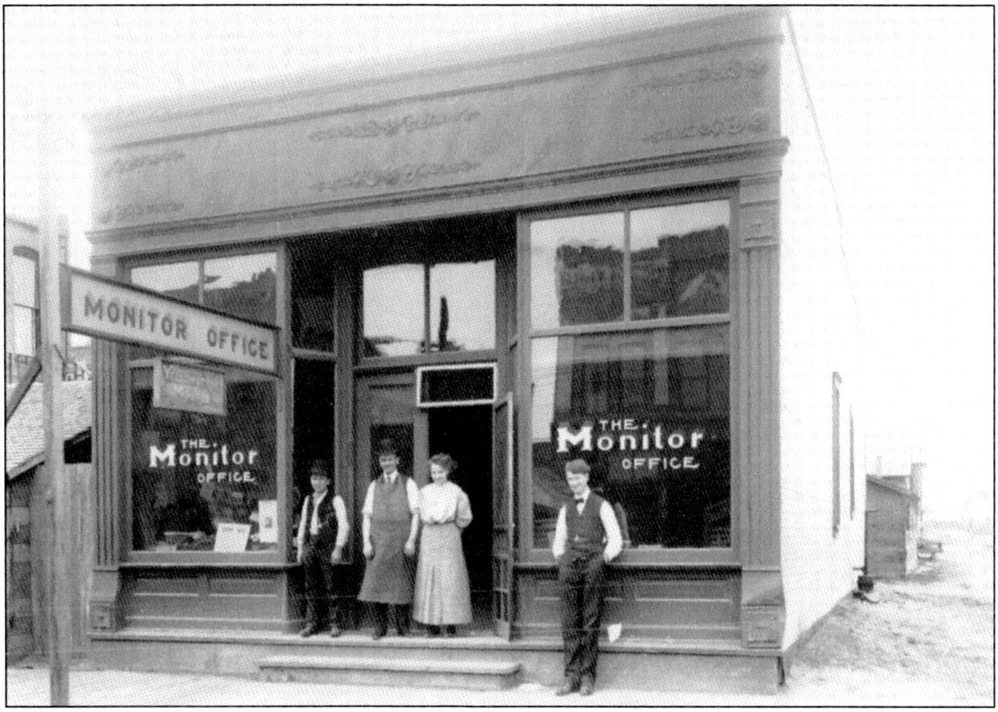

The *Yellowstone Monitor* newspaper office was located at 111 West Bell Street in 1913. Barely visible on display in the left window is a human skull. (Hoole Collection.)

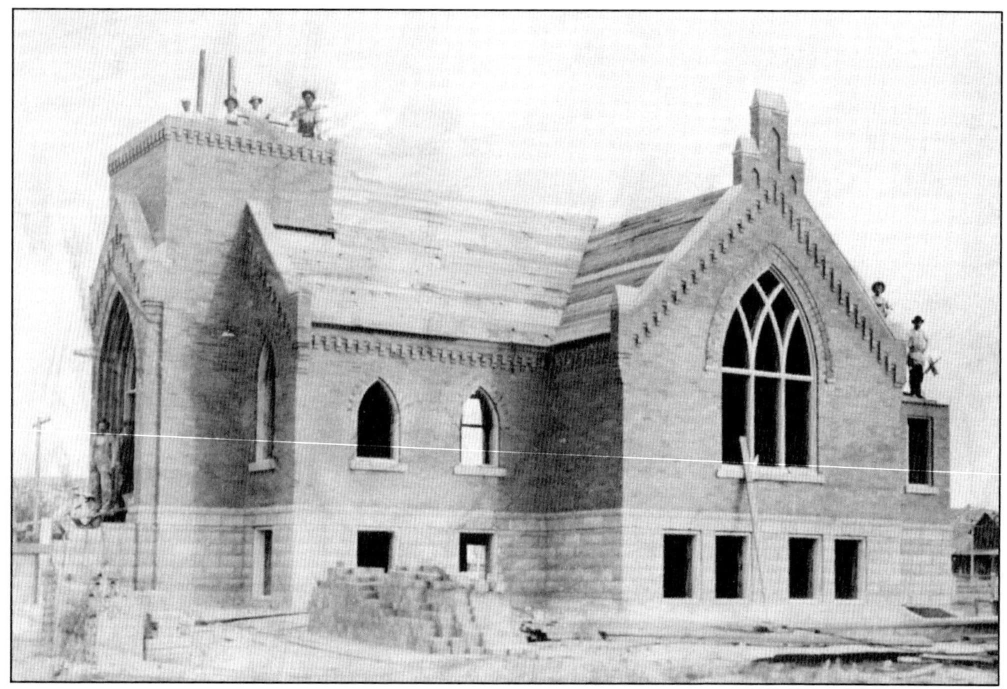

Religion has played a prominent role in the cultural fabric of Glendive since the early 20th century. Immigrants to the area often brought their native styles of worship with them. Pictured here is the Scandinavian Lutheran Church under construction in 1908. It later became home to the Church of Jesus Christ of Latter-day Saints in 1955 and United Pentecostal Church in 1979. Today, the structure is a private residence.

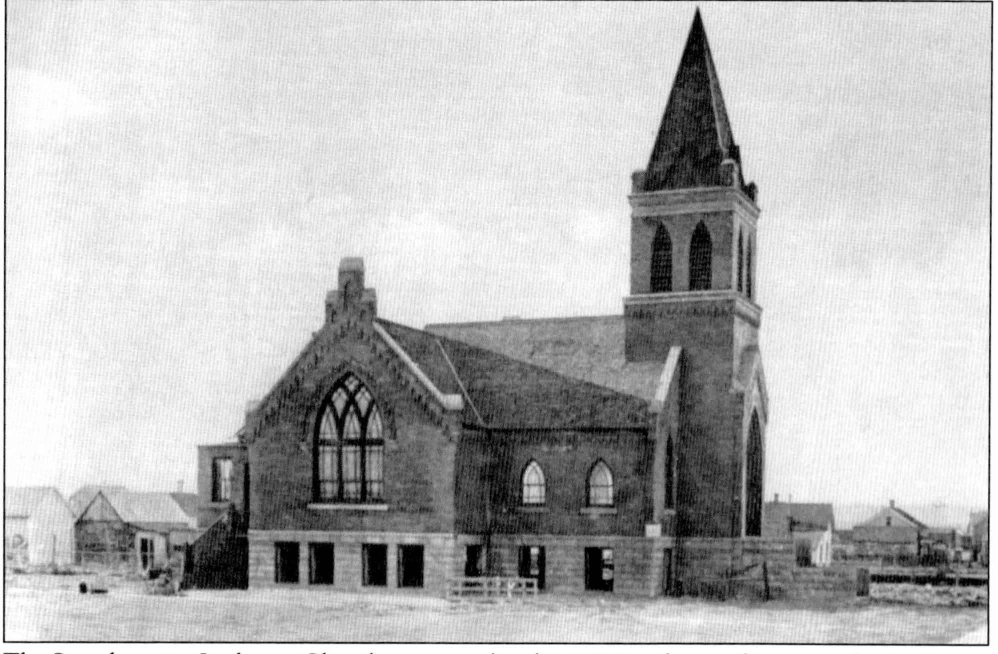

The Scandinavian Lutheran Church was completed in 1908 and was a fixture on the landscape of Glendive until 1955.

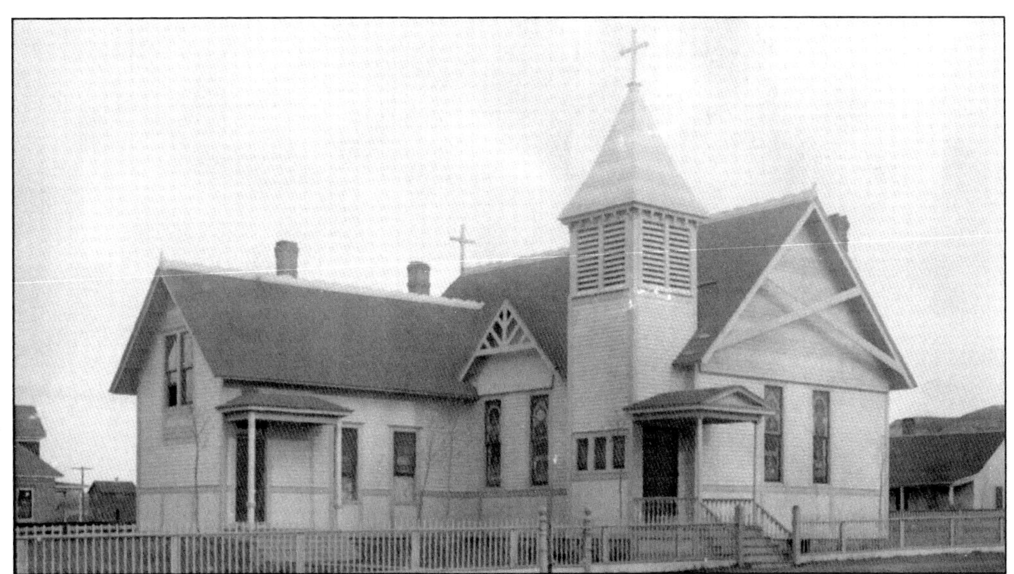

Roman Catholicism has long been the most popular faith in Montana. One of the earliest Roman Catholic congregations in Glendive was St. Juliana Catholic Church. This photograph shows the building in 1908.

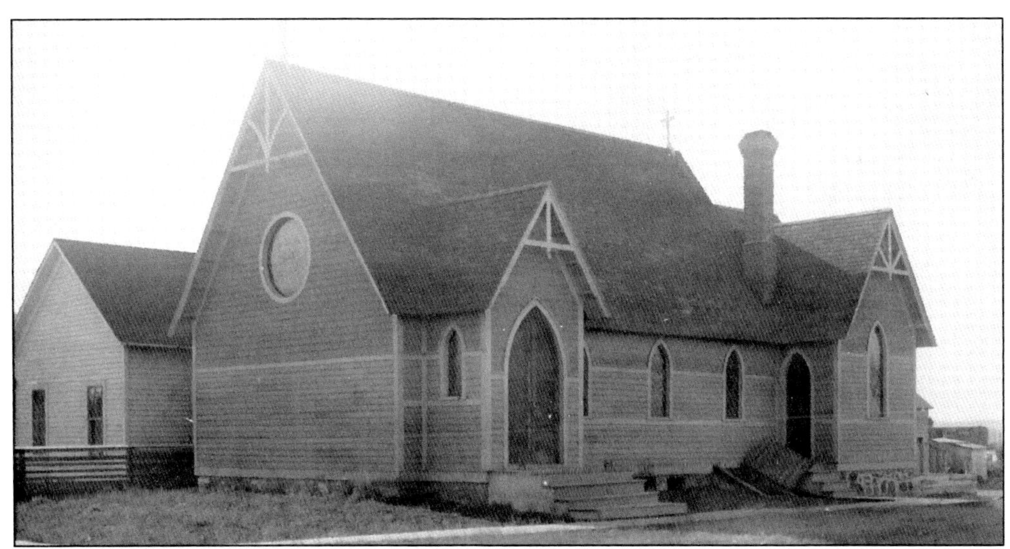

This photograph shows St. Matthews Episcopal Church in 1909. The church membership rolls indicate that there were 75 members of the congregation in 1909.

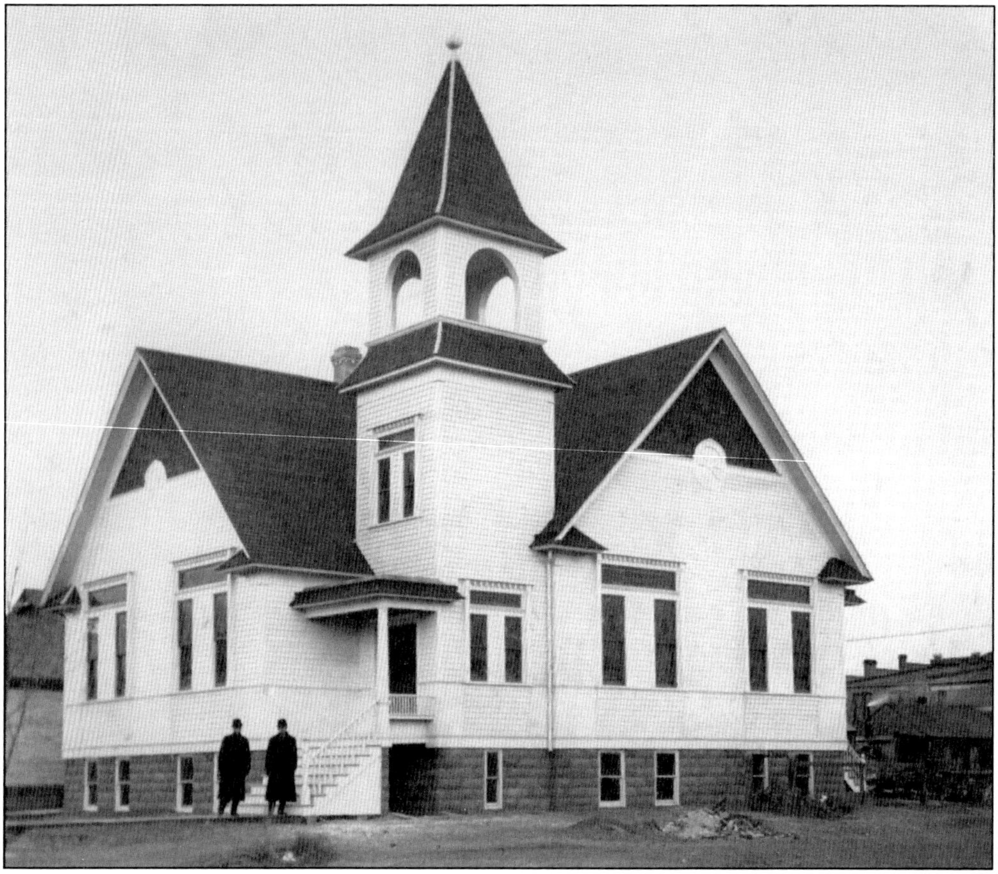

This photograph shows the Glendive Congregational Church at the beginning of the 20th century.

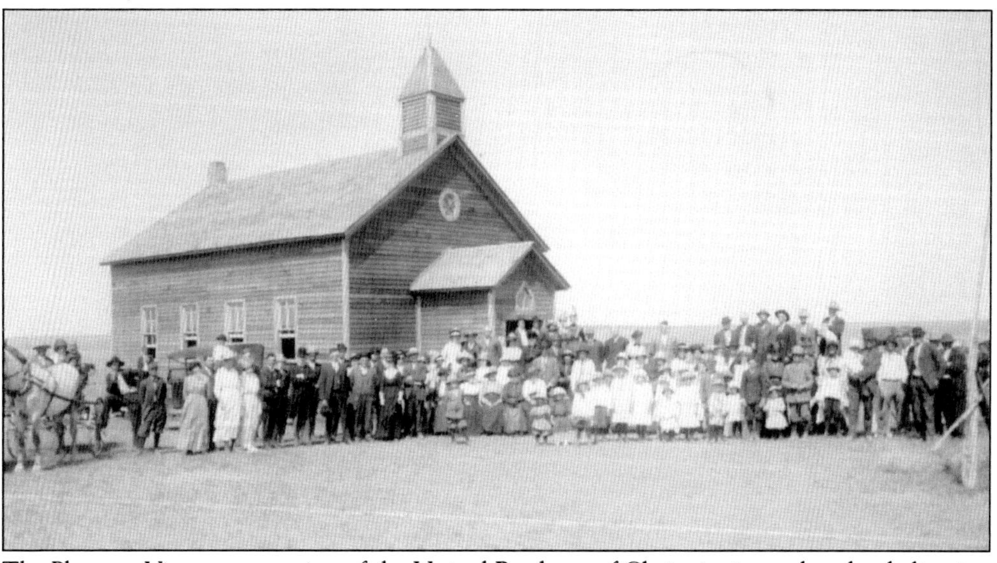

The Pleasant View congregation of the United Brethren of Christ is pictured at the dedication of their new church on May 13, 1914.

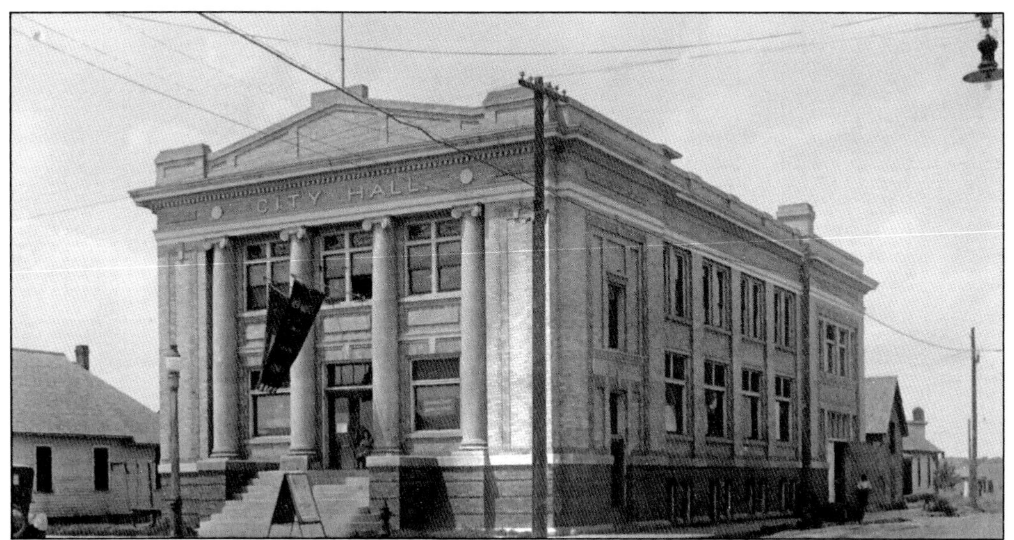

Constructed in 1914, the Neoclassical-style Glendive City Hall was designed by influential Miles City architect Brynulf Rivenes. (M.I. Hatch Collection.)

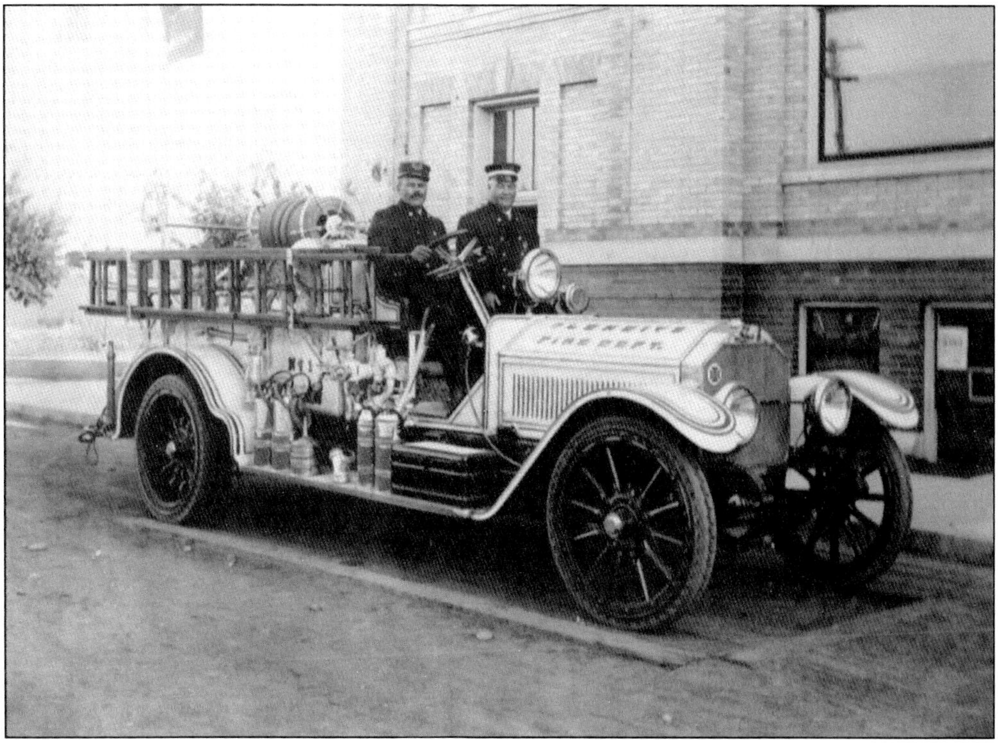

The Glendive City Fire Department was established in 1901. Prior to that time, Glendive relied on a volunteer force to fight fires. In this photograph, two firemen show off their shiny new American LaFrance fire truck parked next to city hall in 1916.

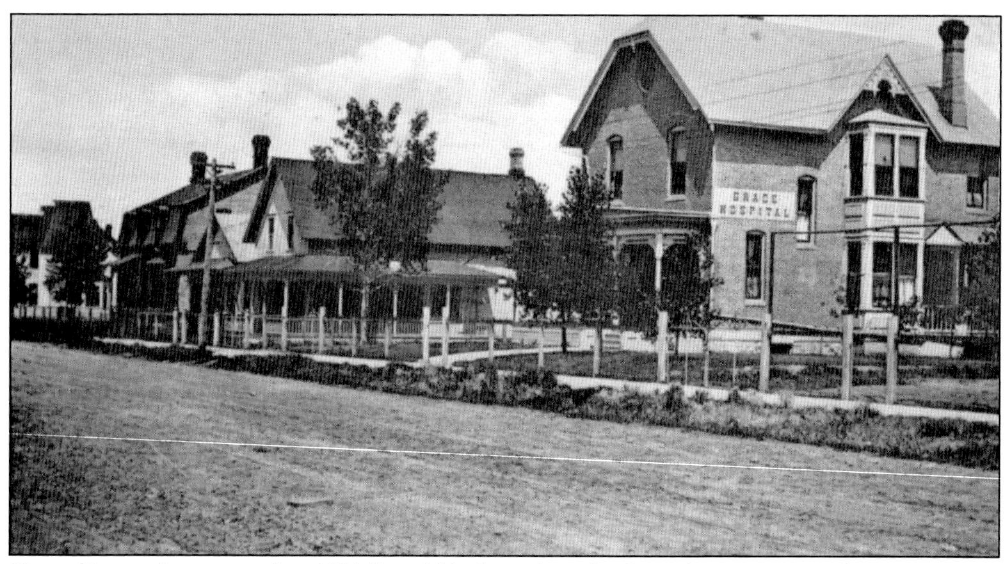

Grace Hospital is pictured in 1914. Local blacksmith and talented construction foreman Morris Cain built Grace Hospital in 1905.

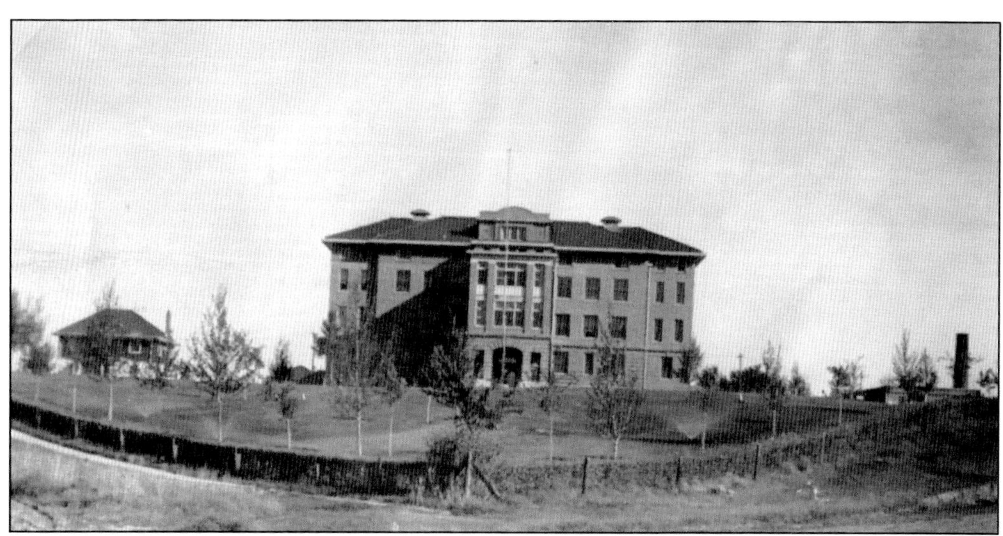

The Northern Pacific Beneficial Association financed the Northern Pacific Hospital in Glendive in 1913. Organized in 1882, the association provided medical, surgical, and hospital care for Northern Pacific employees with the creation of seven hospitals located in major railroad towns in Minnesota, Montana, and Washington.

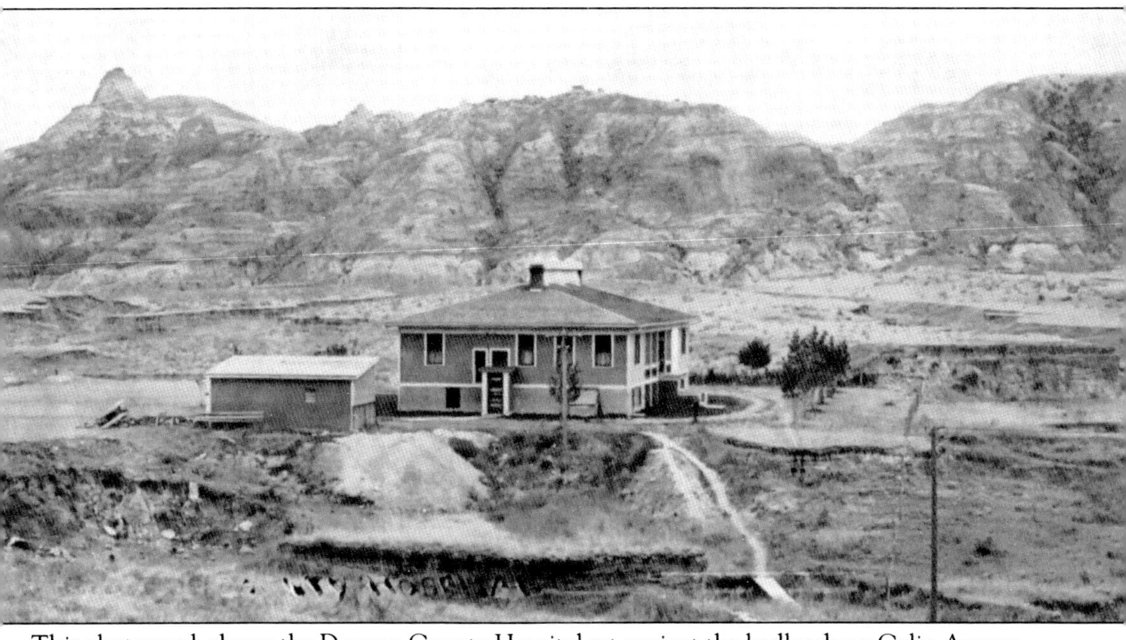

This photograph shows the Dawson County Hospital set against the badlands on Colin Avenue in 1925.

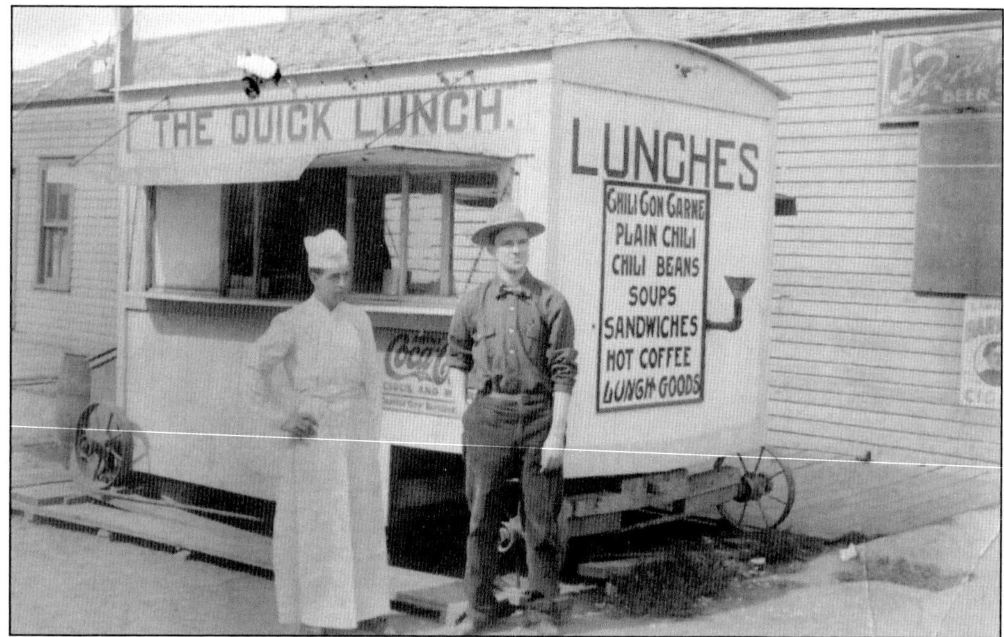

This photograph by L.A. Foster shows an early incarnation of the food truck. The Quick Lunch mainly catered to Northern Pacific employees and featured chili con carne, plain chili, chili beans, soups, sandwiches, coffee, and Coca-Cola.

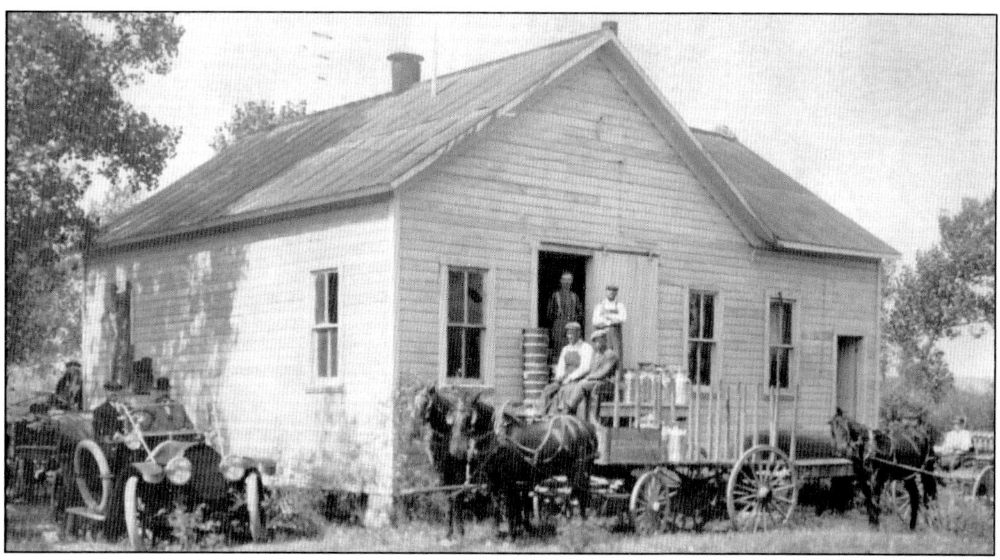

L.A. Foster snapped this photograph of workers at the Gate City Creamery just before a delivery run in 1915.

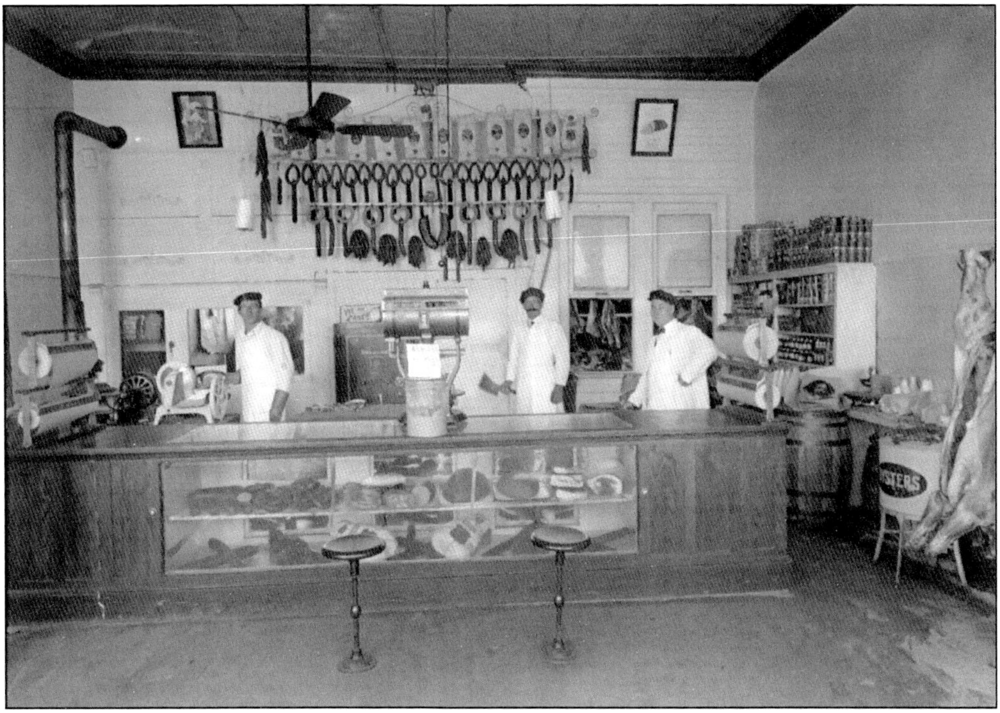

The interior of Schmidt's Butcher Shop is pictured in 1915. Schmidt's was one of several butcher shops in Glendive and was a local favorite until it closed in the 1940s.

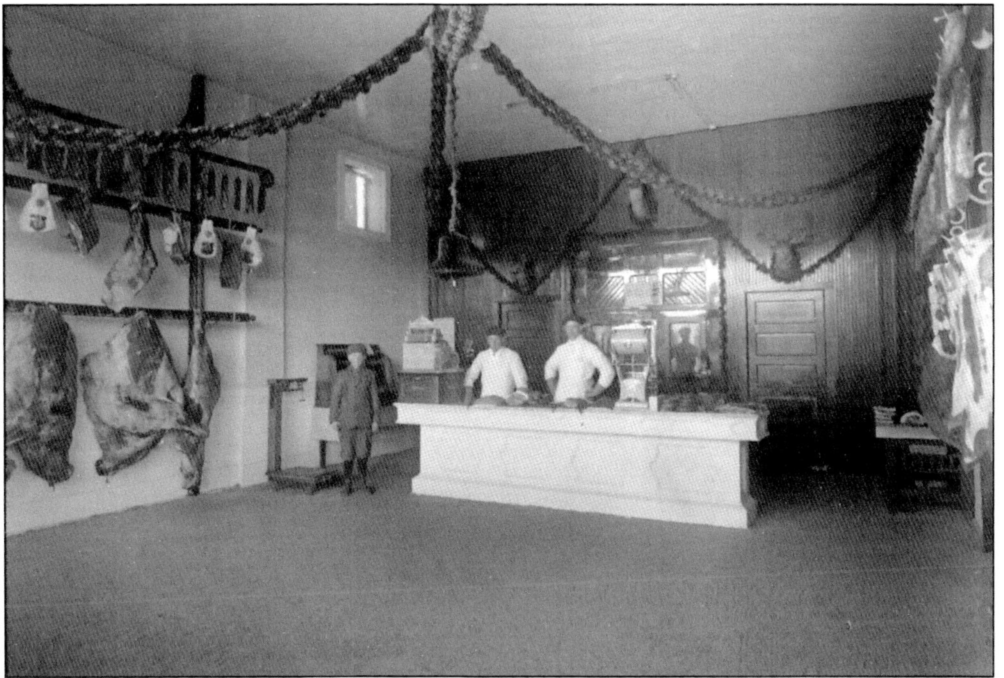

This photograph was taken inside Brinkman's Butcher Shop during the Christmas season. Decorative bunting and festive bells are pictured hanging from the ceiling above freshly raked sawdust on the floor.

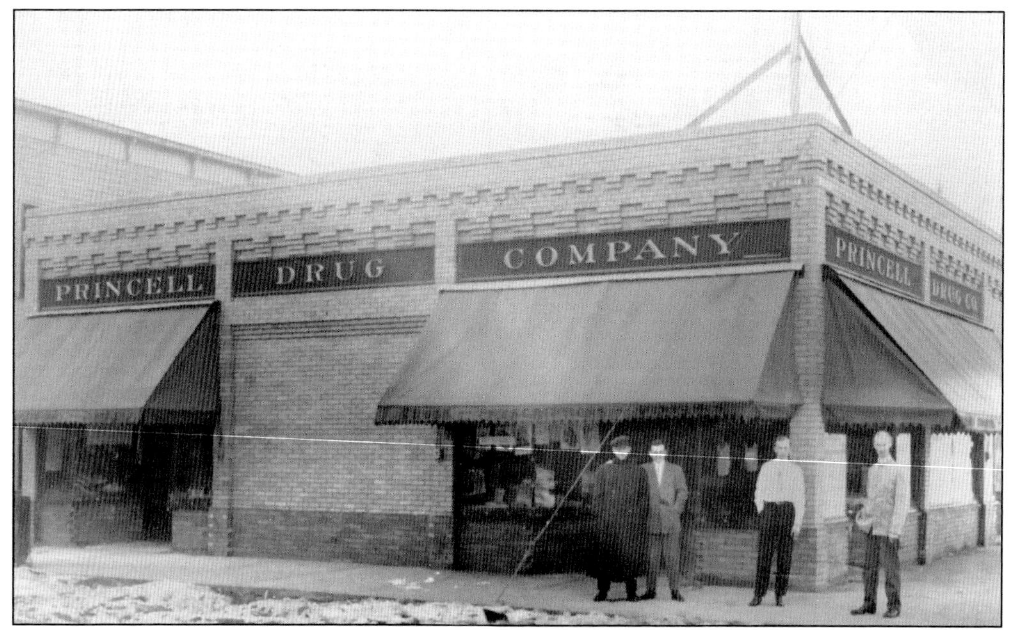

Here, the staff members of Princell Drug Company pose for a picture during the winter of 1916. Princell Drug Company was located at 301 North Merrill Avenue.

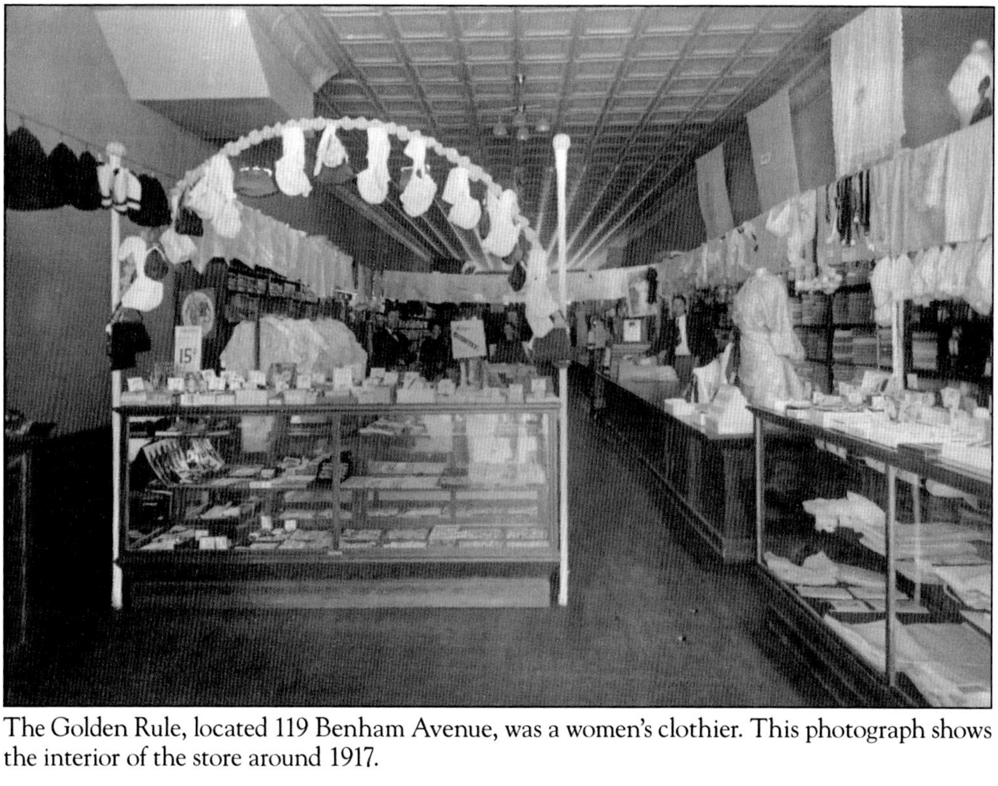

The Golden Rule, located 119 Benham Avenue, was a women's clothier. This photograph shows the interior of the store around 1917.

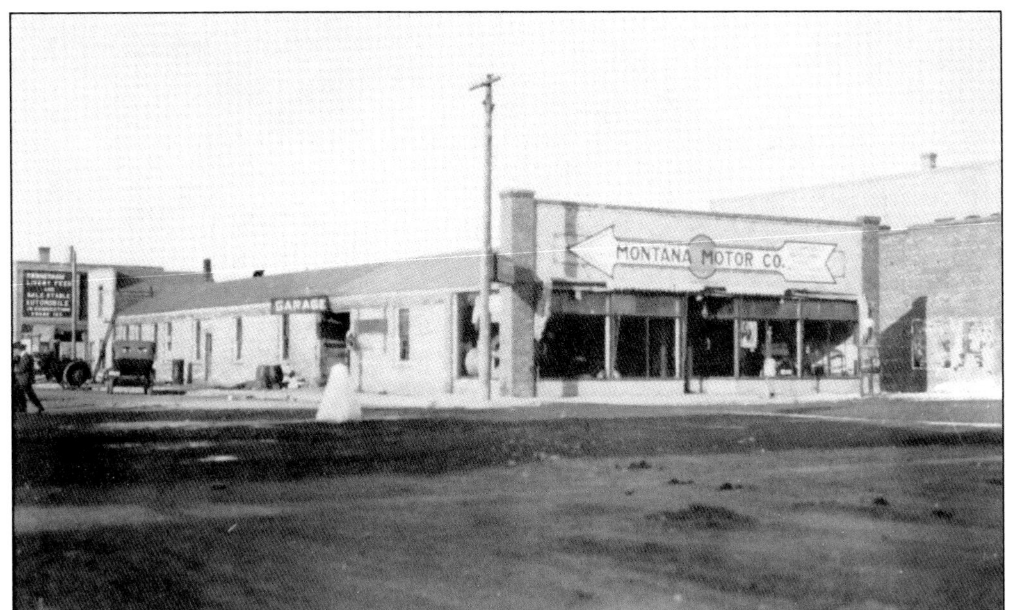

As elsewhere in America, the popularity of the automobile resulted in radical changes to the urban environment of Glendive. The Montana Motor Company, pictured here in 1915, provided Glendivians with an opportunity to get their cars serviced by trained professionals.

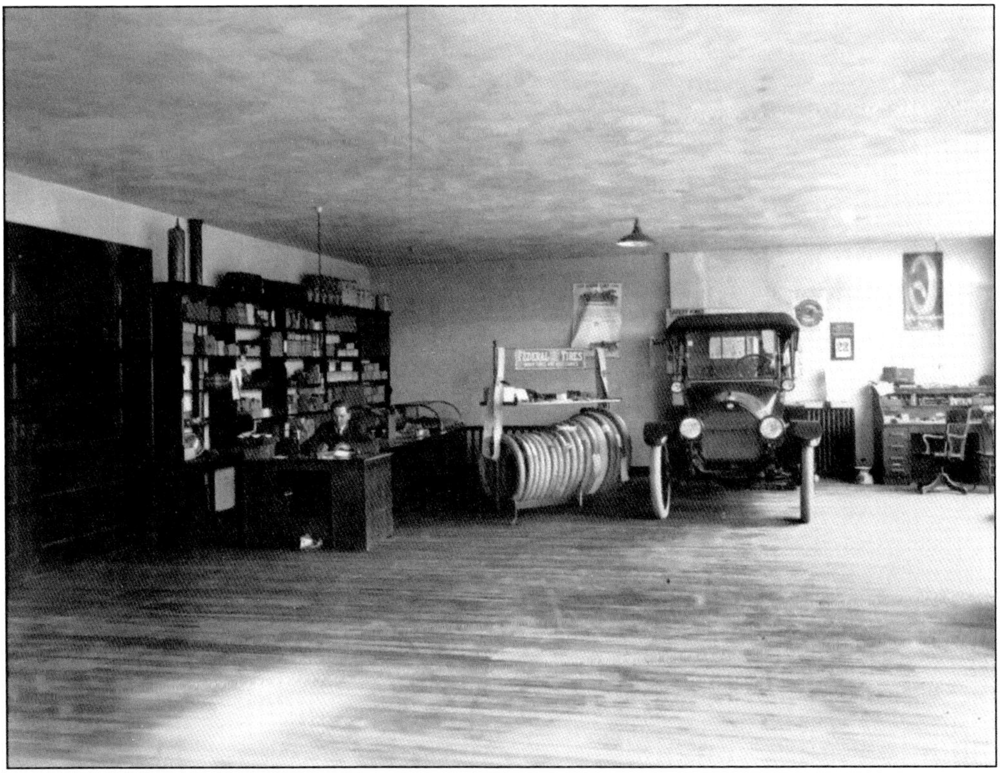

The interior of the Glendive Vulcanizing and Rubber Company is pictured around 1919.

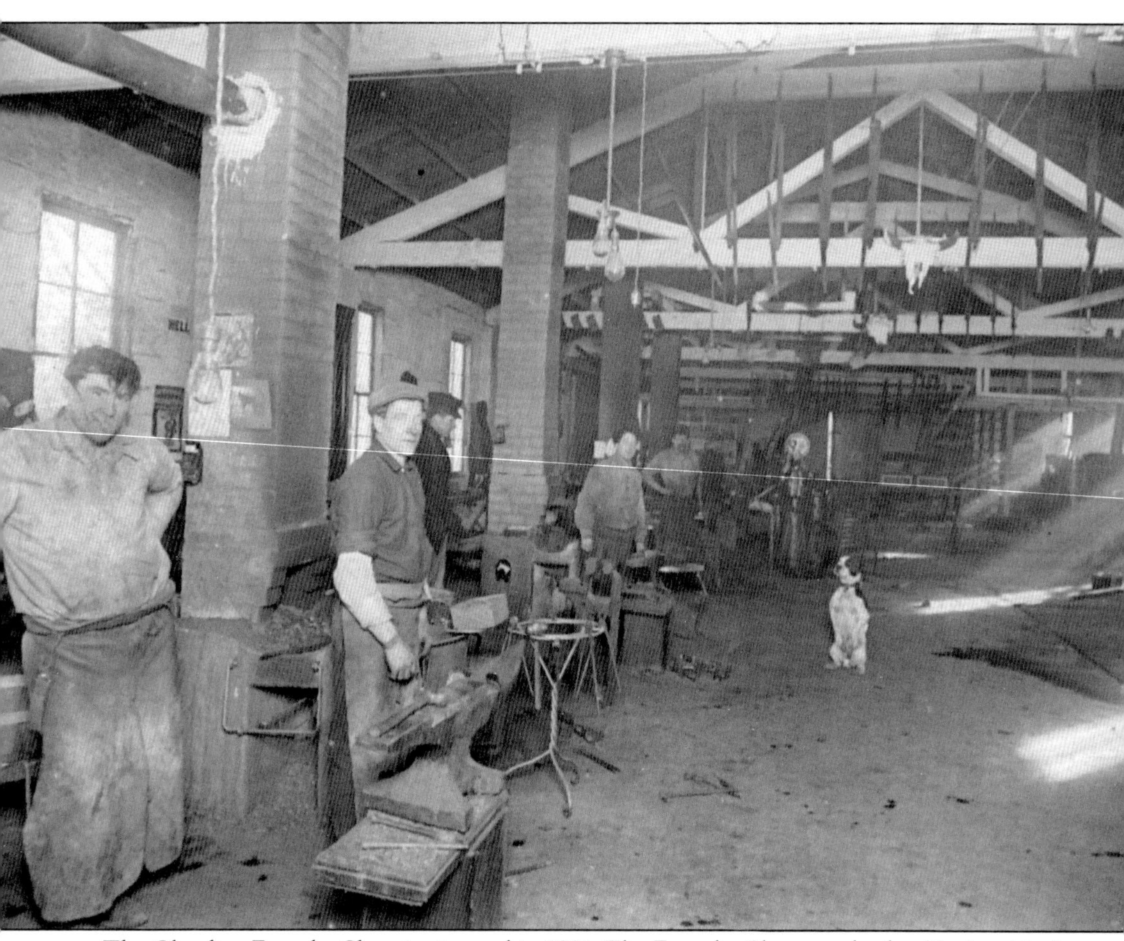

The Glendive Founder Shop is pictured in 1921. The Founder Shop was both a blacksmith shop and wagon repair shop. A dog poses on his hind legs for the picture.

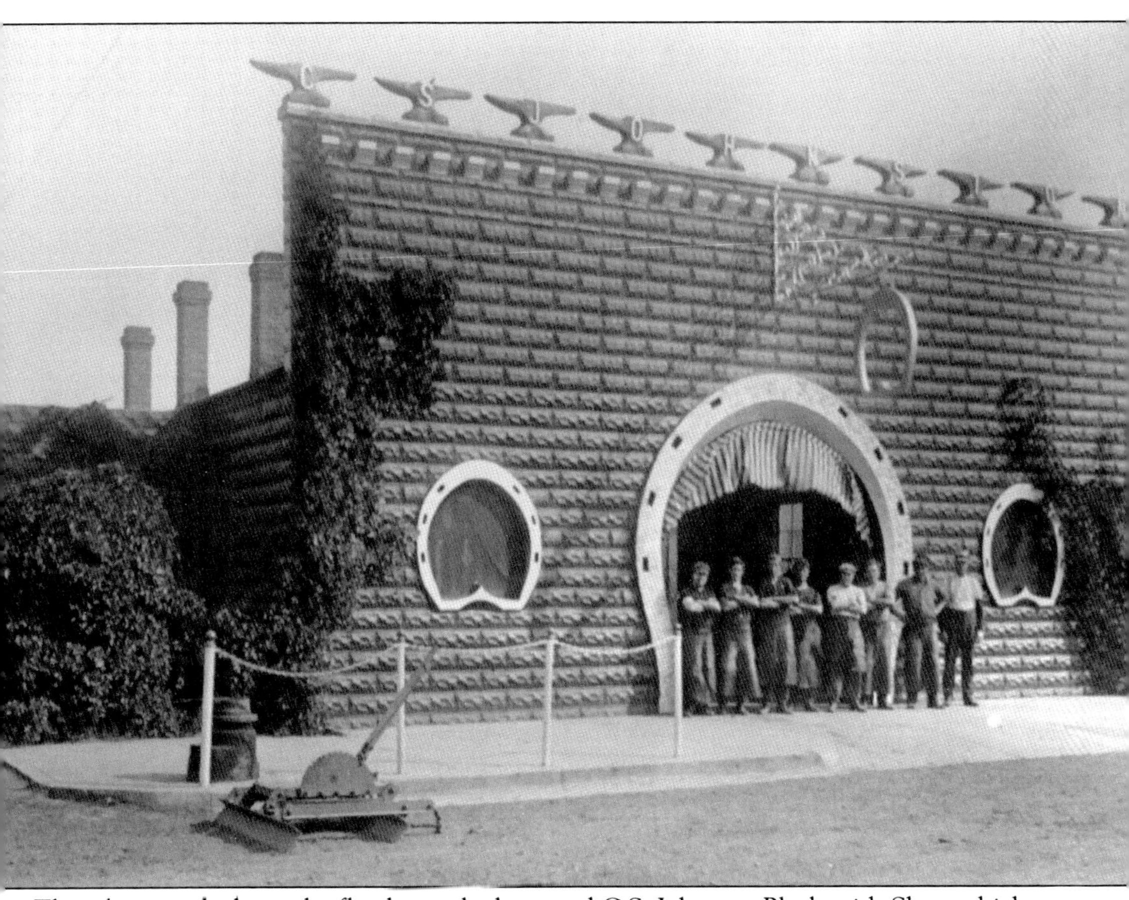

This photograph shows the flamboyantly decorated C.S. Johnston Blacksmith Shop, which was located at 115 South Kendrick Avenue. The window frames and entryway are shaped like horseshoes, and the business's sign on the top of the building is composed of multiple anvils. A pile of horseshoes on the left stands almost as high as the building.

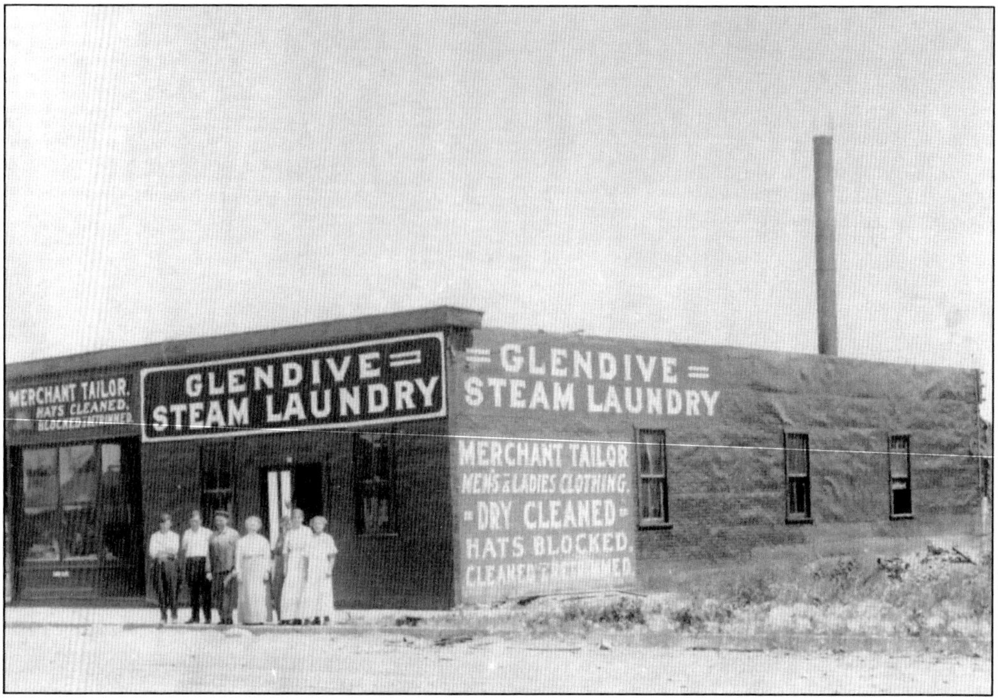

Single male Northern Pacific workers provided a solid clientele for the Glendive Steam Laundry in the early 20th century. Here, some of the laundry staff members pose for a picture outside of their workplace in 1917.

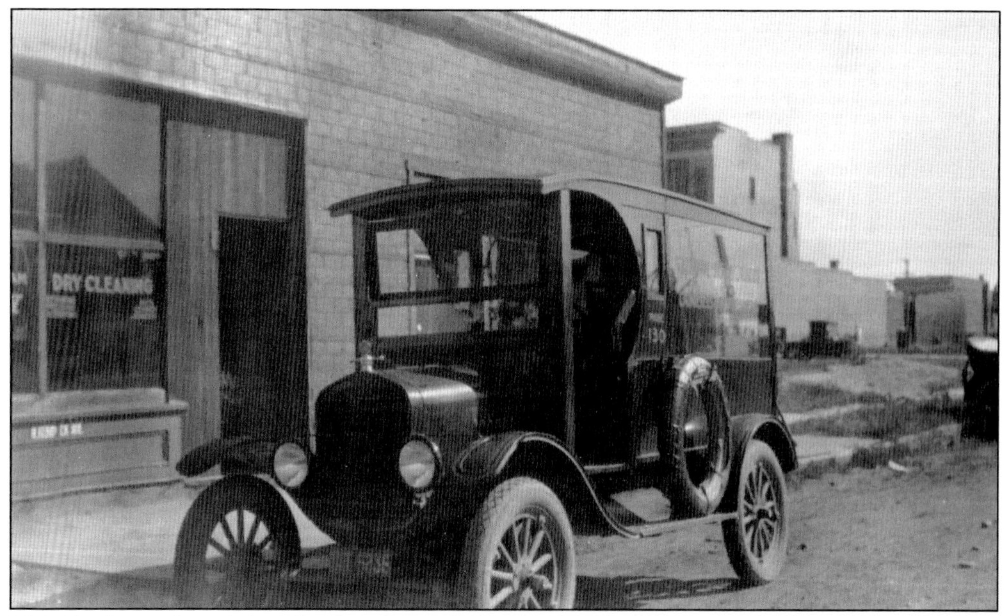

N.A. Healy purchased the Glendive Steam Laundry in 1907, and it stayed in business for the next 65 years. Pictured here is a Glendive Steam Laundry delivery truck around 1916.

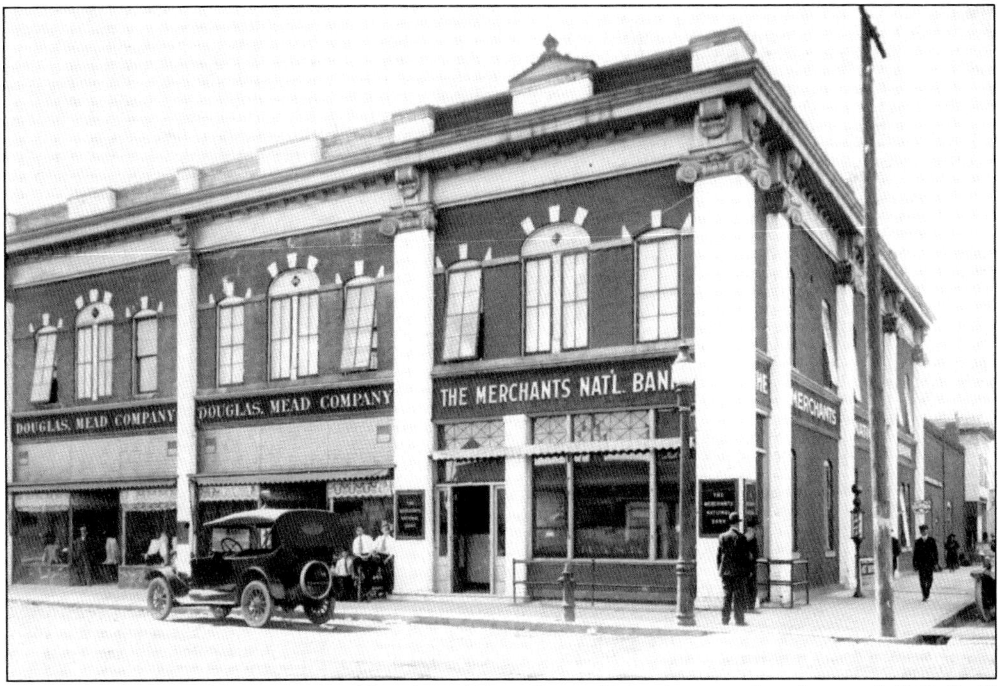

The facade of Merchants National Bank and Douglas and Mead was updated around 1920. Bold Corinthian columns, along with modern tile work and lettering, were designed to symbolize modernity and progress.

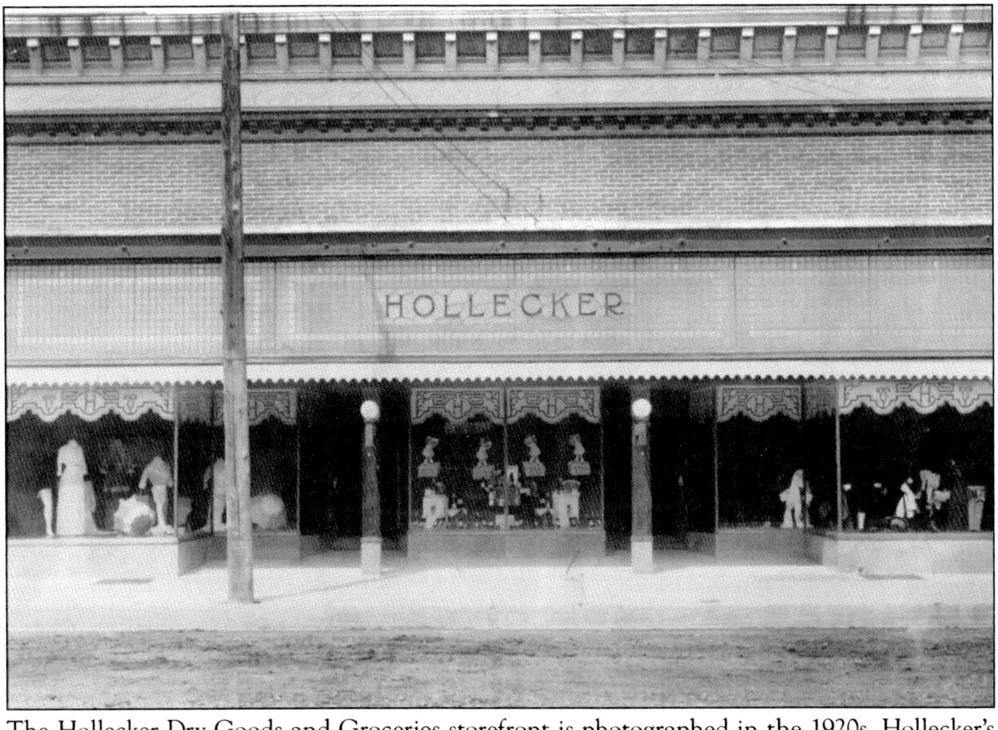

The Hollecker Dry Goods and Groceries storefront is photographed in the 1920s. Hollecker's store was located at 107 North Merrill Avenue.

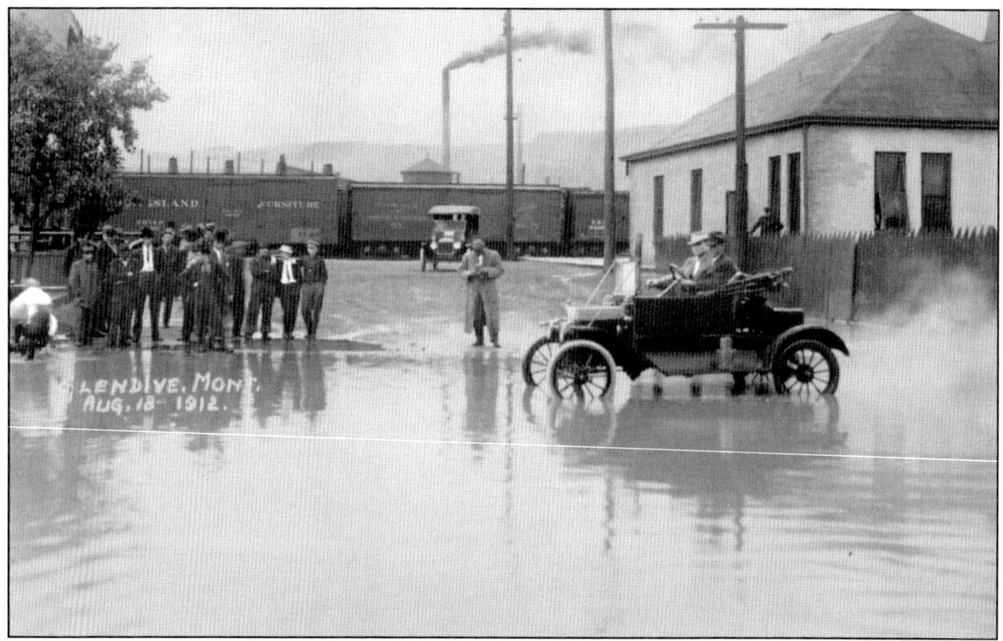

Prior to paved streets in Glendive, heavy summer rains often caused considerable flooding and damage to the roads. This was the case on Merrill Avenue on August 18, 1912, as these two photographs reveal. (Betty Lou T.H. Anderson Collection.)

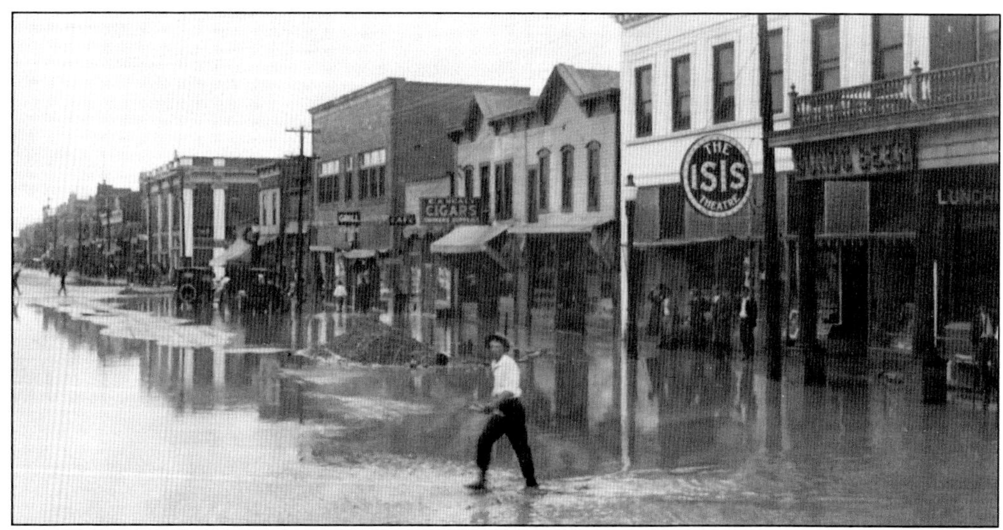

Eastern Montana is a land of extreme weather. Here, Merrill Avenue is a flooded, muddy mess after a summer thunderstorm in 1916.

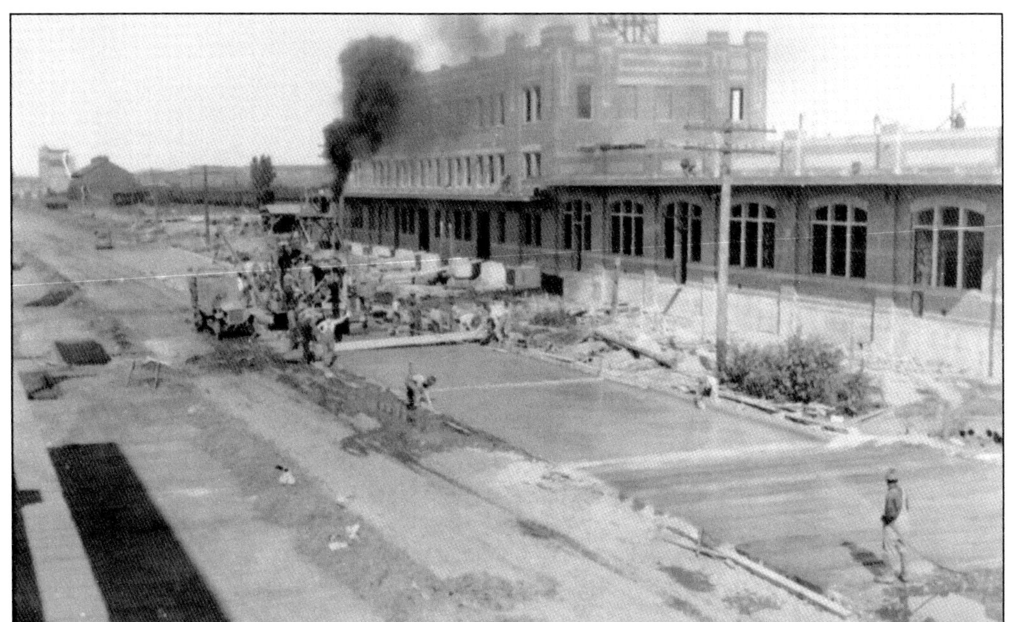

As more Glendivians acquired automobiles, there came a need for improved roadways. This photograph shows the paving of Merrill Avenue in front of the Northern Pacific Passenger Depot in 1922.

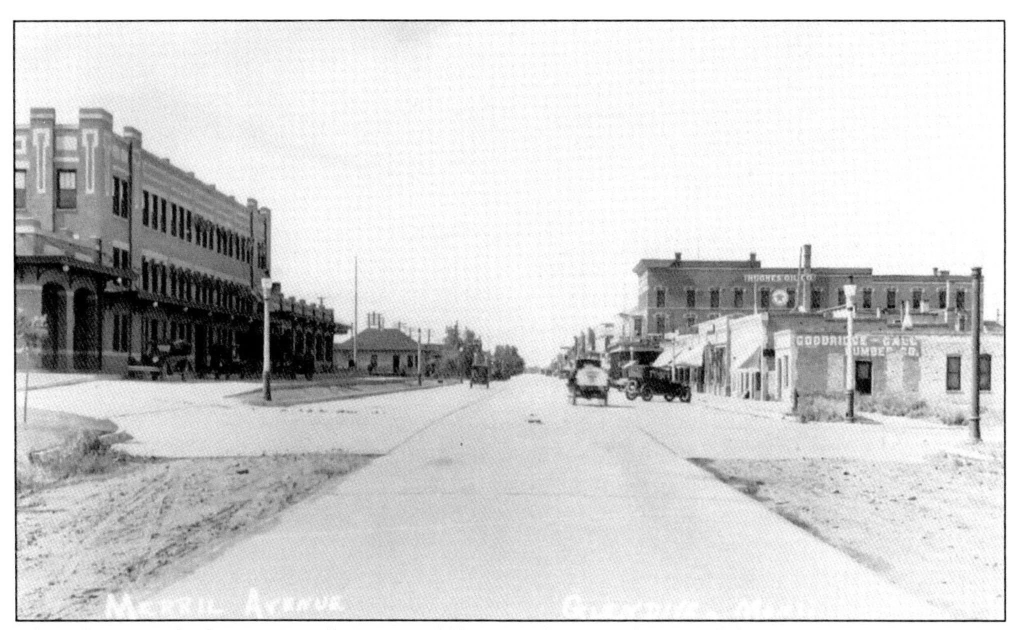

This photograph shows Merrill Avenue following the completion of the paving project in 1922.

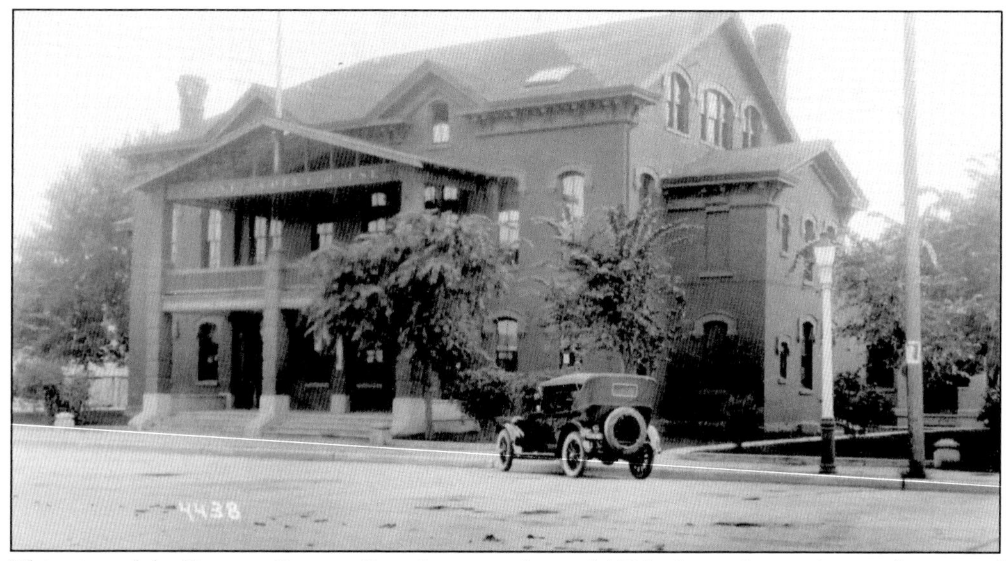

This view of the Dawson County Courthouse in the mid-1920s shows the newly paved streets of Glendive. The tower that topped the courthouse in decades past was removed.

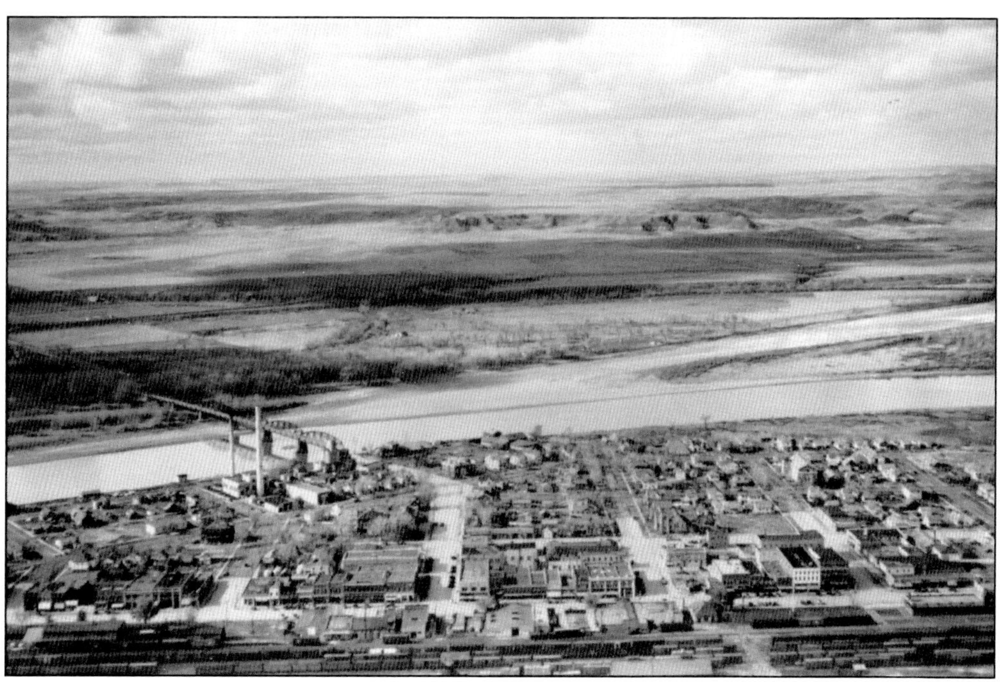
This aerial photograph taken in 1930 shows the contrast between the highly developed east bank of the Yellowstone River and still rural west bank.

Three

The Enlarged Homestead Act and Dry Farming

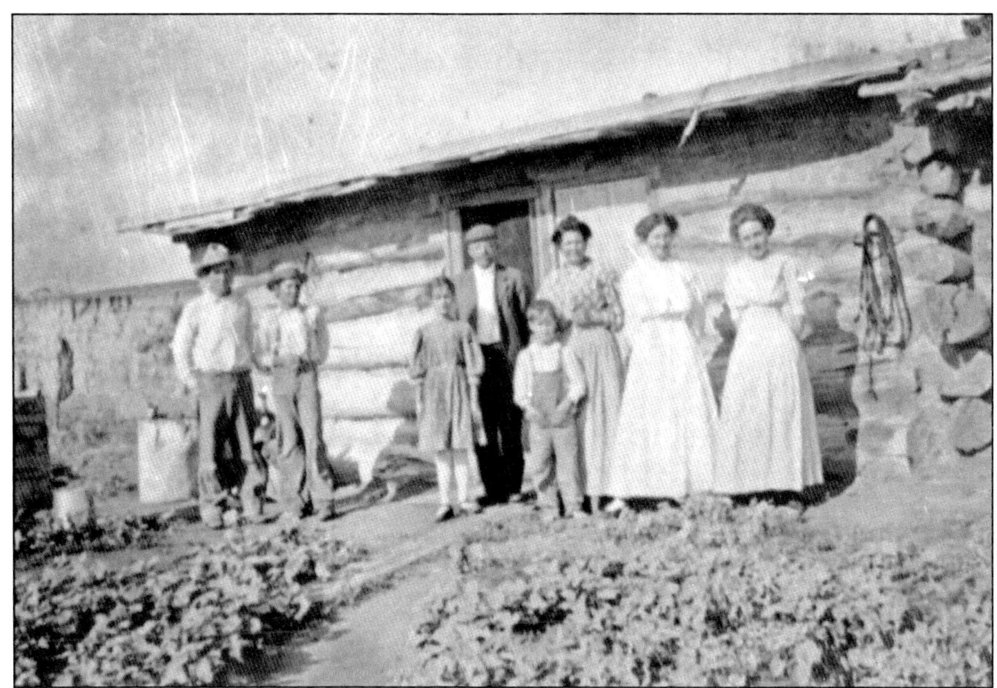

This photograph shows the Arnold and Amy Griffin homestead in 1883. Arnold and Amy Griffin arrived in Glendive in 1881 to homestead, and Arnold worked for the Northern Pacific Railroad. He is credited with helping to build many early roads in the Glendive area. (Griffin Family Collection.)

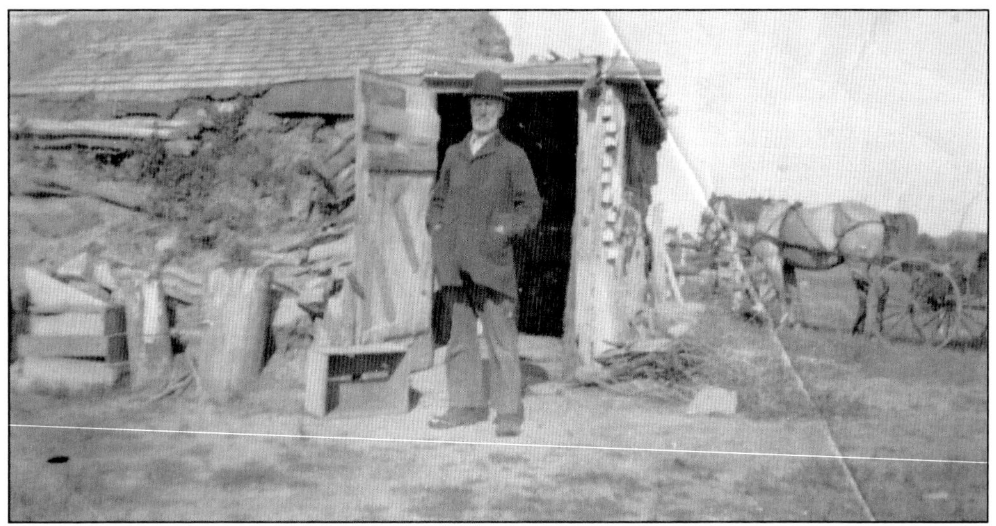

Early homestead cabins in the Montana Badlands, such as this one owned by J. Haggerty, were usually very primitive structures built of a combination of wood, mud, sod, and, eventually, tarpaper.

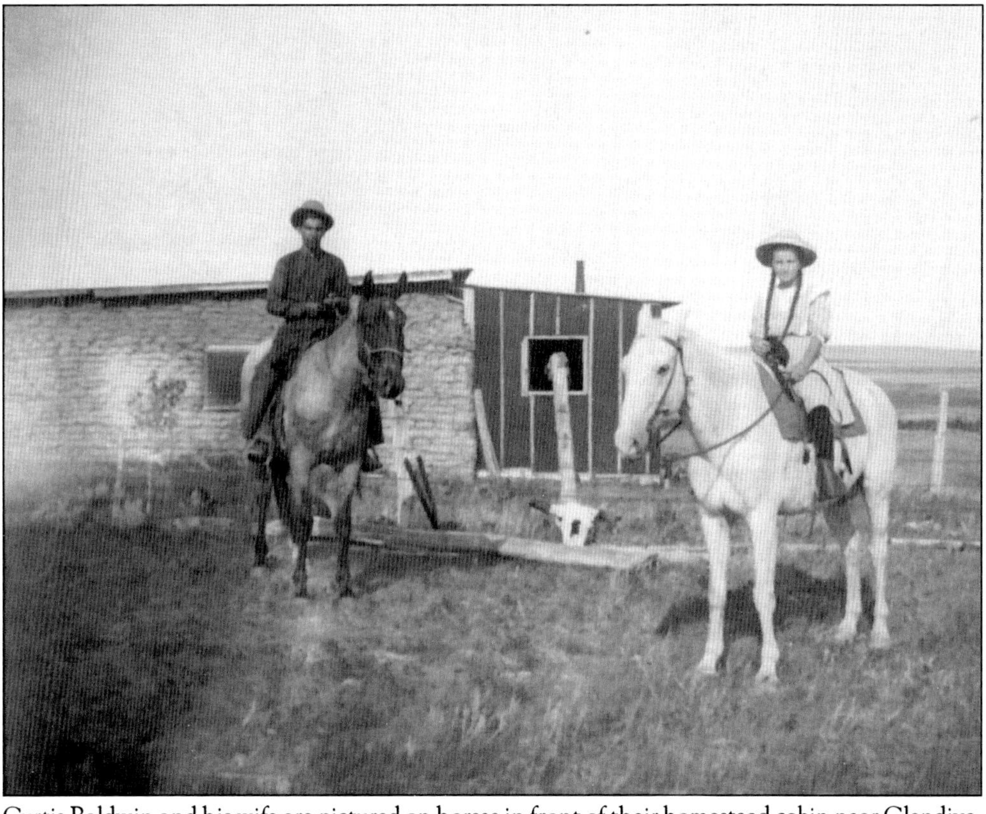

Curtis Baldwin and his wife are pictured on horses in front of their homestead cabin near Glendive. The cabin was initially constructed with sod, but they later built an addition made of tarpaper. (Charles and William Kelly Banker Collection.)

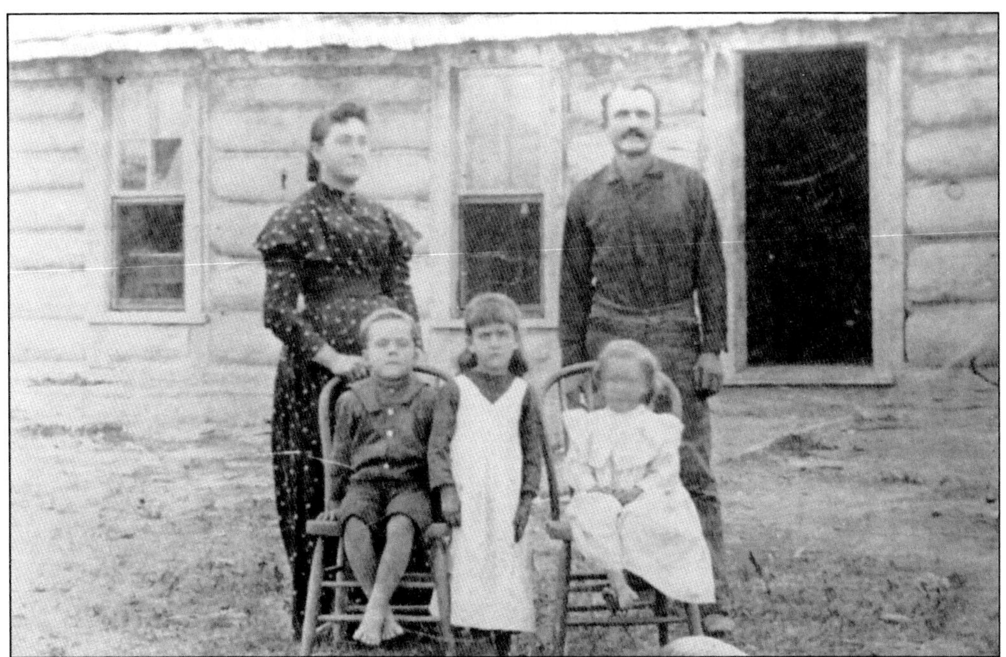

Nora Sartin and Charlie Stielie are pictured here with their children Charlie Jr., Aileen, and Alice in front of their homestead cabin near Glendive around 1900.

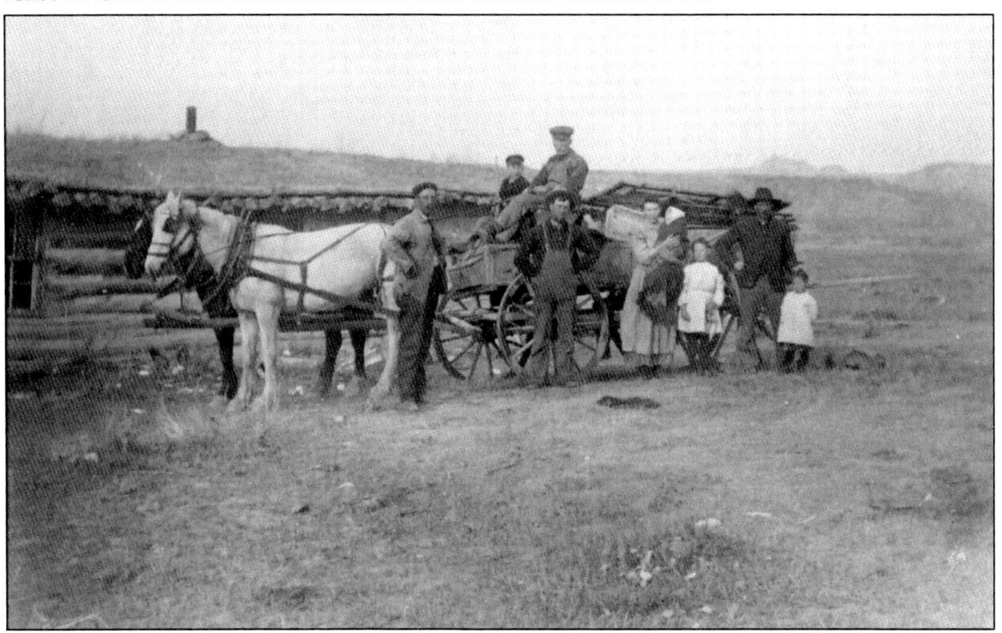

The Enlarged Homestead Act of 1909, along with an aggressive advertising campaign by the Northern Pacific Railroad to lure homesteaders to the region, attracted many Americans and Europeans alike. This photograph taken by Earl Sanford shows the Montana homestead of German immigrants Adolphus and Margaret Kent. Their homestead was located on Lower Seven Mile Creek. Here, they are preparing for a trip into Glendive for supplies in 1910. From right to left are Eivind Kalberg, Walter Reinart, Margaret Kent (holding Eve Kent), Hazel Kent, Adolphus Kent, and Maude Kent.

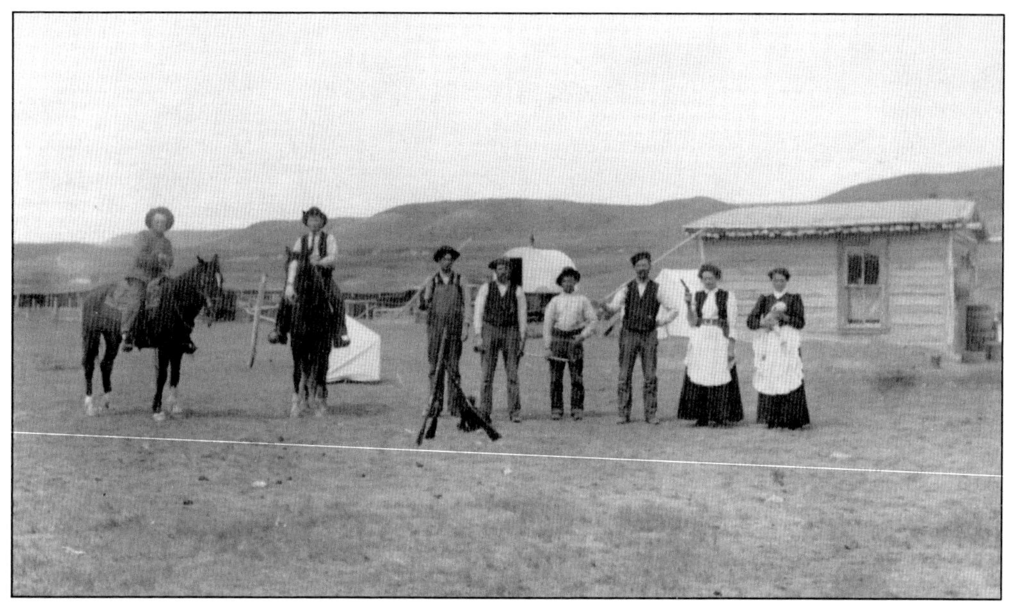

This photograph is of the Sven and Lisa Oftedal homestead on Whoopup Creek in 1909. The Oftedals were Norwegian immigrants from Stavanger, Norway, who migrated to the United States in 1892. They moved the Glendive area in 1895, after farming in Minnesota for two years. The Oftedals raised sheep and often hired newly arrived Norwegian immigrants as ranch hands. From left to right are Tom Dahl, Christ Vaule, Abel Kyllingstad, Haus Oftedal, Andy Highland, Sven Oftedal, Lisa Oftedal (holding pistol), and Ingra Oftedal (holding lamb).

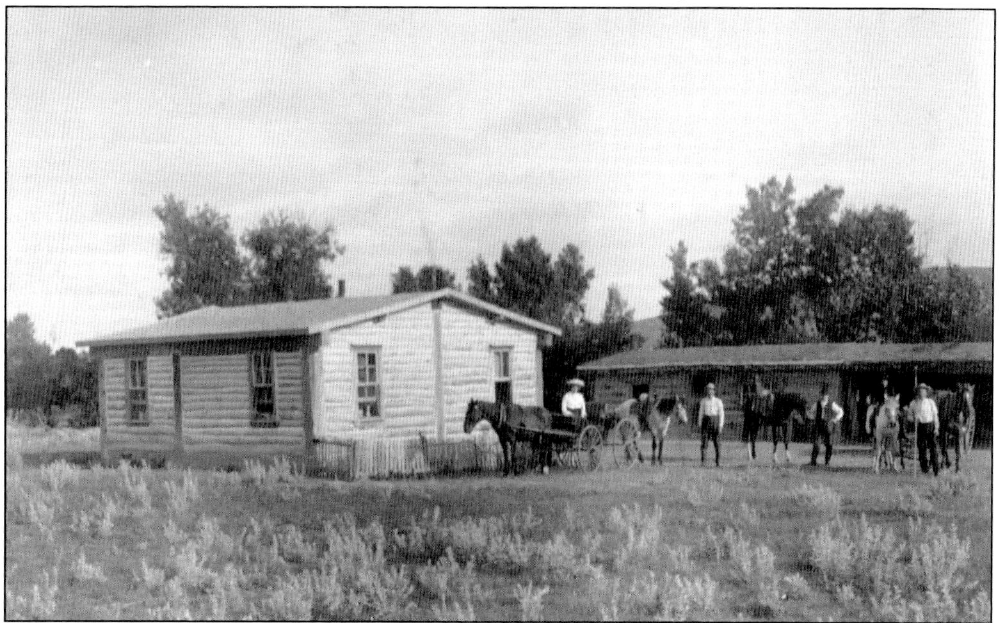

A considerable number of Scandinavian immigrants made their way to Glendive to homestead during the early 1900s. In 1913, 228 individuals became citizens of the United States in Dawson County, and over half of them were Scandinavian. The cultural impact of Scandinavians, like the Oftedal family, is still felt in the region today. This photograph shows the Oftedals at their homestead on Whoopup Creek.

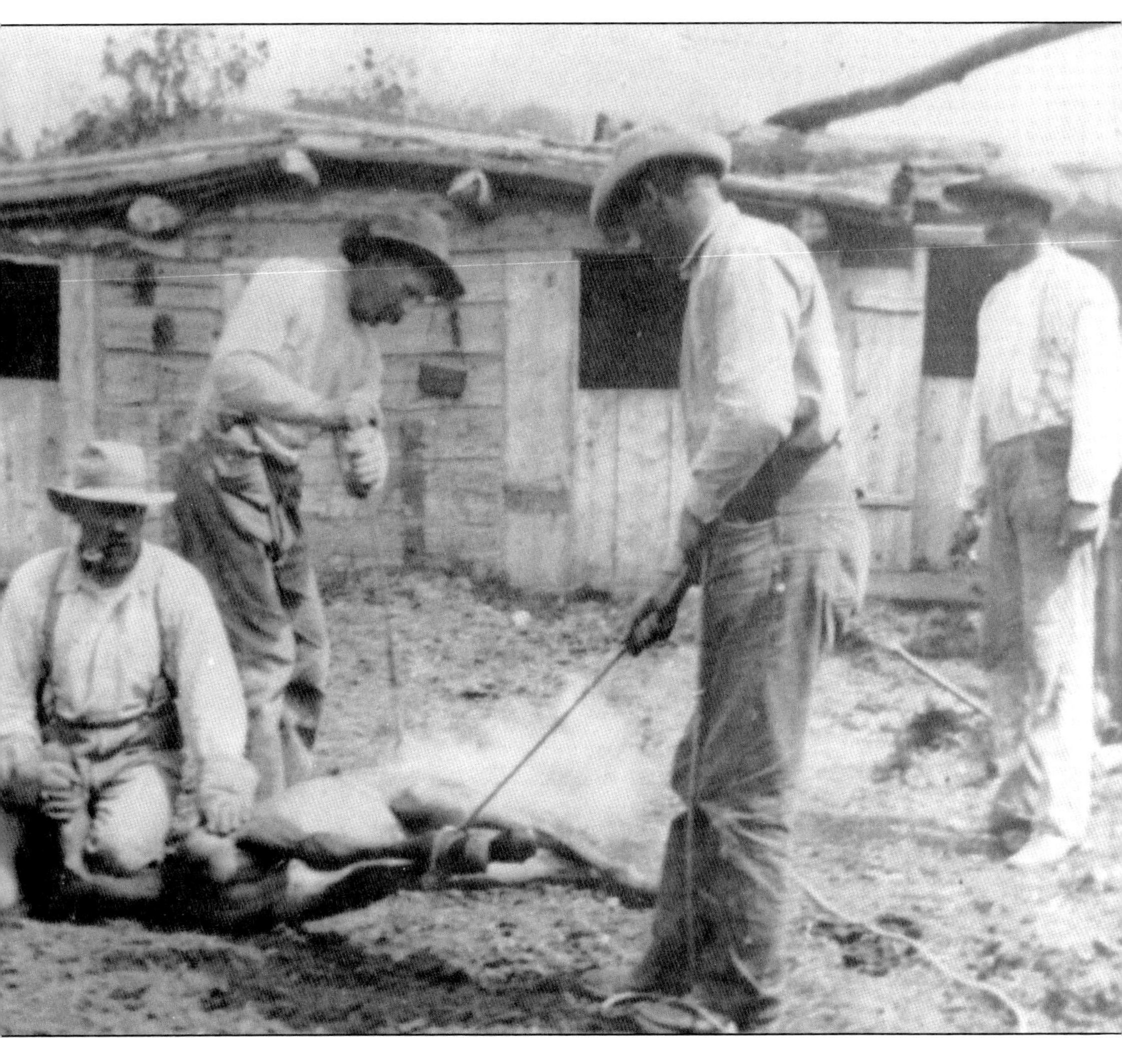

In this photograph, colts are being branded at Sven Oftedal's homestead. In eastern Montana, "branding" constitutes a season. Spring brandings are communal events, where local farmers, ranchers, neighbors, and friends gather at a given ranch to help with the process of branding calves and colts. These temporary cowboys and ranch hands are paid in food that is prepared by the ranch wives. Here, Hans Oftedal is pictured holding down a colt, while Sven Oftedal does the branding. The technique used in this photograph has changed very little.

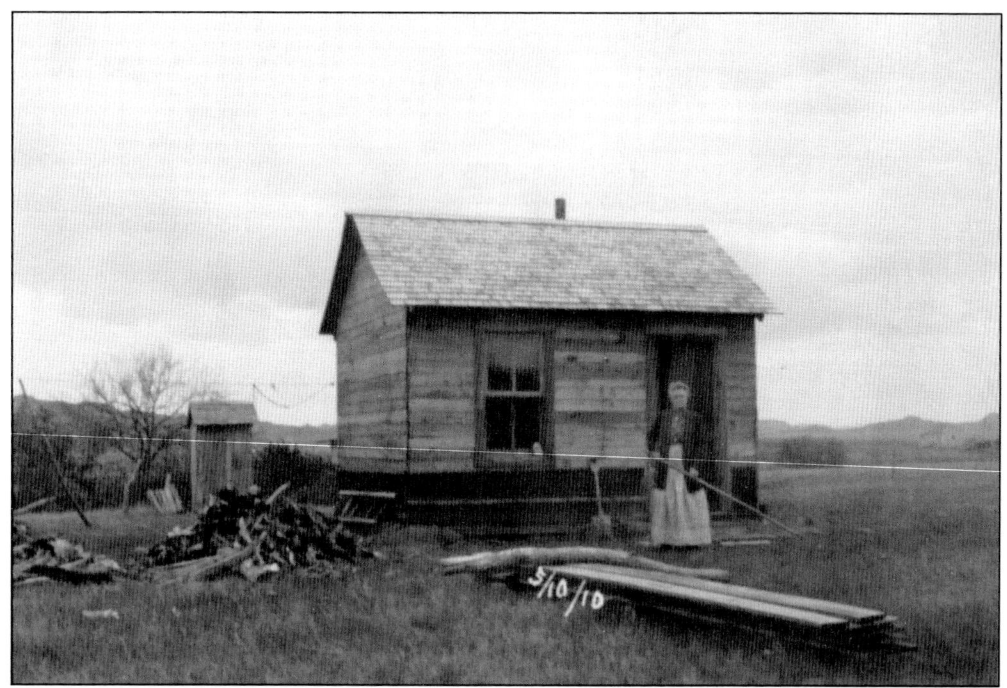

The Sanford family took advantage of the opportunity to homestead in Dawson County during the Enlarged Homestead Act period. Earle Sanford's wife is pictured in front of their cabin in March 1910. (Earle Sanford Collection.)

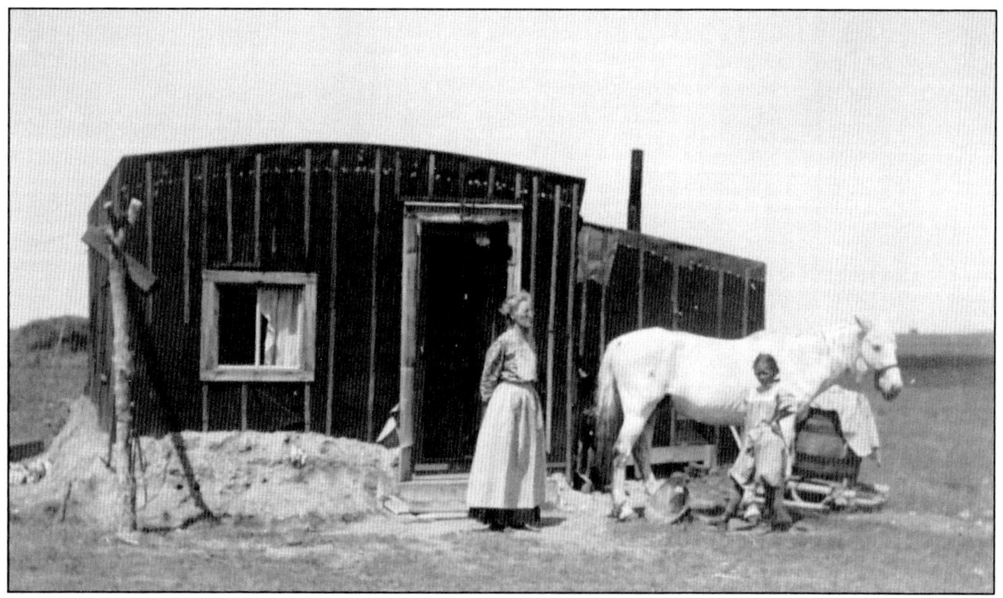

Homesteading on the northern plains in the early 1900s was extremely difficult because of the harsh and unpredictable climate. Mostly passed over by earlier trappers and gold prospectors, the dryland frontier of the Northern Plains was considered by most to be worthless for agriculture. This photograph shows the Ed Smith homestead, located just northeast of Bloomfield. Mrs. Smith stands stoically with her daughter outside of their primitive tarpaper shack. This simple photograph illustrates the difficulty of everyday life on the dryland frontier. (Earl Sanford Collection.)

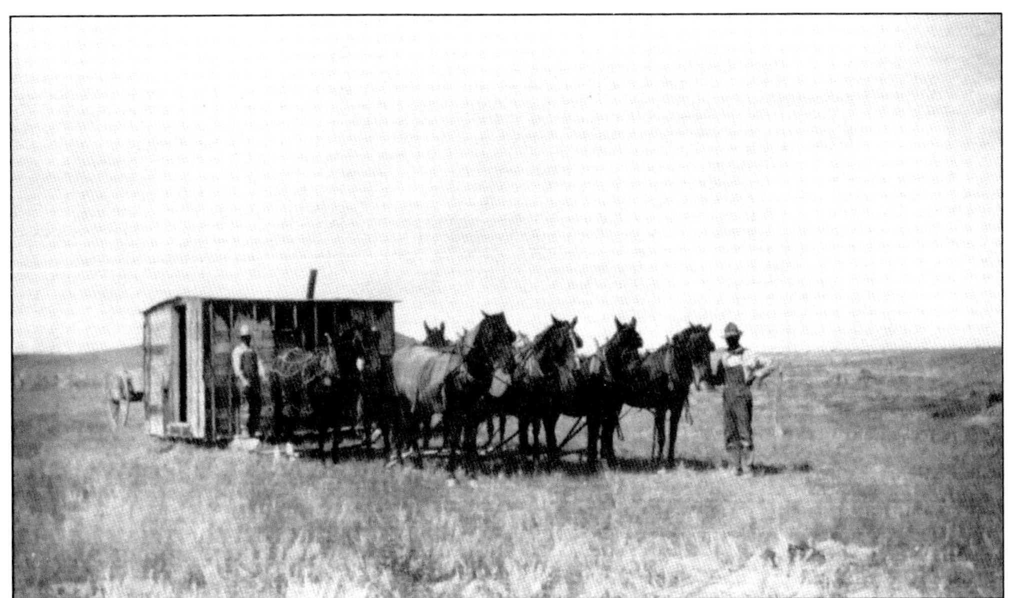

Homestead cabins sometimes had to be moved for various reasons. This photograph shows homesteaders in the process of moving a cabin to a new location using a team of six horses. (Buller Collection.)

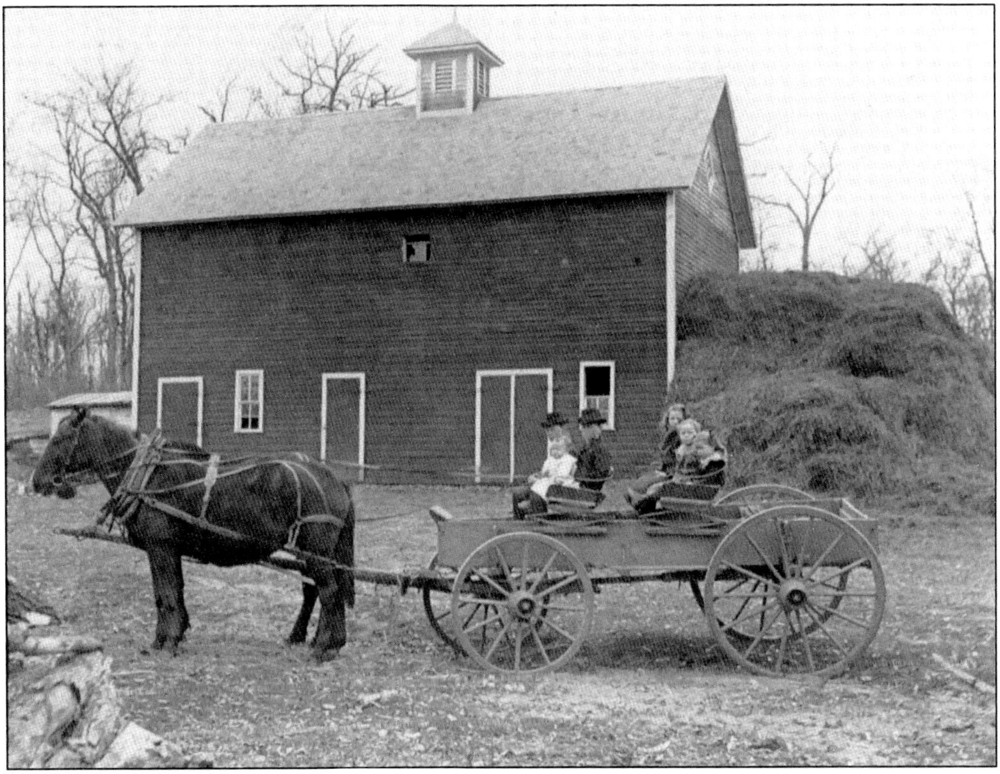

This photograph was taken on the Jonas homestead in late autumn around 1910. Pictured in the front of the wagon are Henry, Herman, and Ben Jonas. In the back sit Emma, Agnes, and Lillian Jonas. A large mound of winterfeed is piled on the side of the barn. (Temple Ranch.)

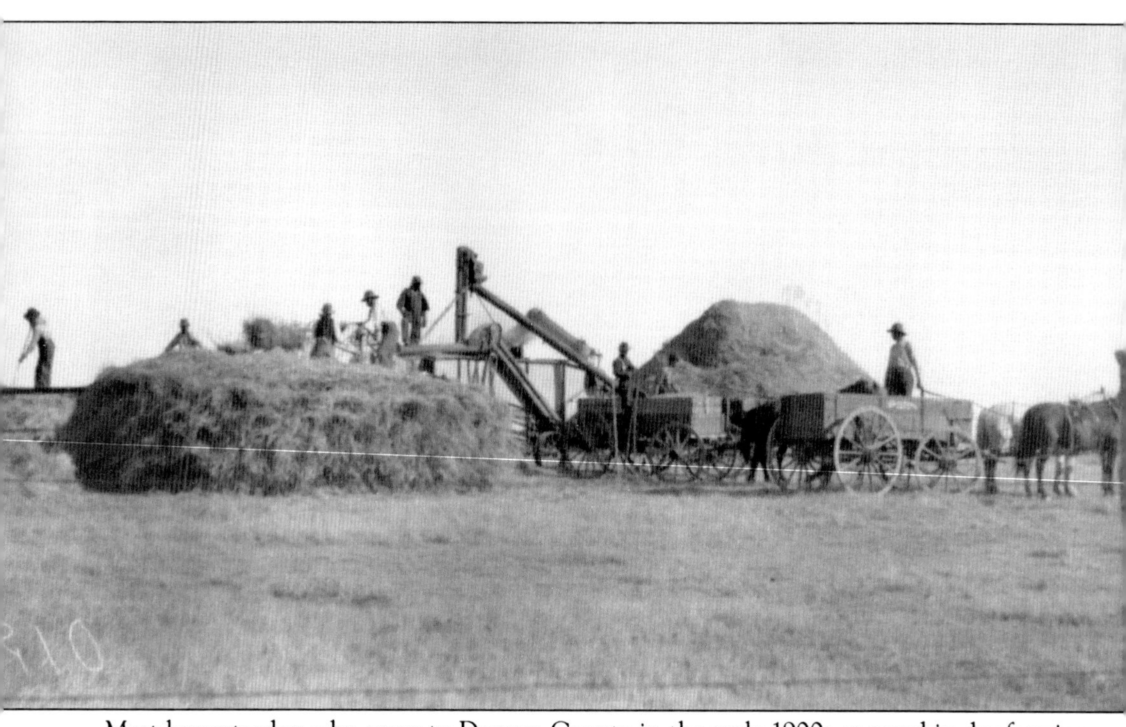

Most homesteaders who came to Dawson County in the early 1900s engaged in dry farming. This photograph shows dryland farmers processing wheat during the harvest of 1910. (Buller Collection.)

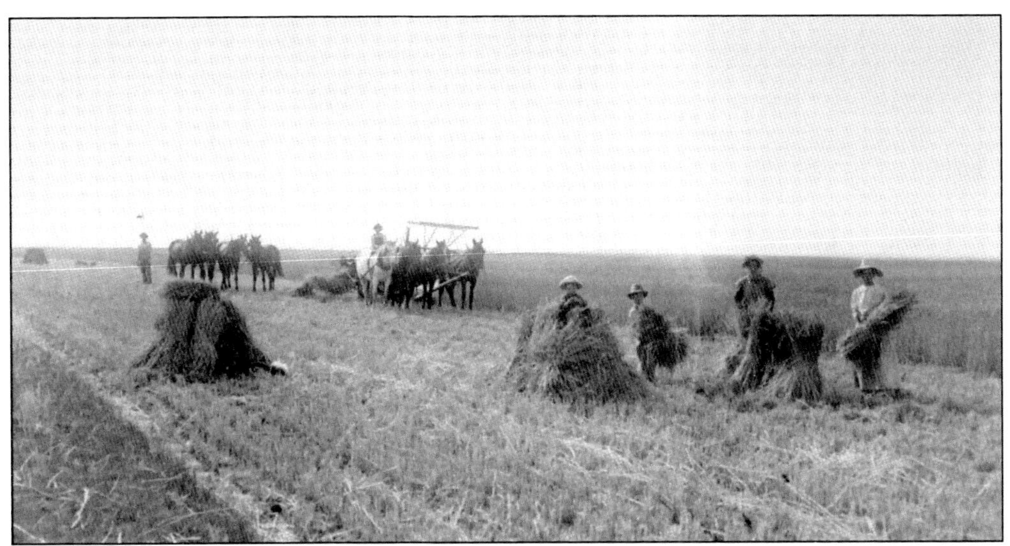

Childhood on a homestead in eastern Montana during the early decades of the 20th century was much different than in the urban enclaves elsewhere in America. From a young age, children were expected to help wherever they were needed. They tended livestock, worked in the fields during planting and harvest, and conducted a variety of chores around the house. This photograph shows children helping their parents with the wheat harvest in 1911.

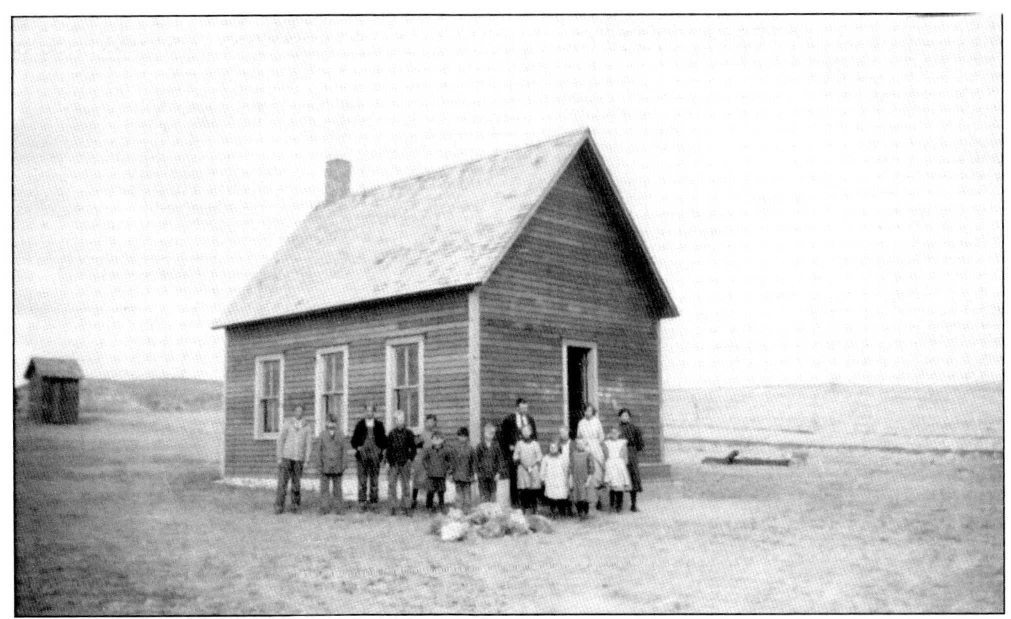

A headmaster and his students pose for a picture outside of their one-room schoolhouse near Glendive. The small structure behind the school is an outhouse. One-room schoolhouses were common in the rural areas around Glendive at the beginning of the 20th century. (Buller Collection.)

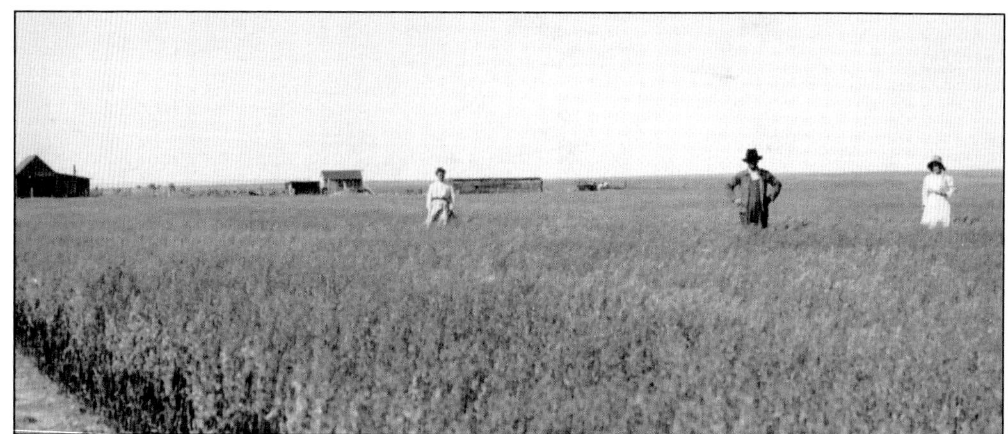

This photograph taken by L.A. Foster shows three dryland farmers standing in their oat field in 1911. (Buller Collection.)

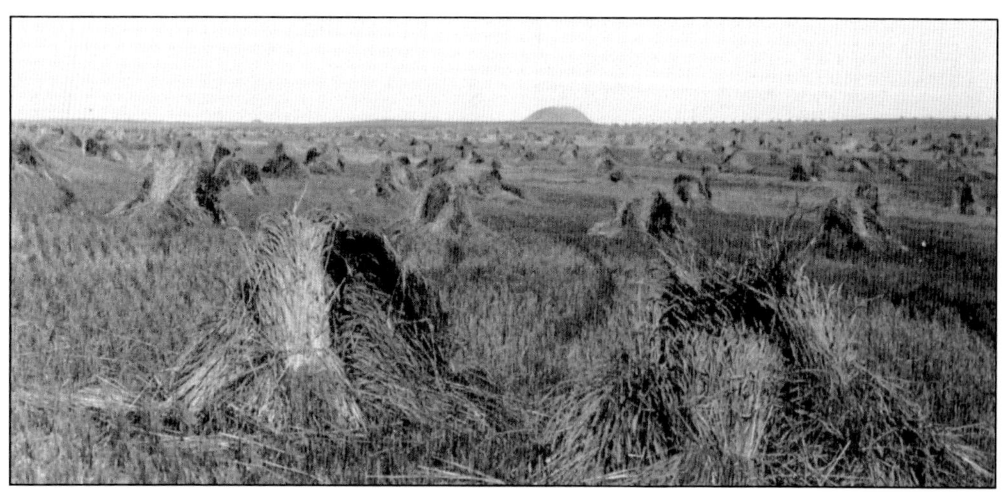

When the weather cooperates, farmers on the northern plains can produce an abundance of corn and cereal grains. This photograph shows the bountiful wheat harvest on Grant Wilson's homestead in 1911. (Buller Collection.)

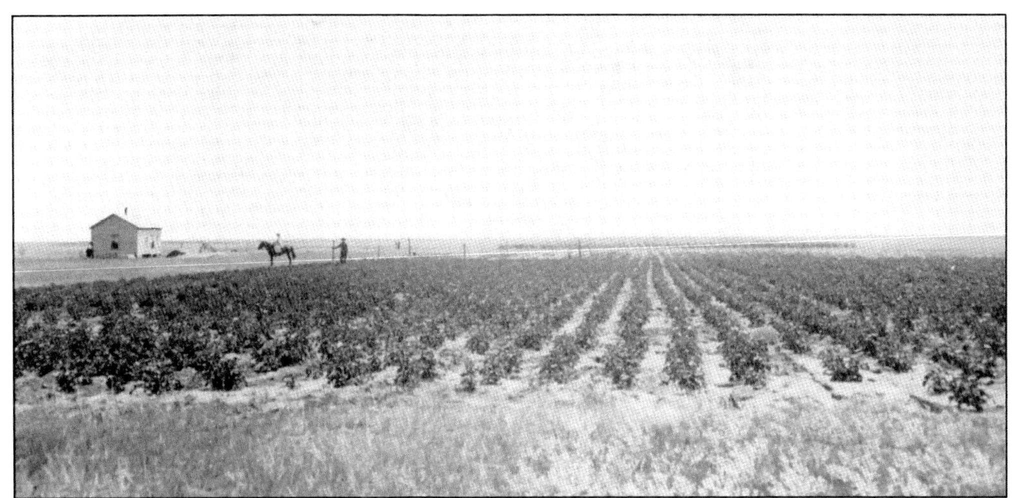
The northern plains are scientifically classified as semiarid, with an average rainfall total of around 14 inches. Homesteaders on the dryland frontier had to grow crops suited to such an environment. These homesteaders near Glendive tried their luck raising potatoes in 1911.

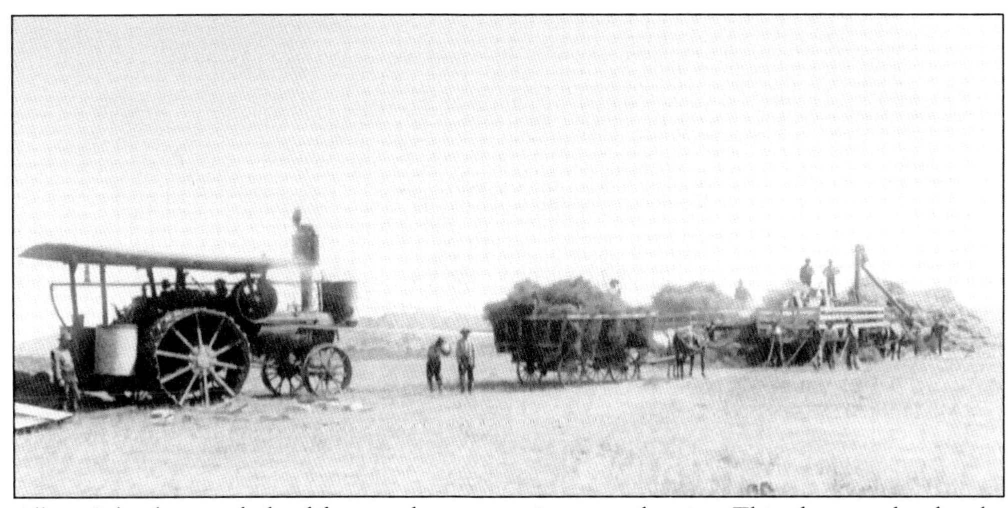
Albert Schaal was a dryland farmer who grew various cereal grains. This photograph taken by L.A. Foster shows Schaal's crew threshing a 1,500-acre crop of flax during the fall of 1911.

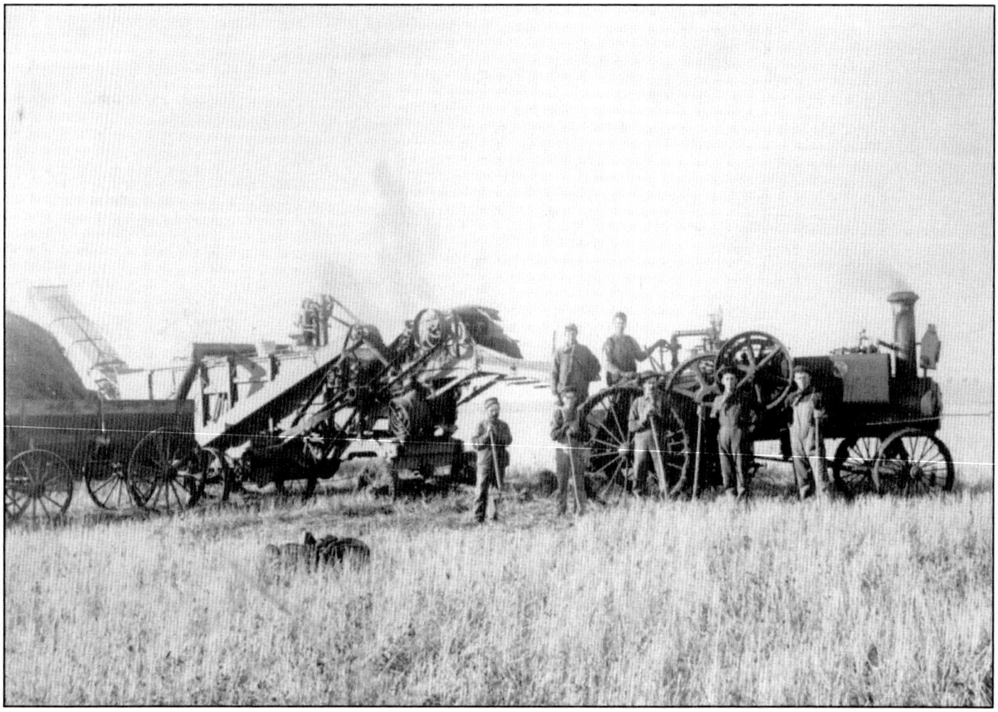

Pictured here are Roy Jackson and George Hardy's threshing machine and crew harvesting wheat near Glendive in 1911.

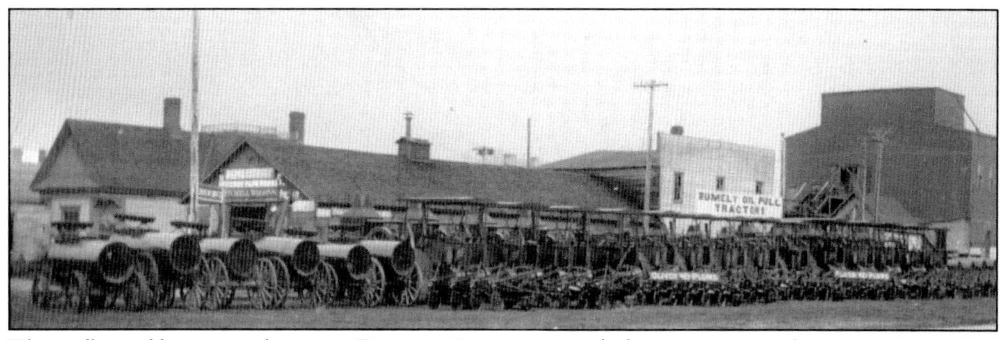

The influx of homesteaders into Dawson County provided opportunities for entrepreneurs to cash in on the agricultural boom. This photograph shows an array of tractors and plows for sale by the Glendive Implement Company in 1912.

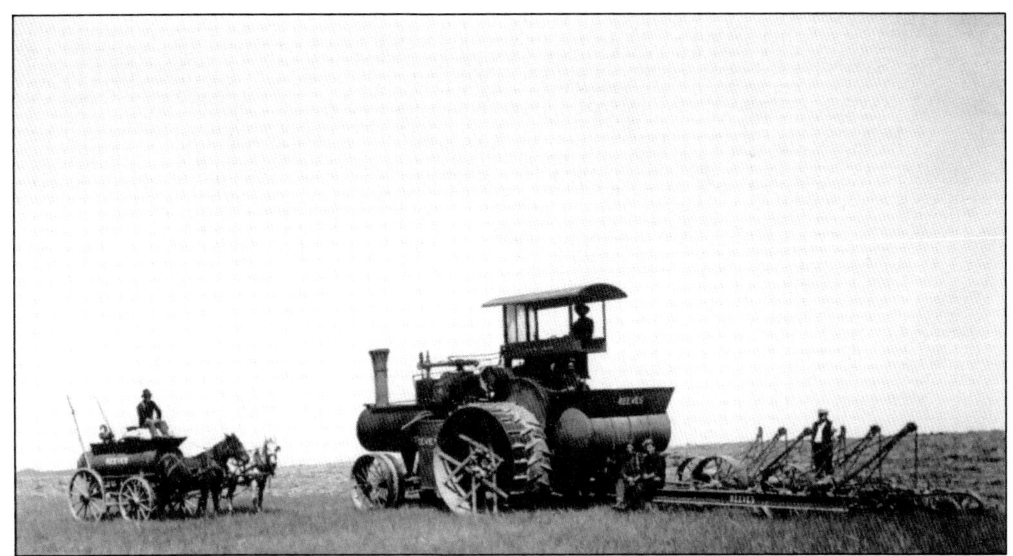

Pictured here is a Reeves and Company 40-140 cross compound steam traction engine breaking ground near Glendive in 1912. It was largest steam-powered traction engine ever made. The two-story engines were often called "road locomotives." Steam-powered tractors were phased out gradually after World War I by internal combustion tractors, which were lighter, faster, and more economical.

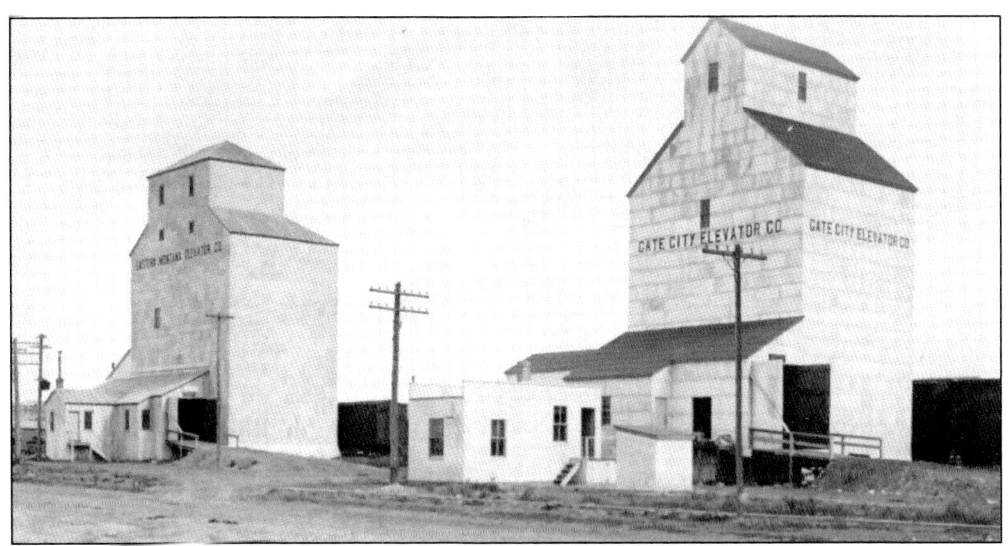

The mechanization of agriculture and proximity to the railroad prompted entrepreneurs in Glendive to open grain elevator companies in the early 1900s. Pictured here in 1910 are the Eastern Montana Elevator Company and Gate City Elevator Company grain elevators, which were located just off of Merrill Avenue.

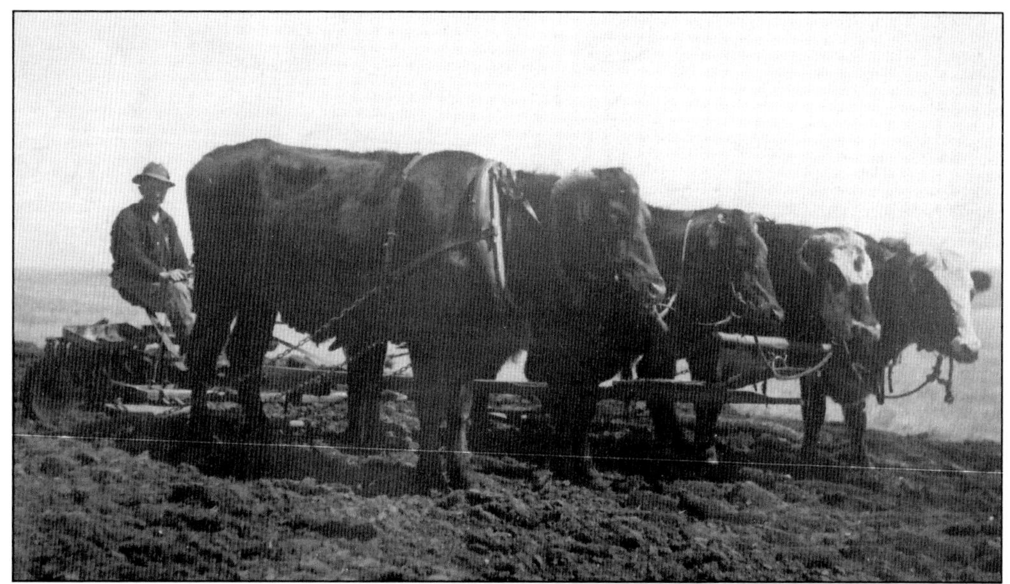

Some homesteaders could not afford mechanization and continued to rely on more traditional methods of farming. In this photograph, homesteader Earle Sanford prepares to plow his field with an ox-drawn plow in 1912.

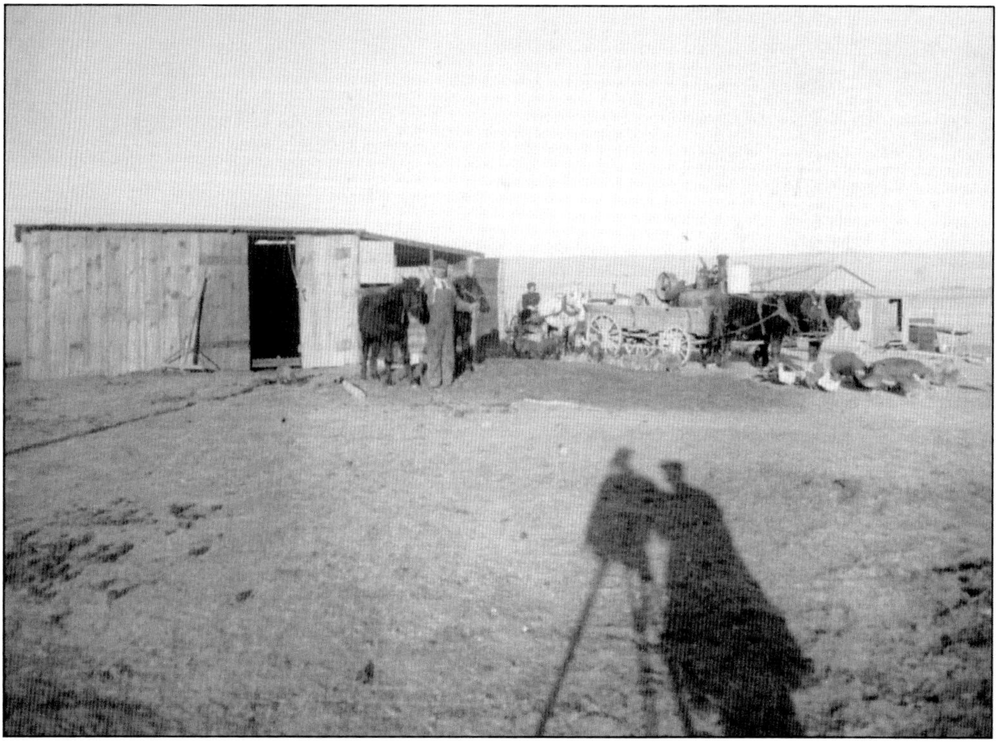

Glendive homesteader George Hardy and his wife proudly pose for a picture with their farming equipment and livestock in 1913.

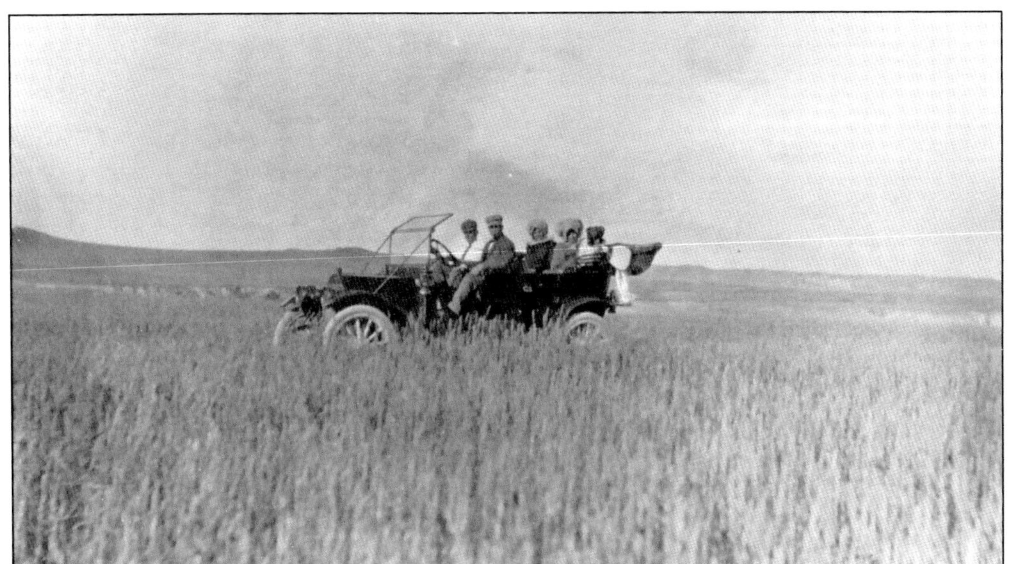

This photograph shows the Lowe family out for a drive in their wheat field.

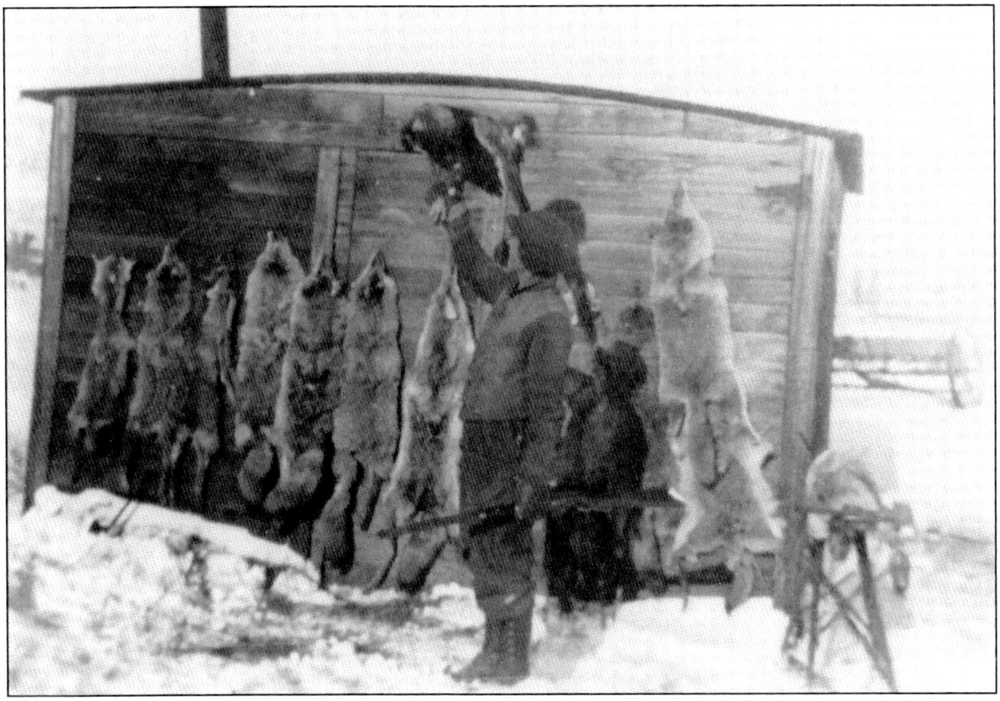

Some homesteaders in eastern Montana supplemented their income by hunting and trapping for furs. Leo Carroll is pictured holding a shotgun in one hand and with a golden eagle perched on his other arm. Displayed on his cabin are coyote furs, which were trapped in the Bryan Plains area around 1920.

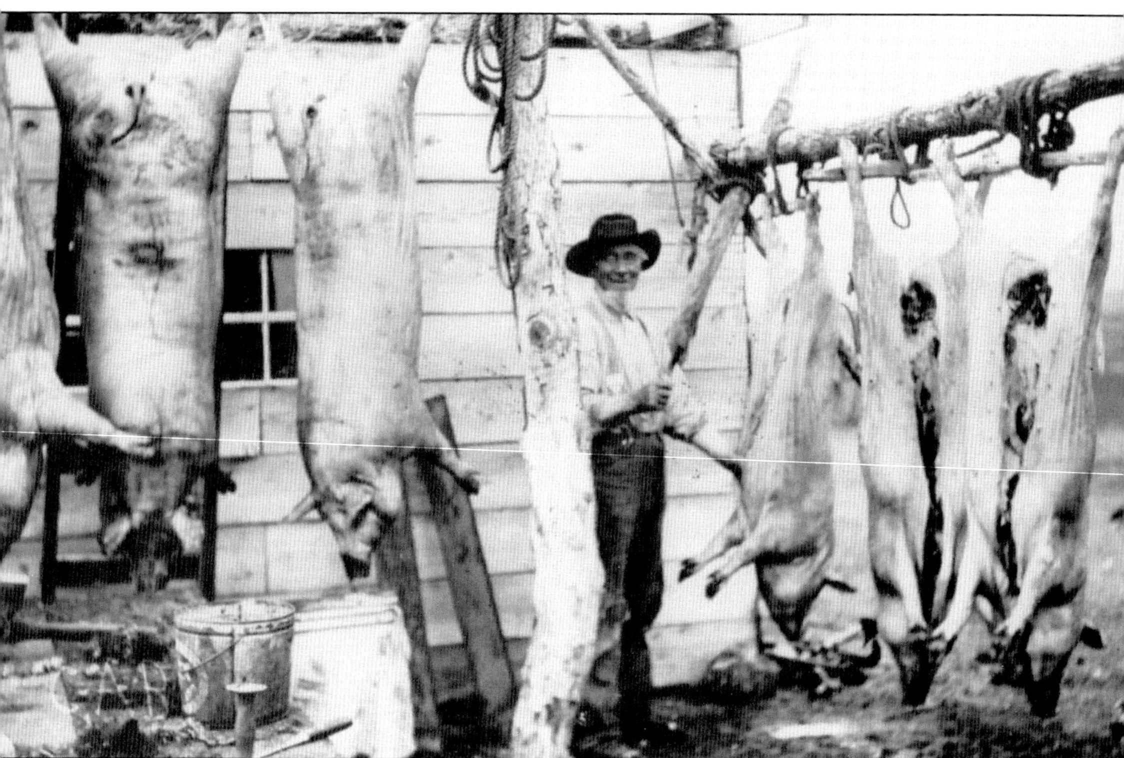

Homesteader Andrew H. Buller supplemented his income by raising hogs and delivering pork to Glendive for 8¢ a pound. This photograph shows Buller in the process of processing hogs at his homestead in 1914. (Buller Collection.)

Four

Ranching, Roundups, and Rodeo

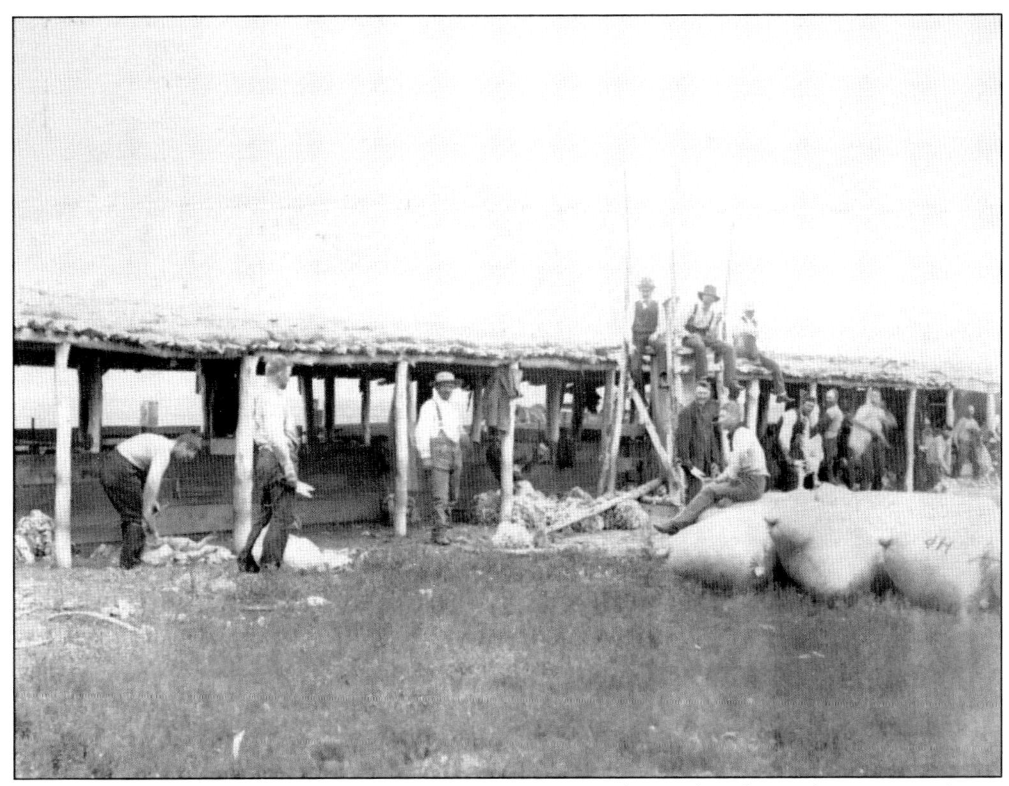

Before cattle became king in eastern Montana, many early ranches focused on raising sheep. The endless open range of the northern plains provided ample feed for thousands of sheep. This photograph shows ranch hands shearing sheep on one of James W. Gilmore's ranches near Glendive in 1885.

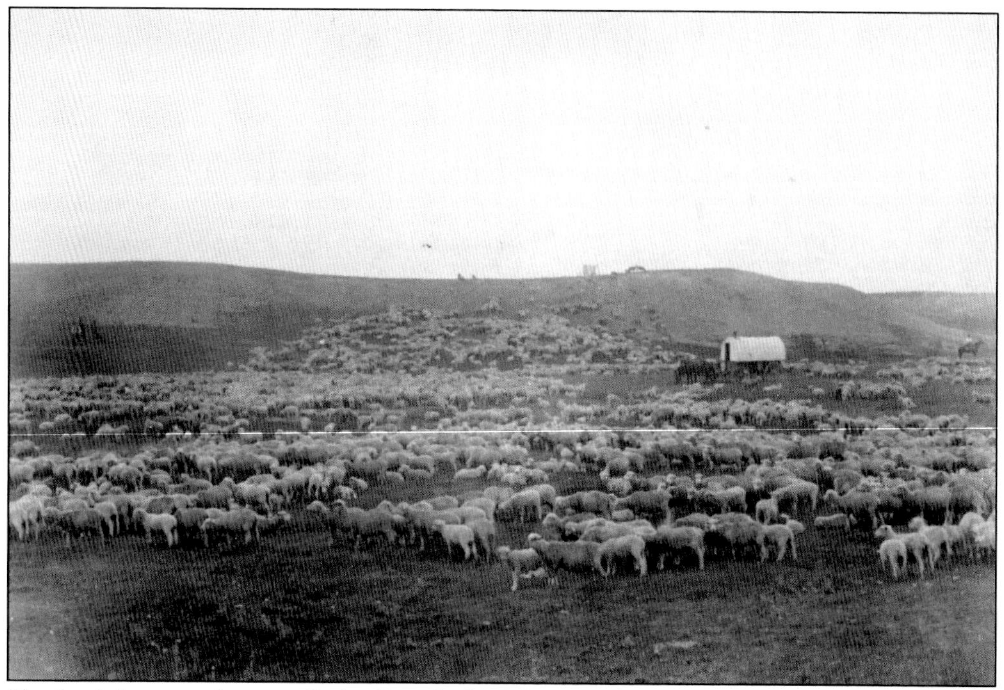

Shepherds keep watch over a flock of hundreds of sheep on the vast plains near Glendive in 1900. Because sheep owners mainly grazed their flocks on the open range, there were always shepherds in tow to protect the sheep from predators and rustlers. (Manegold Collection.)

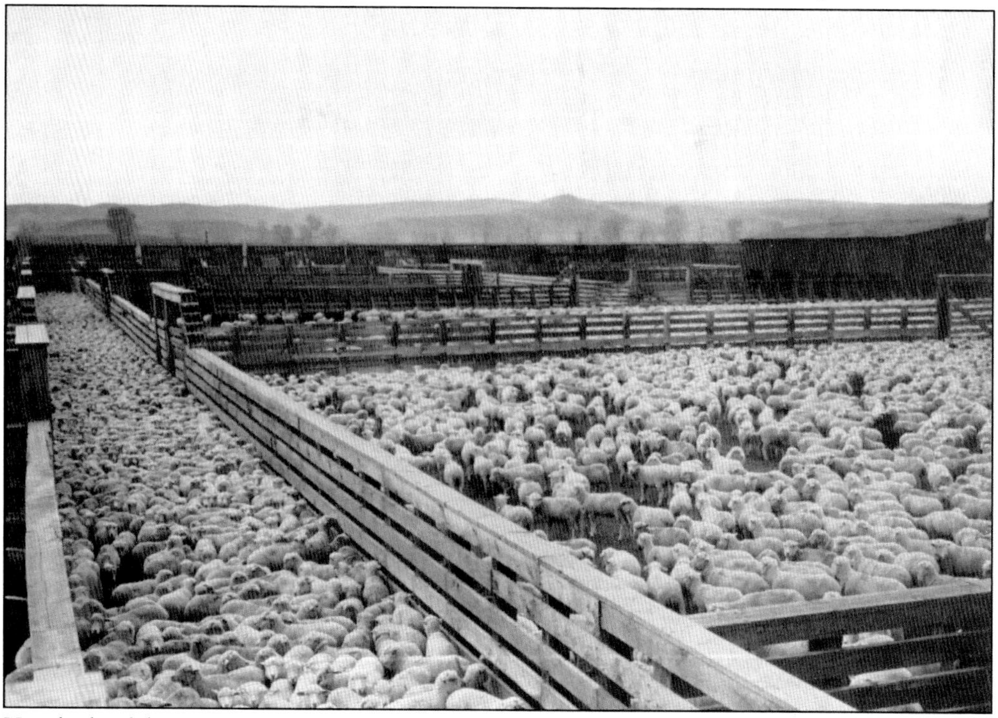

Hundreds of sheep are pictured at the Glendive Stockyards prior to transport to market by rail in 1905.

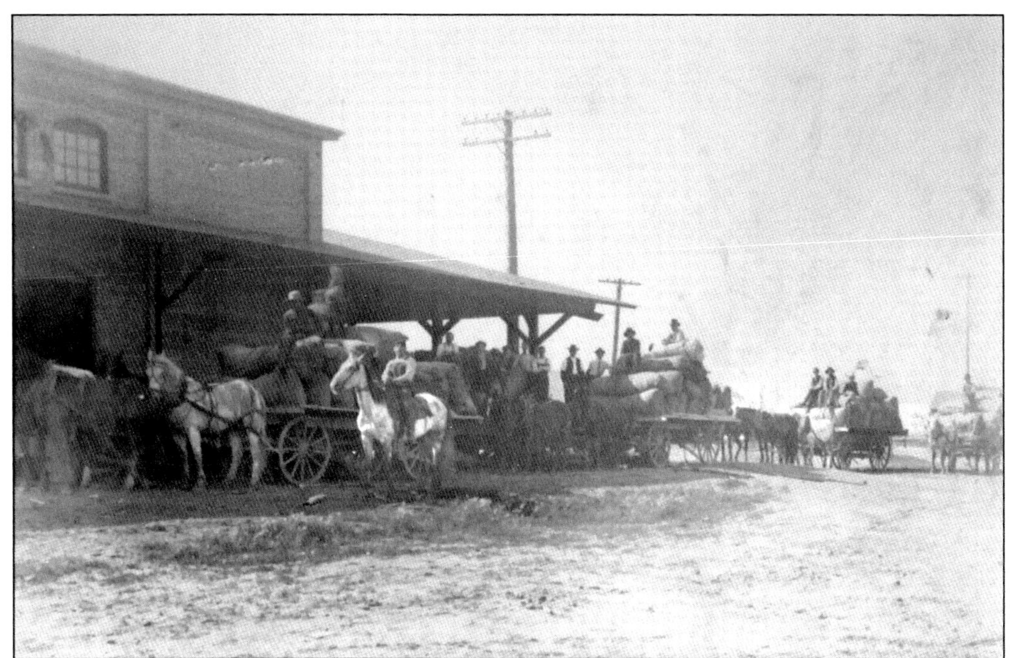

This photograph shows several tons of raw wool being hauled by wagon to the Northern Pacific Railroad Depot in Glendive for shipment to market in 1905.

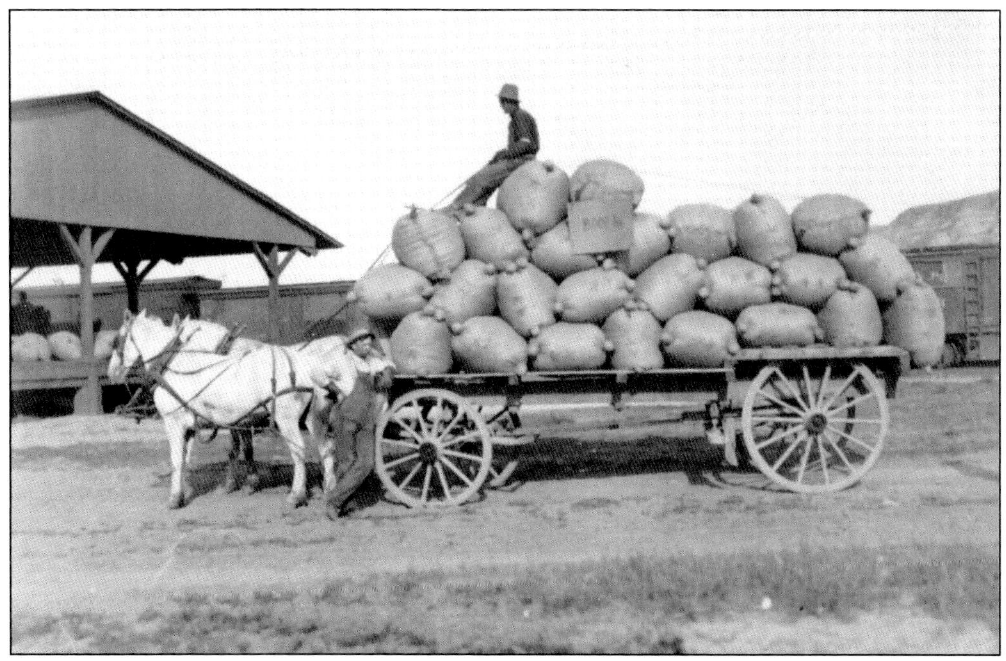

Earl Semines (driving) and an unidentified man proudly pose with four tons of raw wool from Redwater in 1908. (R.H. Foss.)

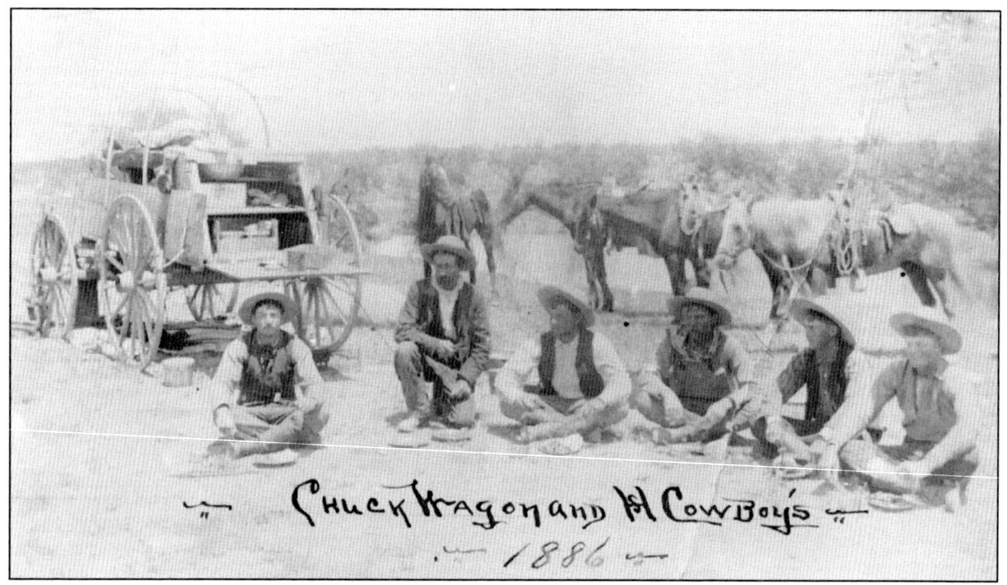

Six range-worn HS Ranch cowboys pose for a photograph in front of their chuck wagon during roundup in the spring of 1886. Absentee owners possessed many large ranches in the Glendive region. Several of the cowboys who worked the range around Glendive never met the owners of these large, sprawling ranches. Cowboys were usually loyal to the brand they worked with rather than the person who owned ranch.

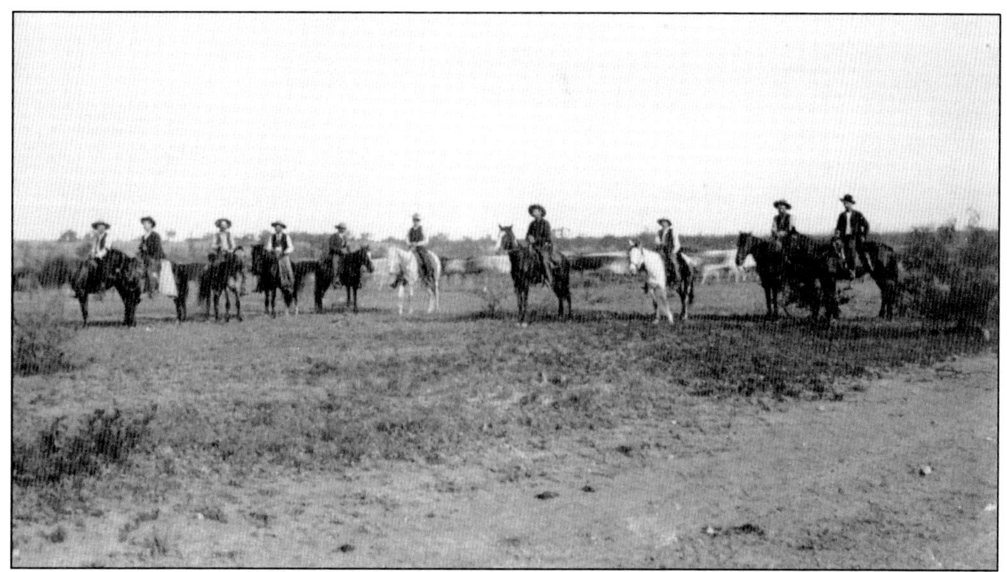

Several HS Ranch cowboys are photographed on horseback in 1888. The Hubbard and Sampson Ranch on the lower Redwater Creek was owned by two millionaires who had hunted in Dawson County in the 1870s and later decided to ranch in the area. The foreman of the HS Ranch, Ed Marron, served as Hubbard and Sampson's hunting guide during their earlier visits to the area. The two men eventually sold the ranch to Douglas and Mead.

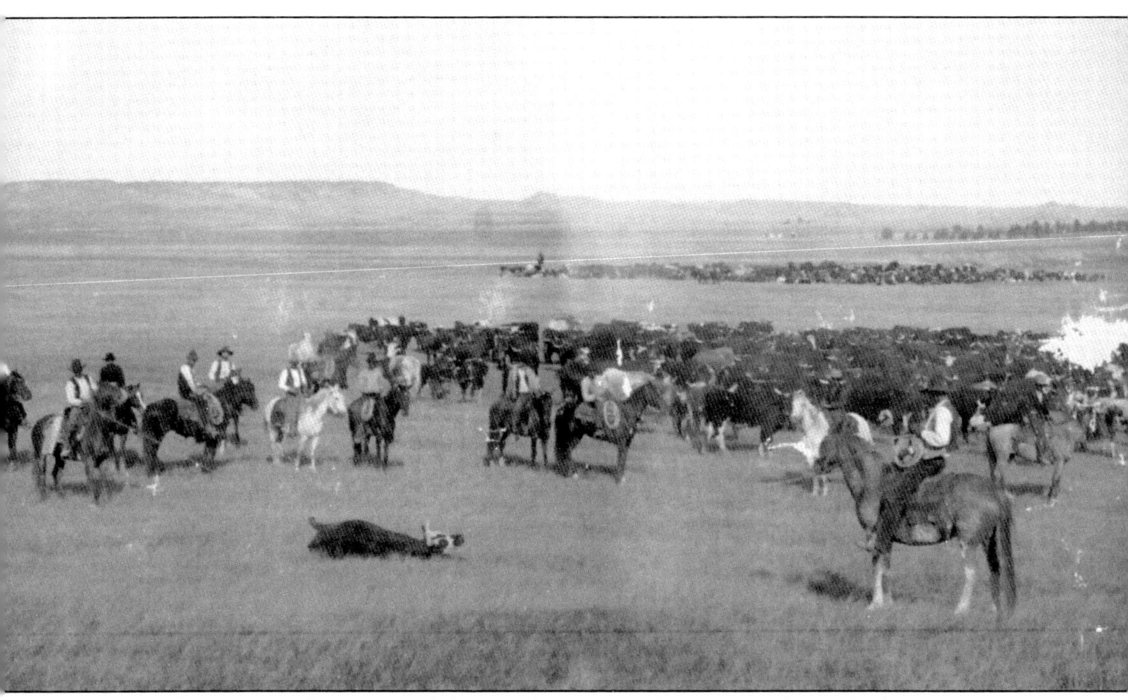

Roundup at the HS Ranch is pictured during the spring of 1889. In order to find young calves for branding and to sort out mature animals intended for sale, cattle ranchers would hold a roundup, usually in the spring. A roundup required a number of specialized skills on the part of both cowboys and horses. Individuals who separated cattle from the herd required the highest level of skill and rode specially taught "cutting" horses, trained to follow the movements of cattle and capable of stopping and turning faster than other horses. Once the cattle were sorted, most cowboys were required to rope young calves and restrain them to be branded and (in the case of most bull calves) castrated.

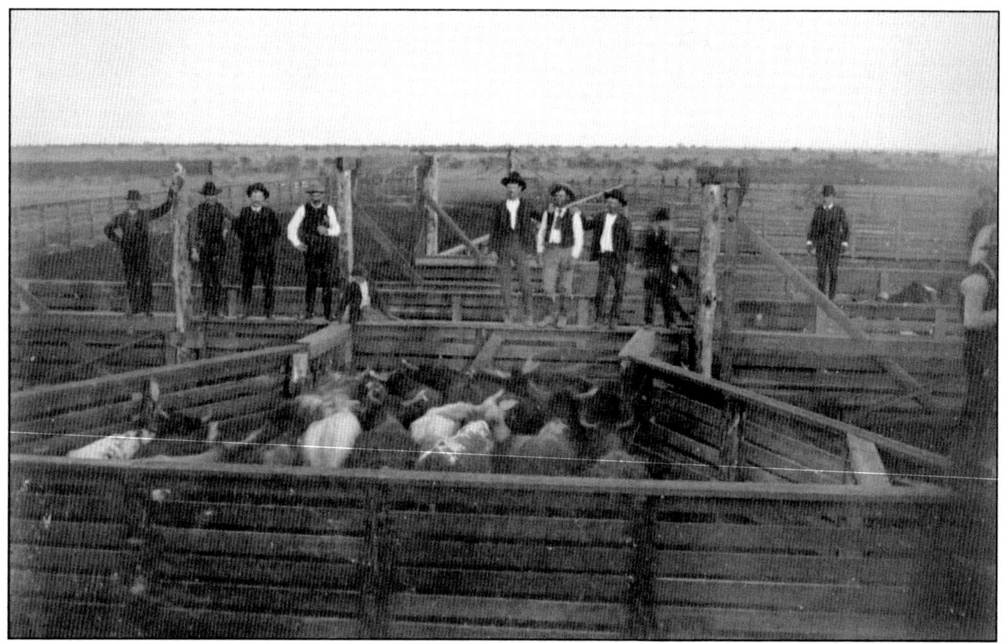

This photograph taken at the Glendive Stockyards shows steers ready to be shipped by rail to slaughterhouses in the Midwest in 1889.

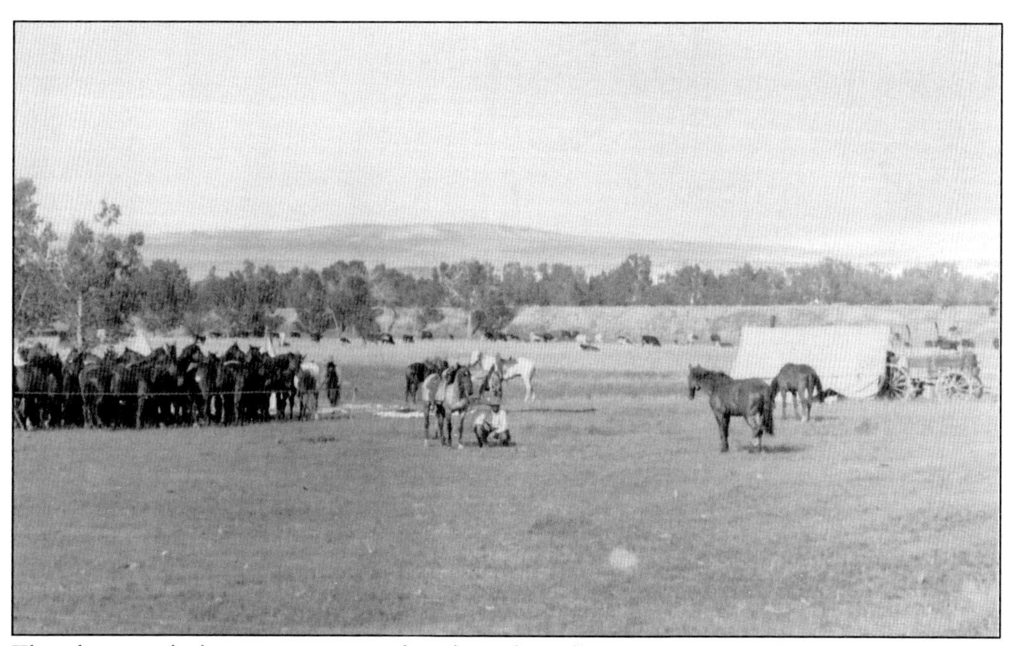

This photograph shows a spring roundup along the Yellowstone River at the L.U. Bar Ranch in the 1890s. The L.U. Bar Ranch was responsible for 12,000 head of cattle and 300 horses. (Bob Petermann Ranch.)

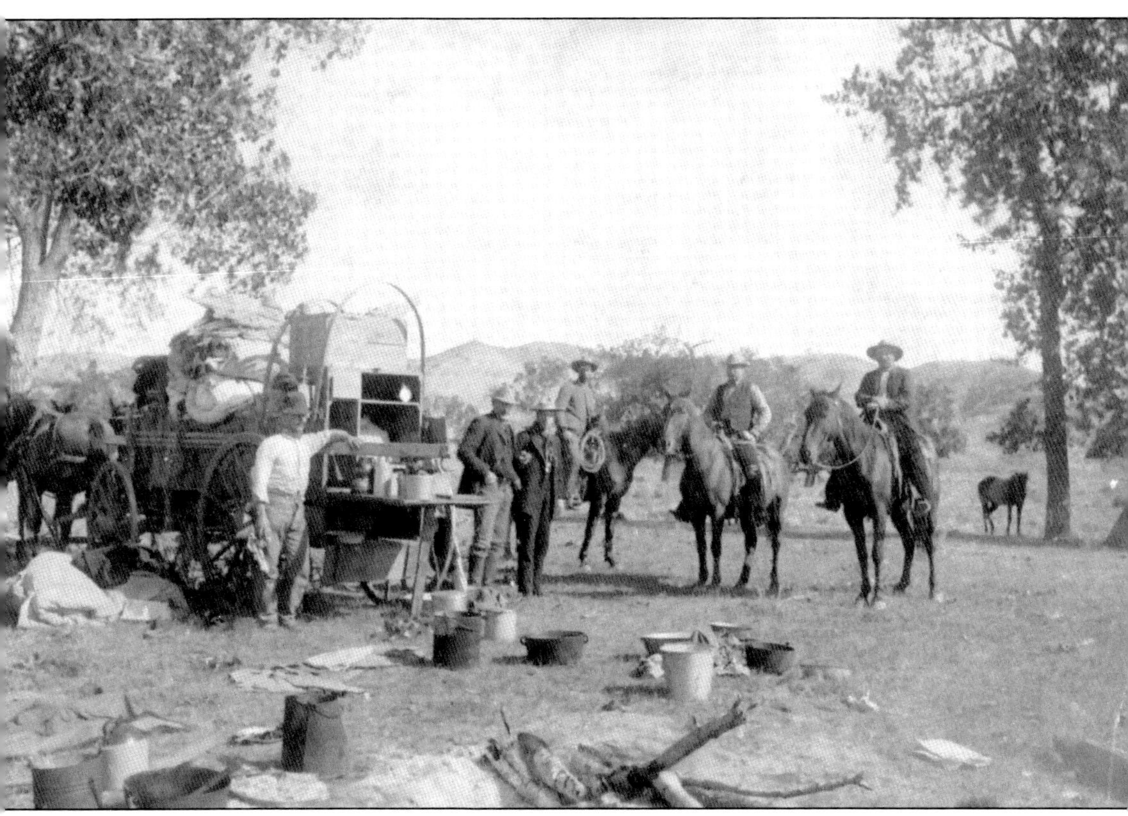

XIT Ranch cowboys, foremen, and the camp cook pause for a break after a long day of work during roundup near Cedar Creek around 1895. The XIT Ranch was a Texas-based cattle operation that had range rights to two million acres in Dawson County. The ranch operated in the region from 1890 to 1909. During this period, XIT was one of the largest cattle ranching operations in the world.

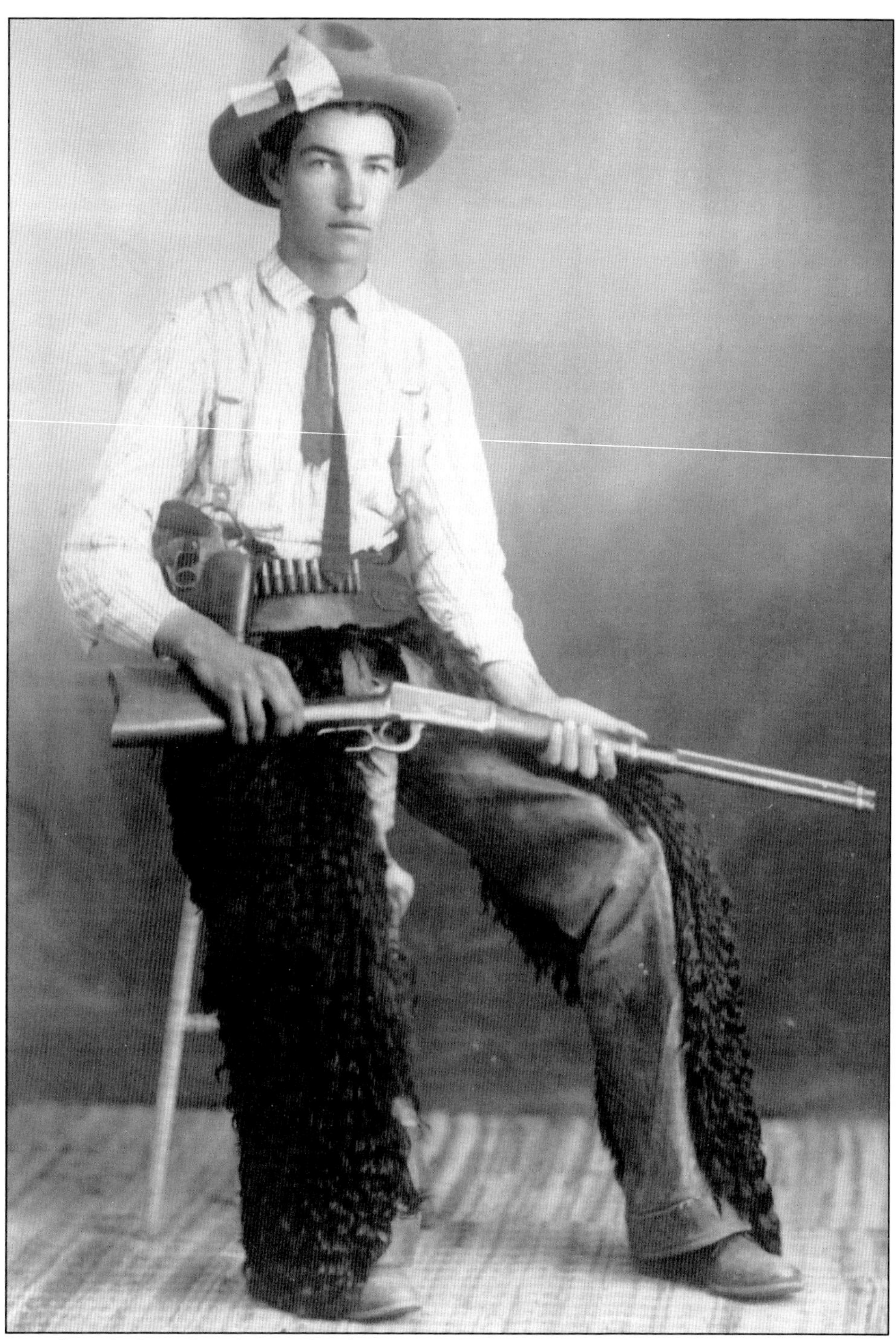

An unidentified cowboy from Glendive poses for a professional photograph with his prized Angora goat fur chaps. Chaps such as these were popular on the northern plains in the late 1800s. Cowboys in states like Montana and North Dakota wore these since the hair repelled not only the rain and snow but kept the wearer warm and comfortable, even in the most torrential downpour or heavy snowstorm.

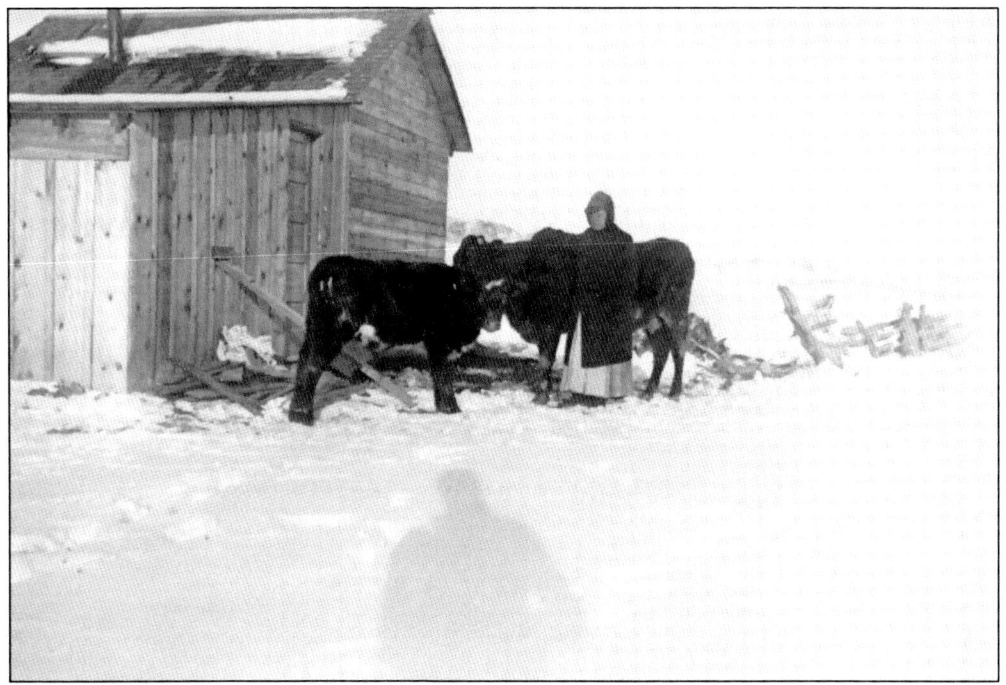

Raising livestock in the Glendive region of Montana was and is a difficult and risky occupation. Brutal winters can take their toll on cattle, horses, and sheep. Mrs. Earle Sanford is shown here at their homestead with cattle during the winter of 1910. (Earle Sanford Collection.)

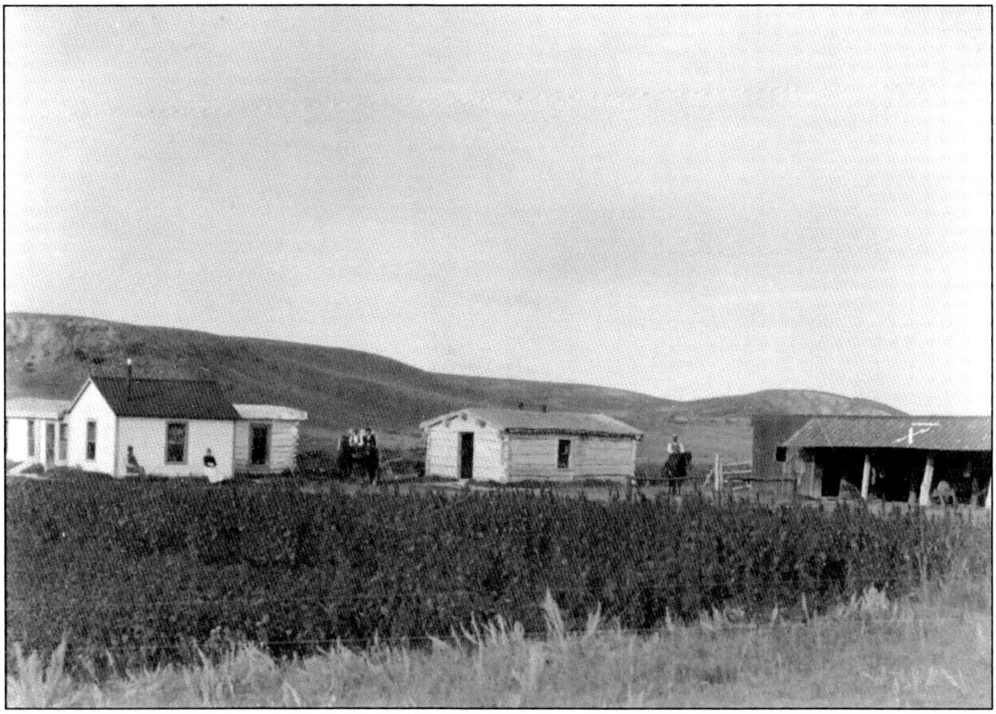

This photograph shows Sampson and Fahnstock's Bar X Ranch on Seven Mile Creek around 1910. Charlie A. Dole was the locally famous foreman of the Bar X. (Verne G. Paulson Collection.)

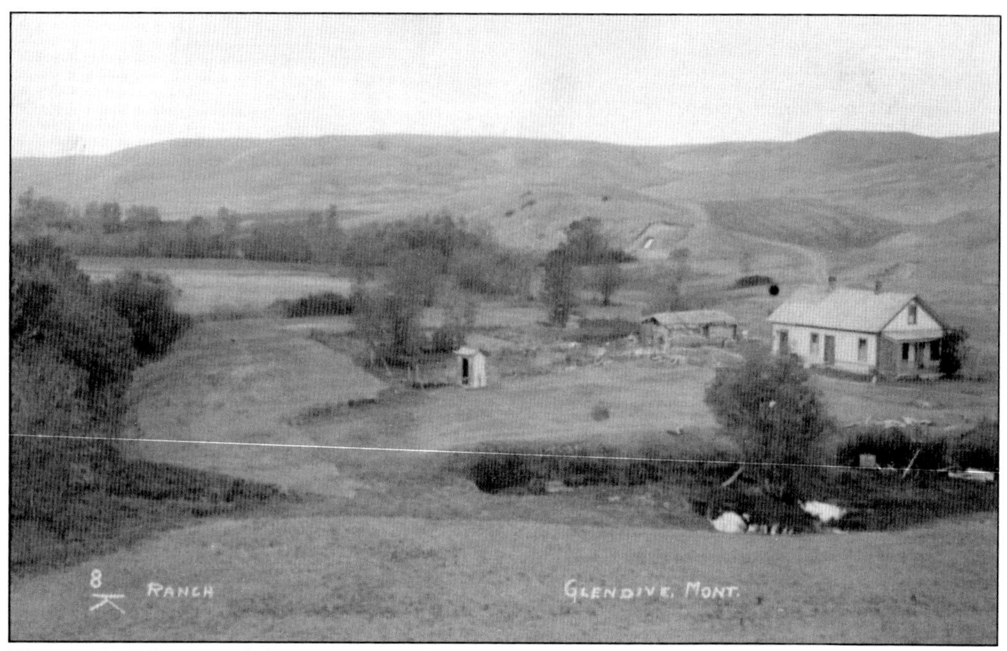

This c. 1910 photograph by L.A. Foster shows the 38 Ranch near Glendive. (Buller Collection.)

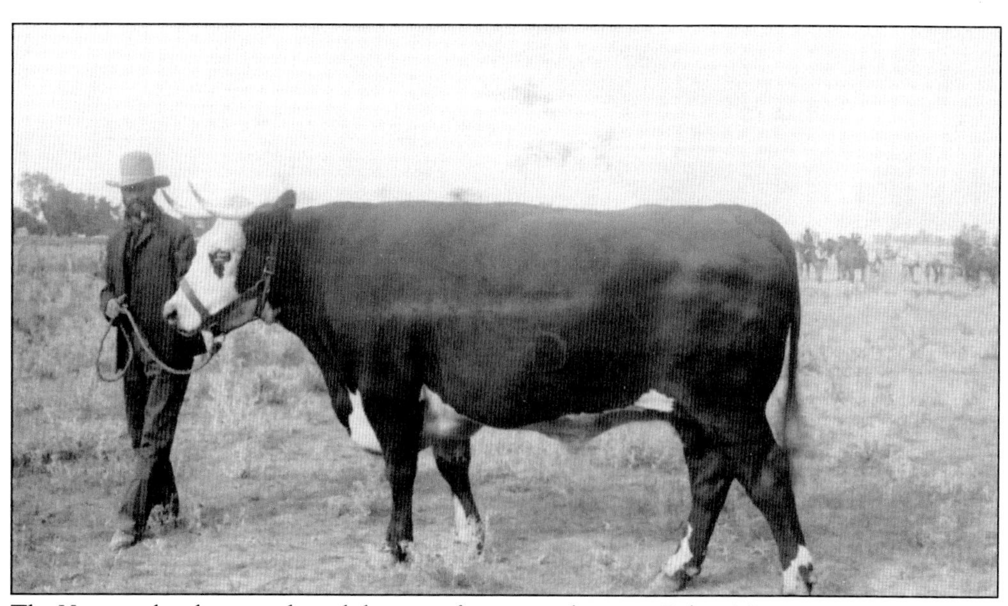

The Harpster brothers purchased this steer from a rancher near Baker, Montana. He was a young calf when purchased and did not show any promise until he took to hanging around the barn and stealing a little grain from the milk cows. Without much help, the steer grew to be the largest of its kind recorded in Dawson County. The man pictured is Fistg Thompson in 1910.

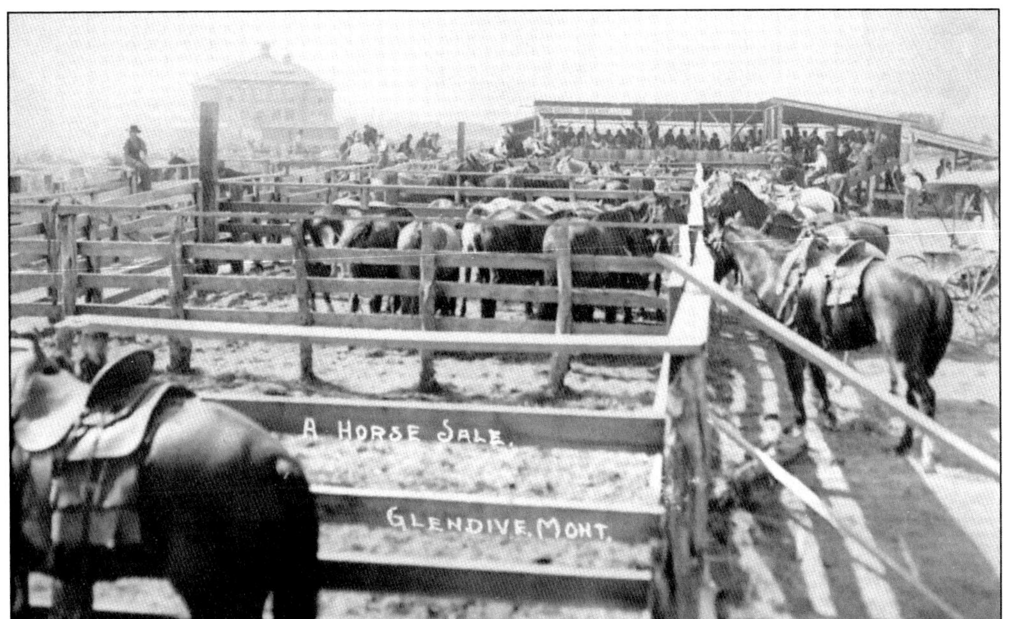

Range horses were also profitable for ranchers in eastern Montana. This photograph shows an auction at the Glendive Stockyards featuring range horses in 1911. (Archie Hamilton Collection.)

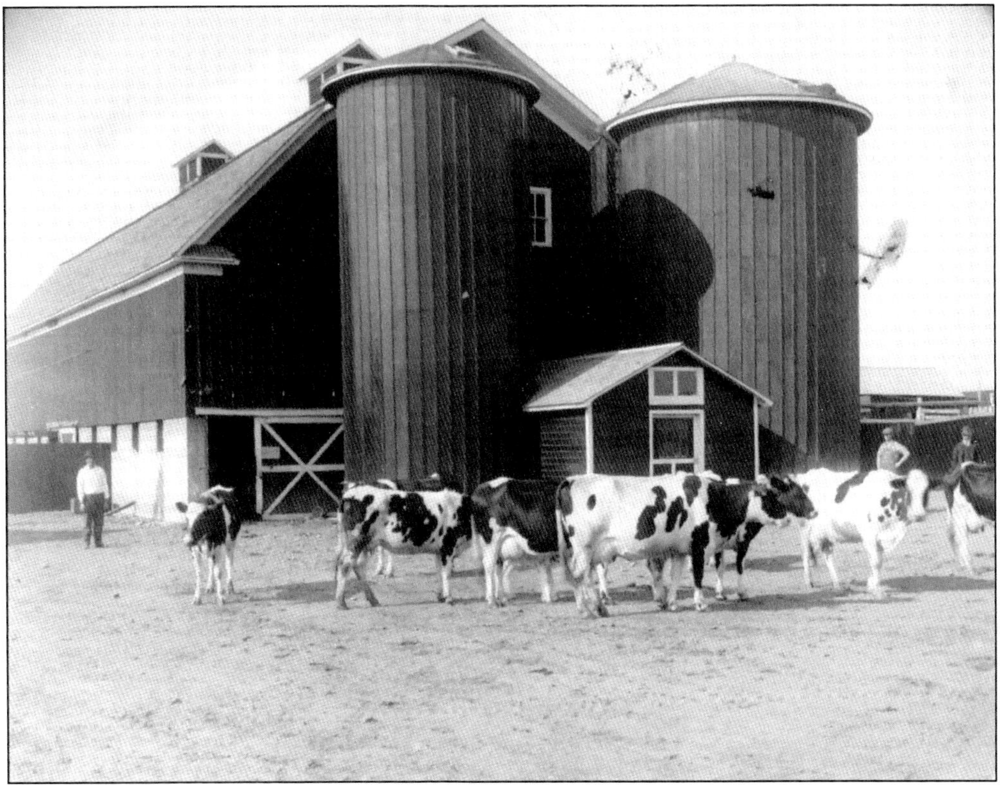

Although uncommon, some ranchers focused on raising cattle for dairy rather than beef. The Pope Ranch supplied fresh dairy products to the town of Glendive in the early 1900s.

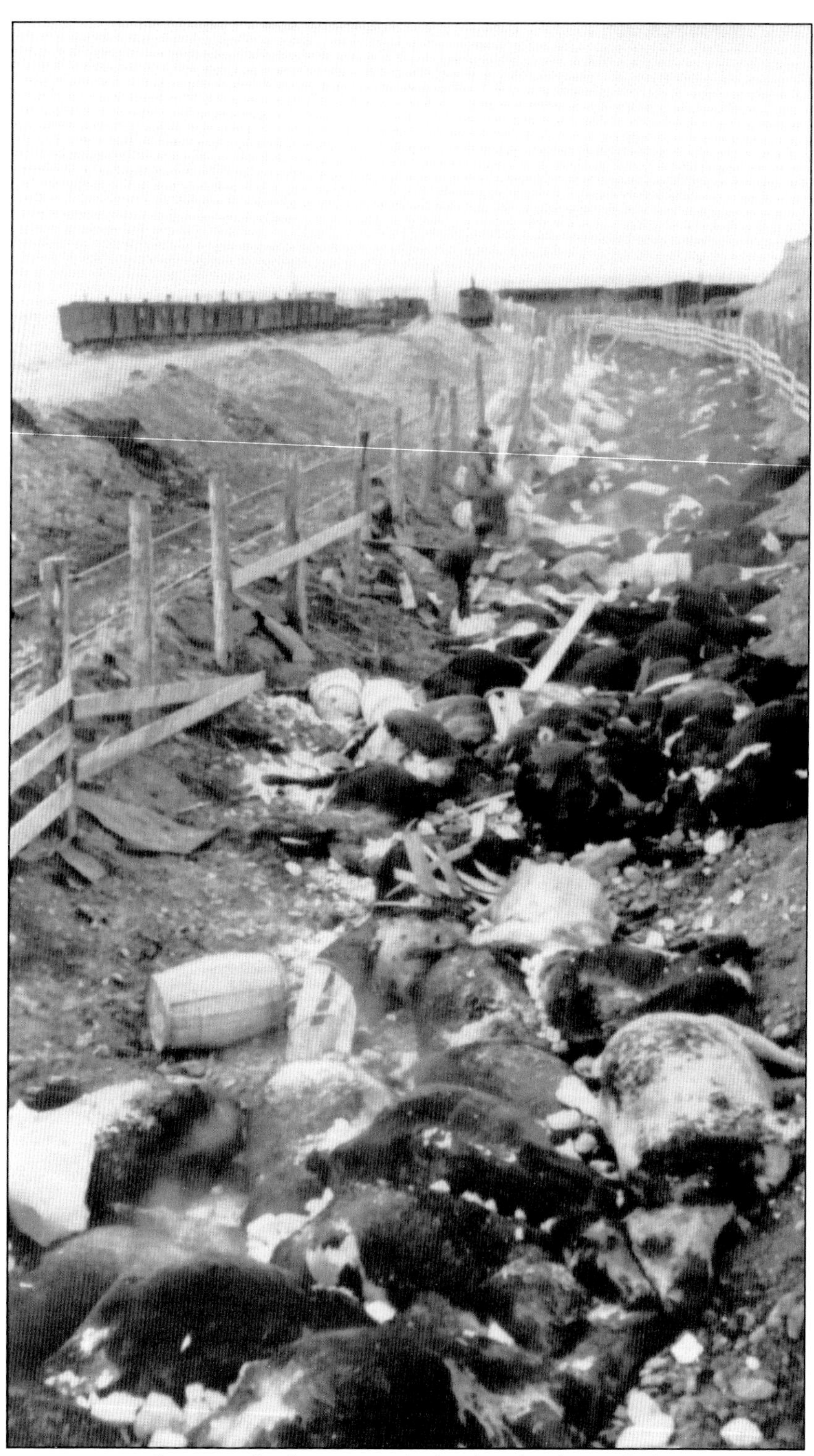

This gruesome image shows cattle that succumbed to hoof-and-mouth disease in the Glendive area in 1914.

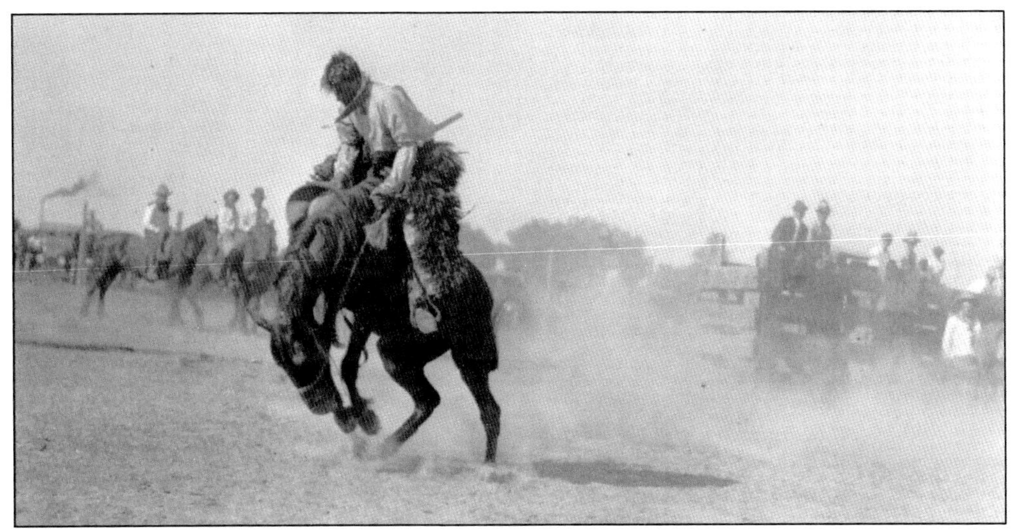

Because of the cowboy culture that dominates life in Glendive, rodeo has always been one of the most popular sports in town. This photograph shows Panama Kid, wearing wooly chaps, riding "Wild Liz" at the Glendive Rodeo in 1917. (Andrew Foss Collection.)

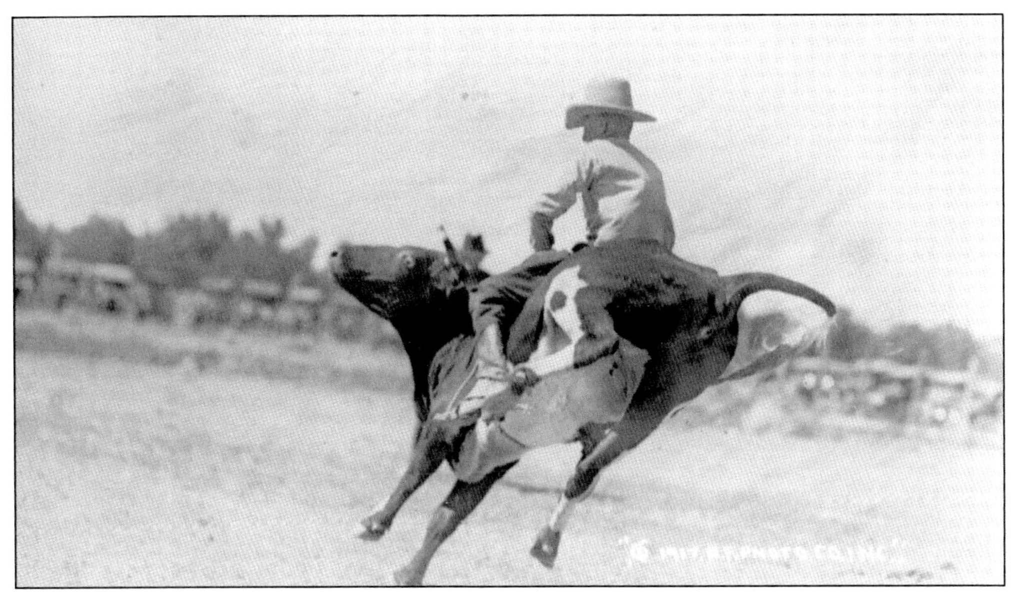

This photograph taken by Andrew Foss shows a cowboy riding a bull at the Glendive Rodeo in 1917. (Andrew Foss Collection.)

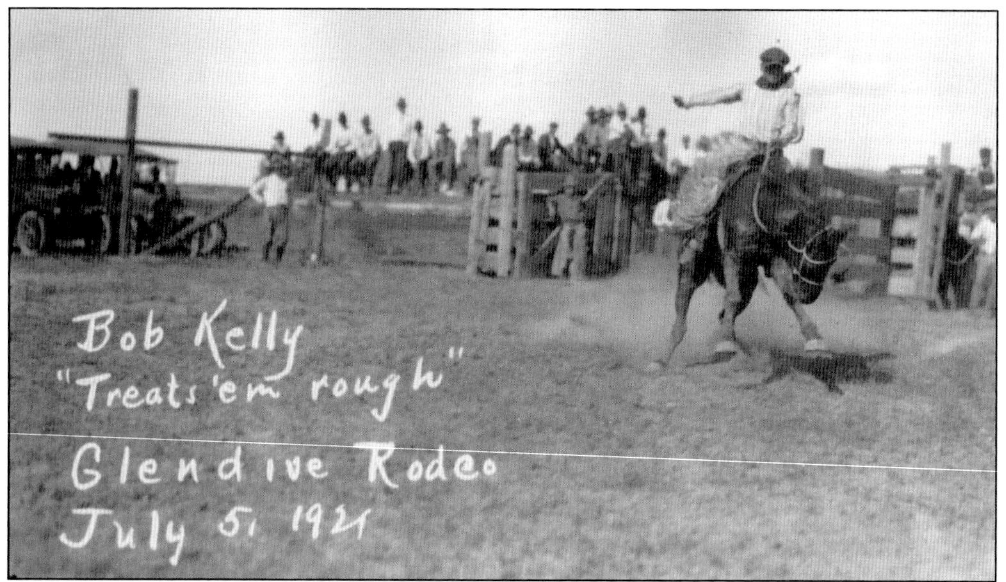

Bob Kelly rides the infamous bronco "Fan Tail" in the Glendive Rodeo of 1921.

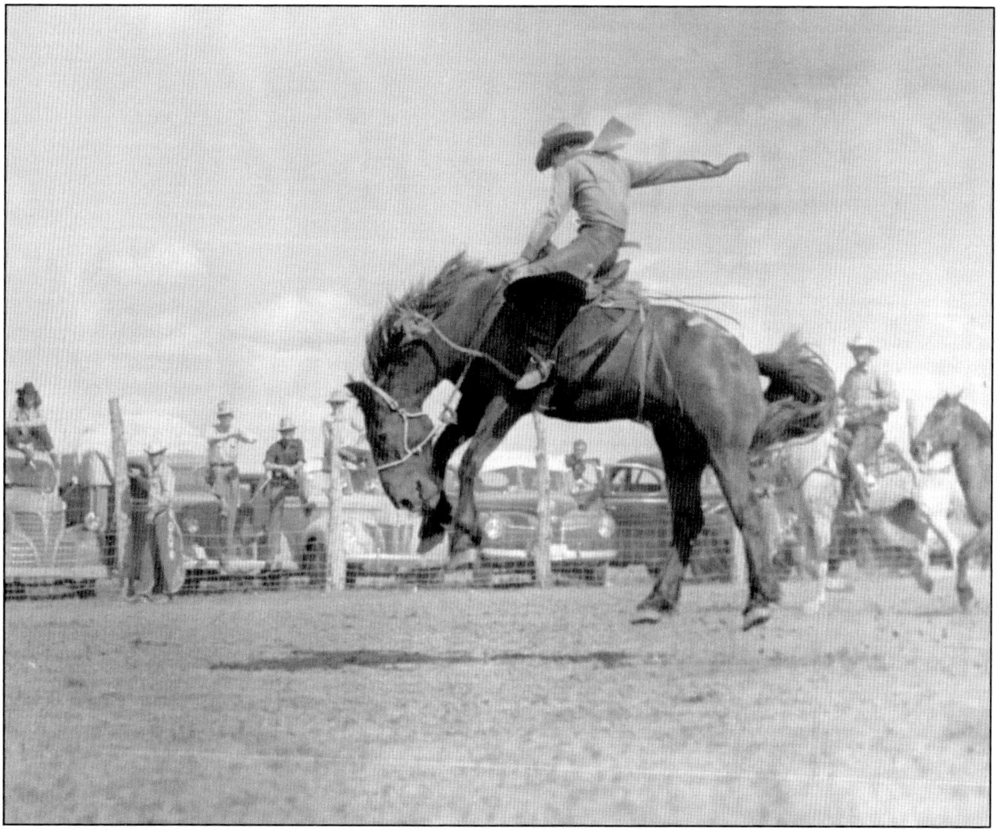

Broc Bradley rides an angry bronco at the Glendive Rodeo during the late 1940s.

Five

The Makoshika Badlands

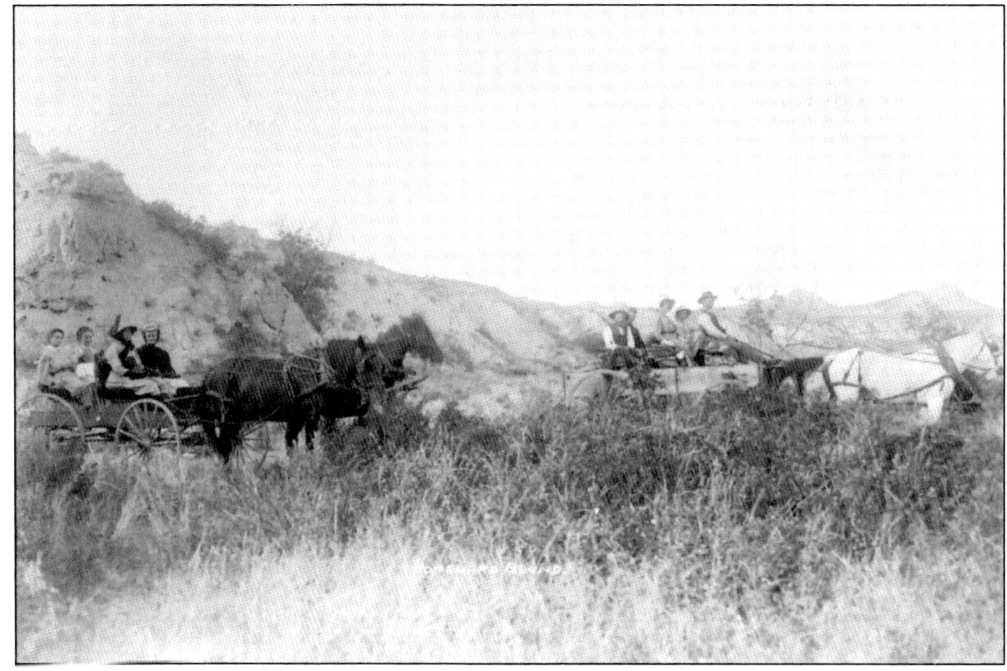

The hauntingly surreal geological formations in the contiguous badlands that border the town of Glendive to the southeast have drawn curious visitors since the late 19th century. This faded photograph shows a couple of local families on a leisurely carriage ride through the badlands in the 1890s.

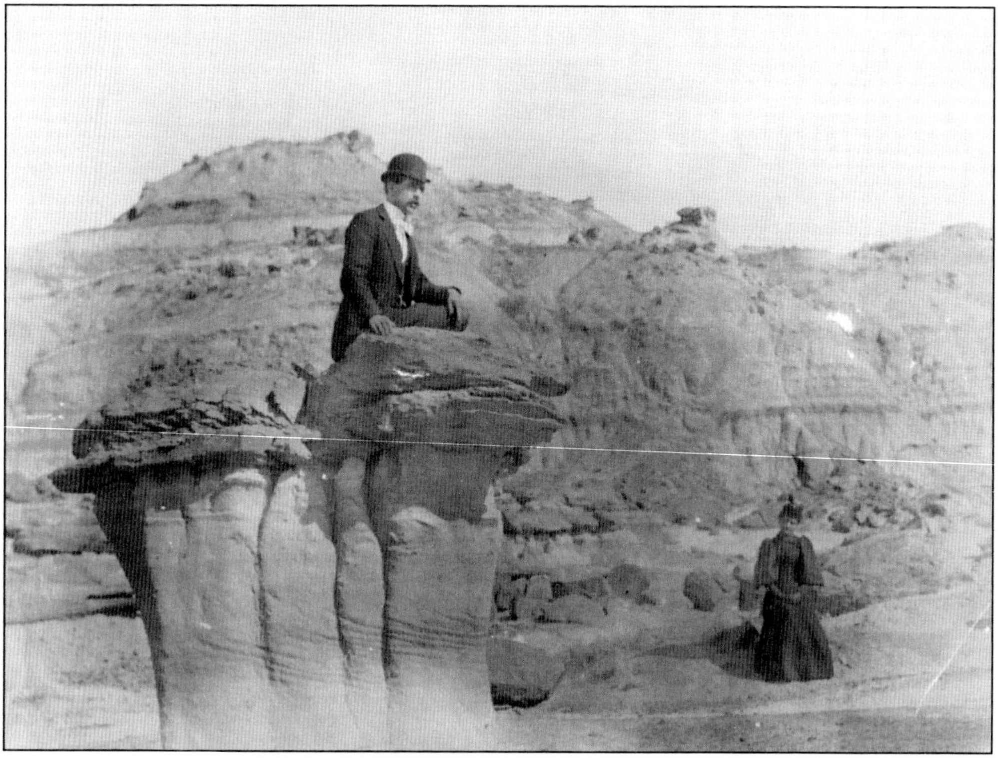

Professor E.O. Busenberg and his wife are pictured in the Makoshika Badlands in the 1890s. *Makoshika* is a variant of a Lakota phrase *Maco Sica*, meaning "Bad Earth." Over time, the badlands of Makoshika have revealed a variety of fossils, including portions of tyrannosauruses and triceratops.

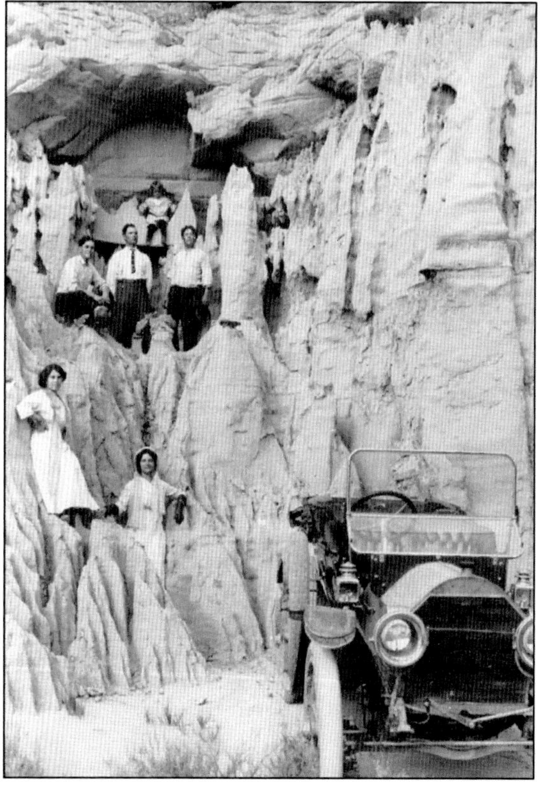

This photograph taken by L.A. Foster in 1912 features a family posing by a formation called the Grotto in what is now Makoshika State Park. (Buller Collection.)

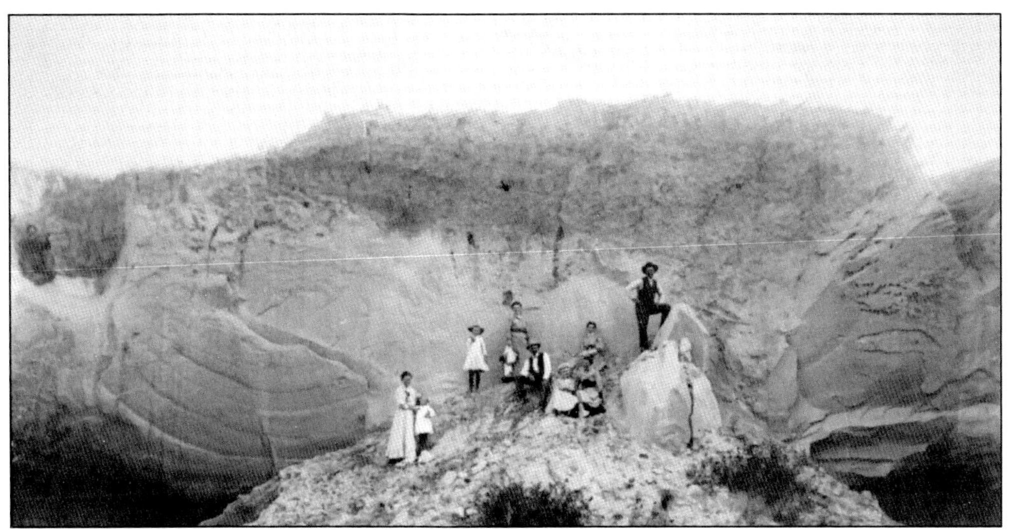

Families pose for a picture next to the geological feature known as Twin Caves at the beginning of the 20th century.

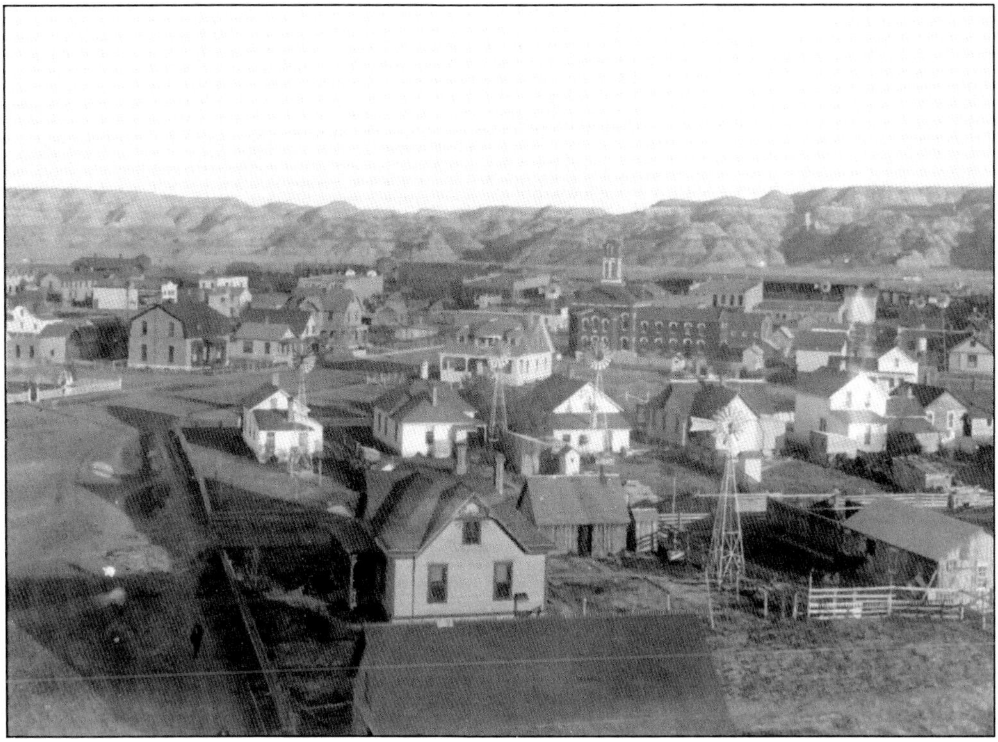

The town of Glendive is pictured around 1900, with the imposing Makoshika Badlands in the background.

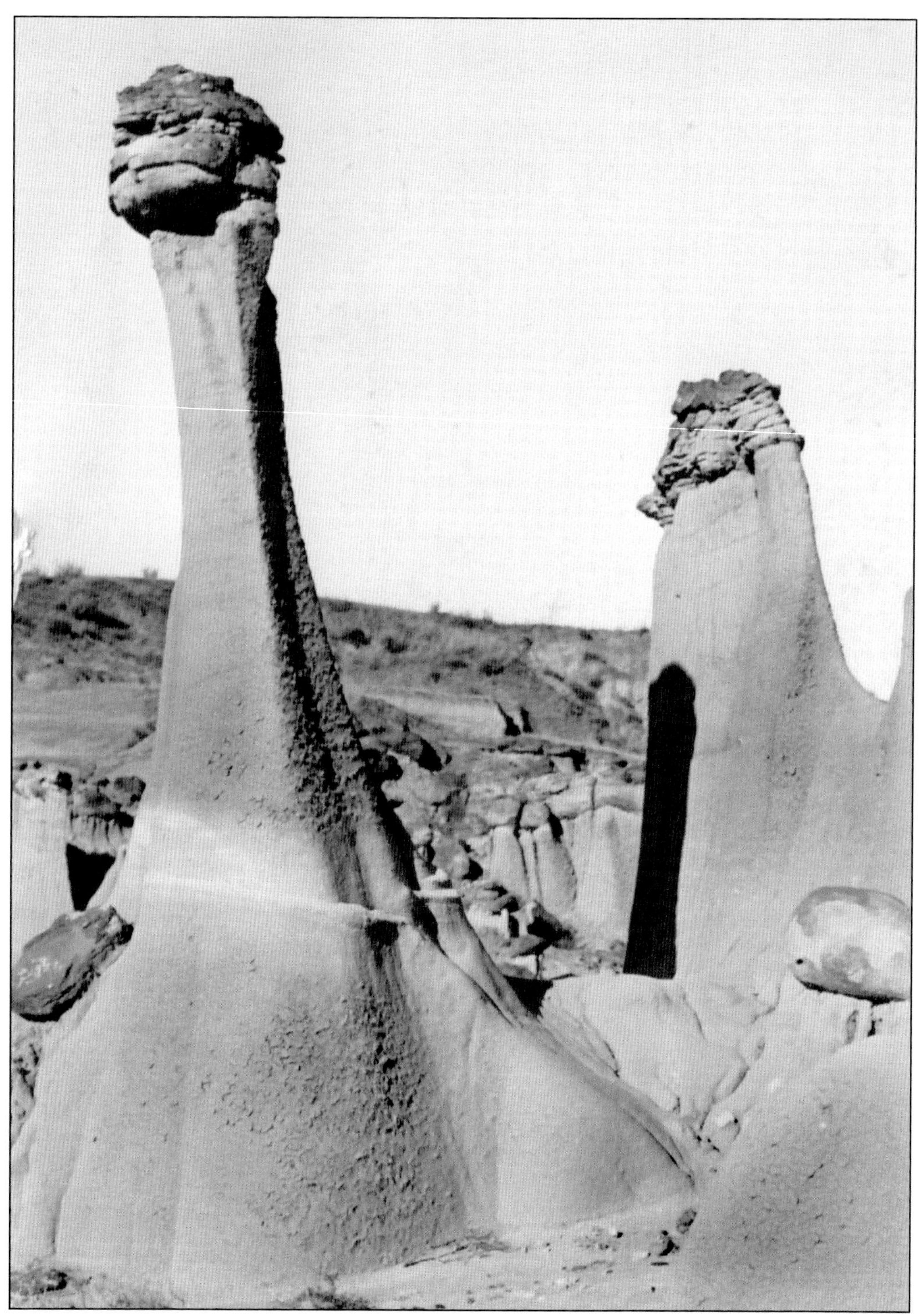

As early as 1893, Andrew Larson promoted the idea that the badlands near Glendive, which have gone by the names *Maco Sica* and Pinnacle Park, should be federally protected. In 1953, Makoshika State Park was officially born and is currently the largest state park in Montana. This photograph of rock-capped pinnacles shows why so many locals wanted to preserve this special place.

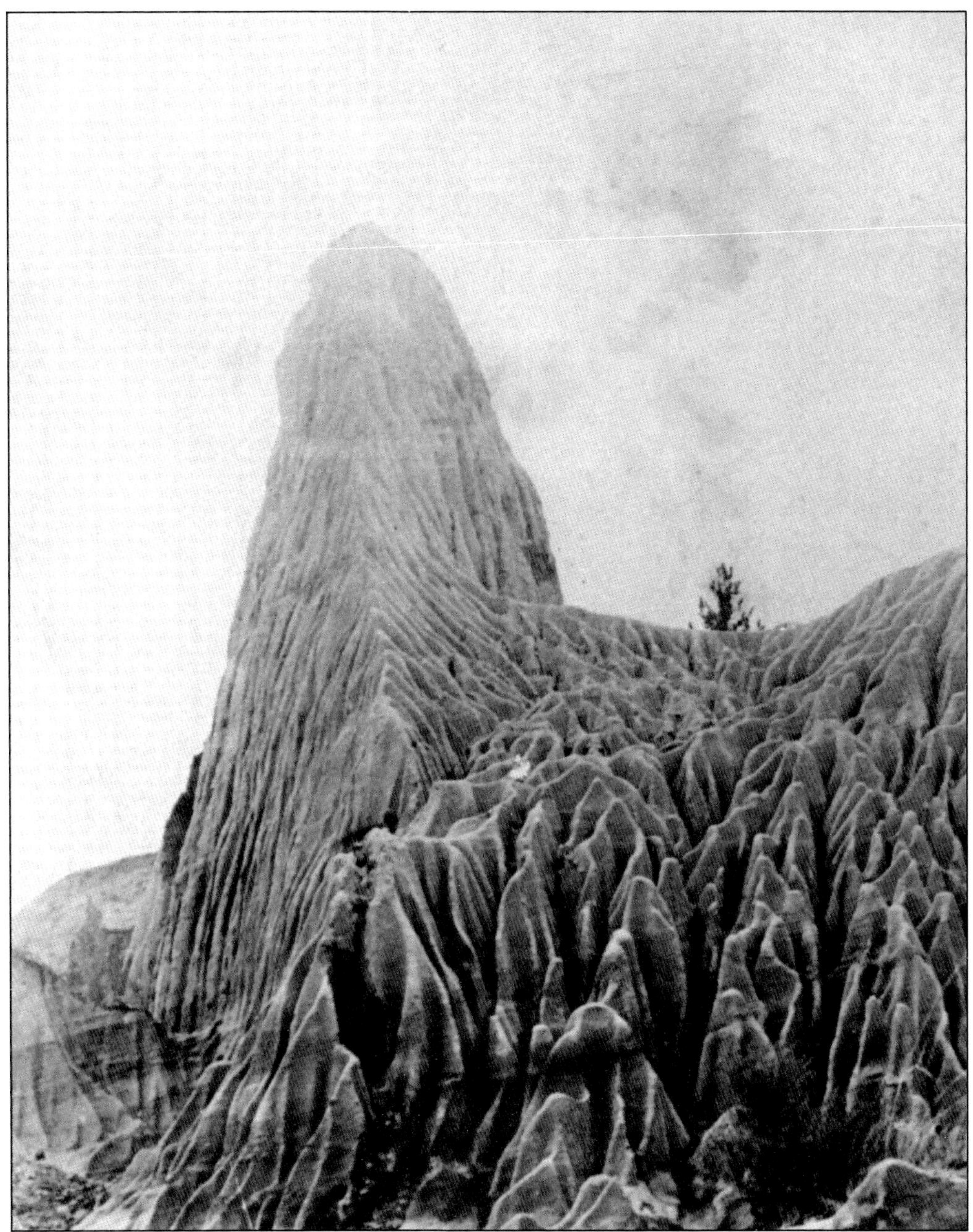

The contours of Icicle Peak in the Makoshika Badlands were formed by a steady barrage of erosion over a long period of time. An amateur photographer took this picture in 1902.

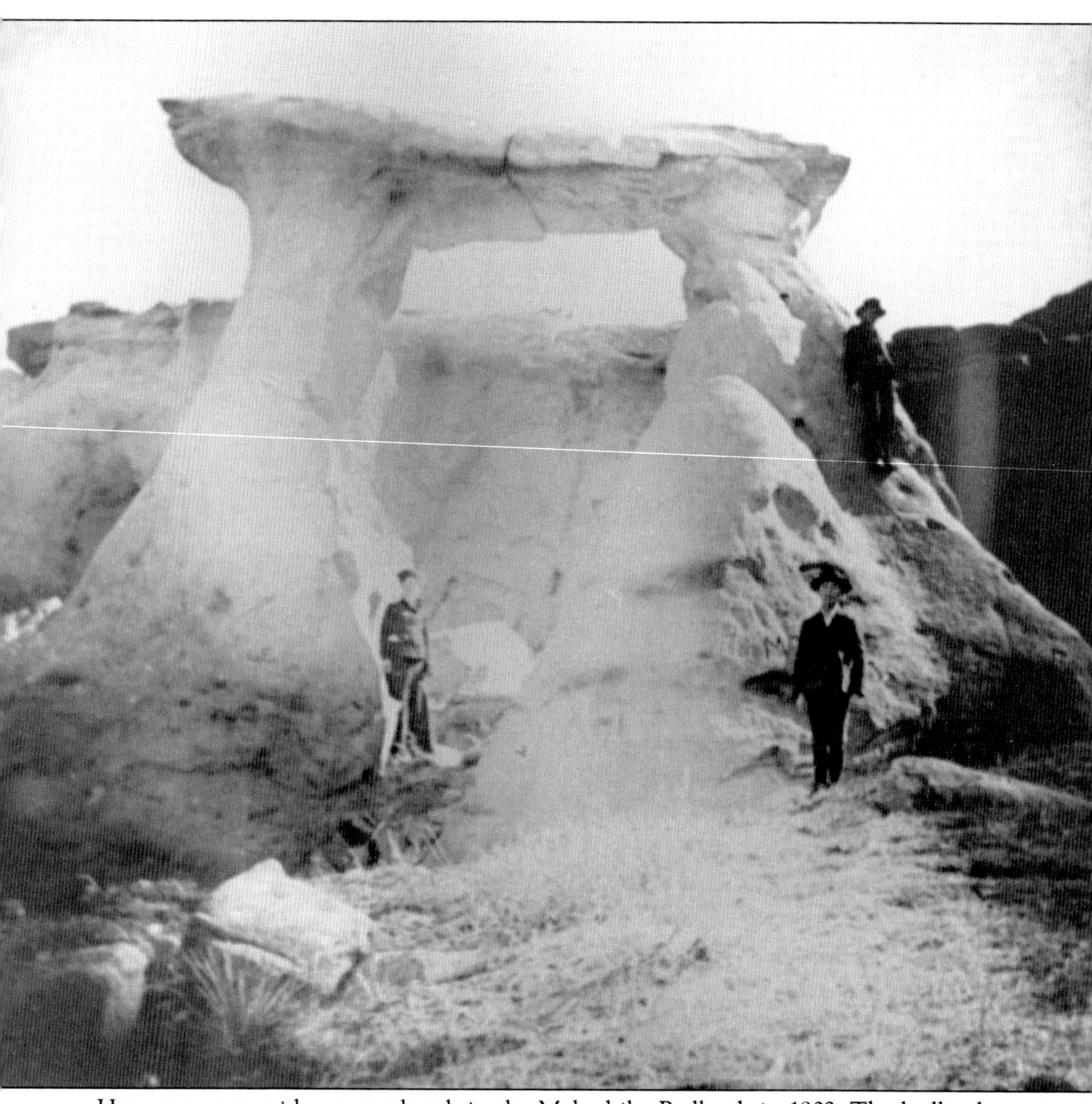

Here, men pose with a natural arch in the Makoshika Badlands in 1902. The badlands are in a constant state of erosion, and many of the geological features that were prevalent during the first half of the 20th century are no longer visible today. This arch has been claimed by nature since this photograph was taken.

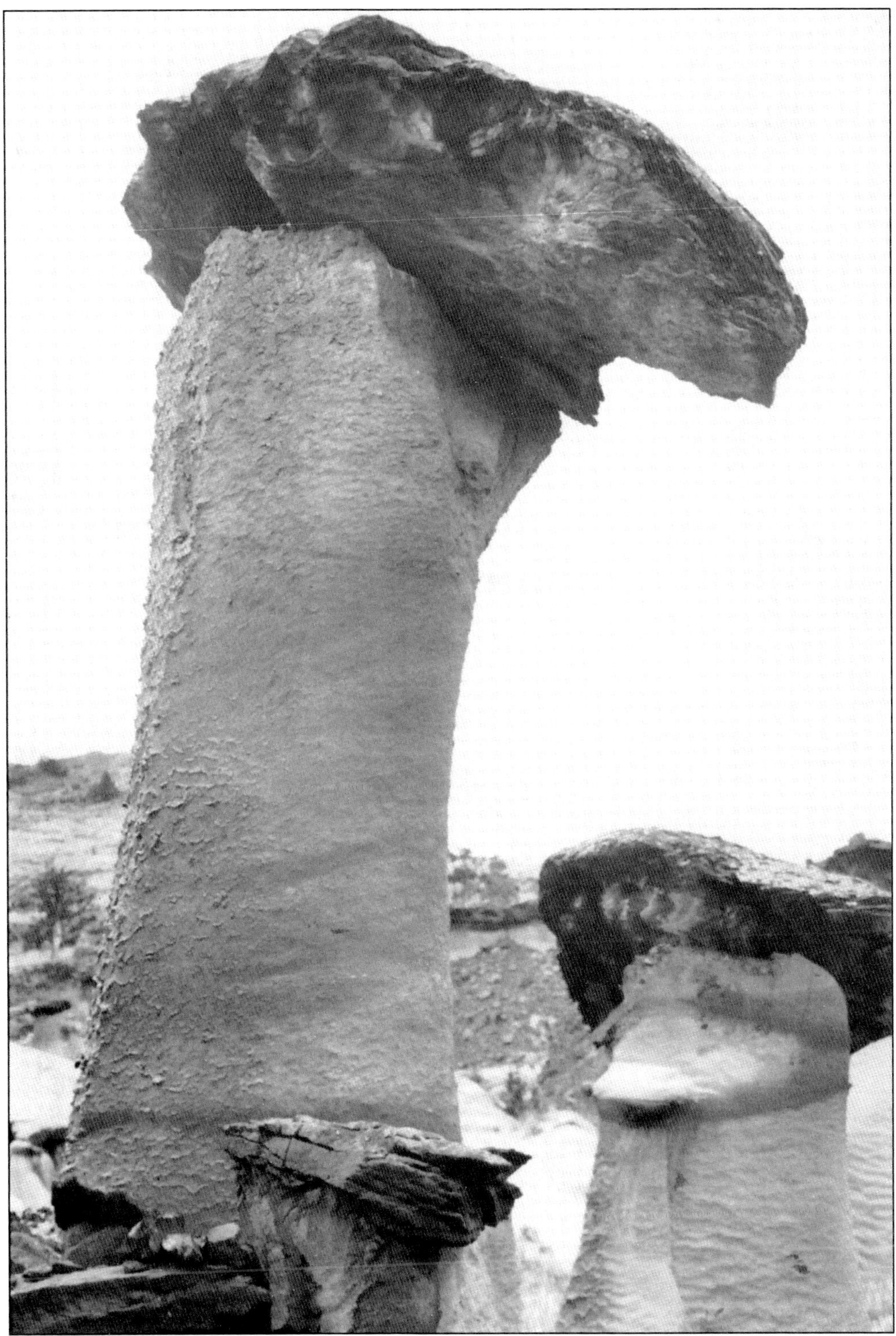
This photograph taken in 1916 shows the rock formation known as Custer's Pillar in the Makoshika Badlands. (Miskimen Collection.)

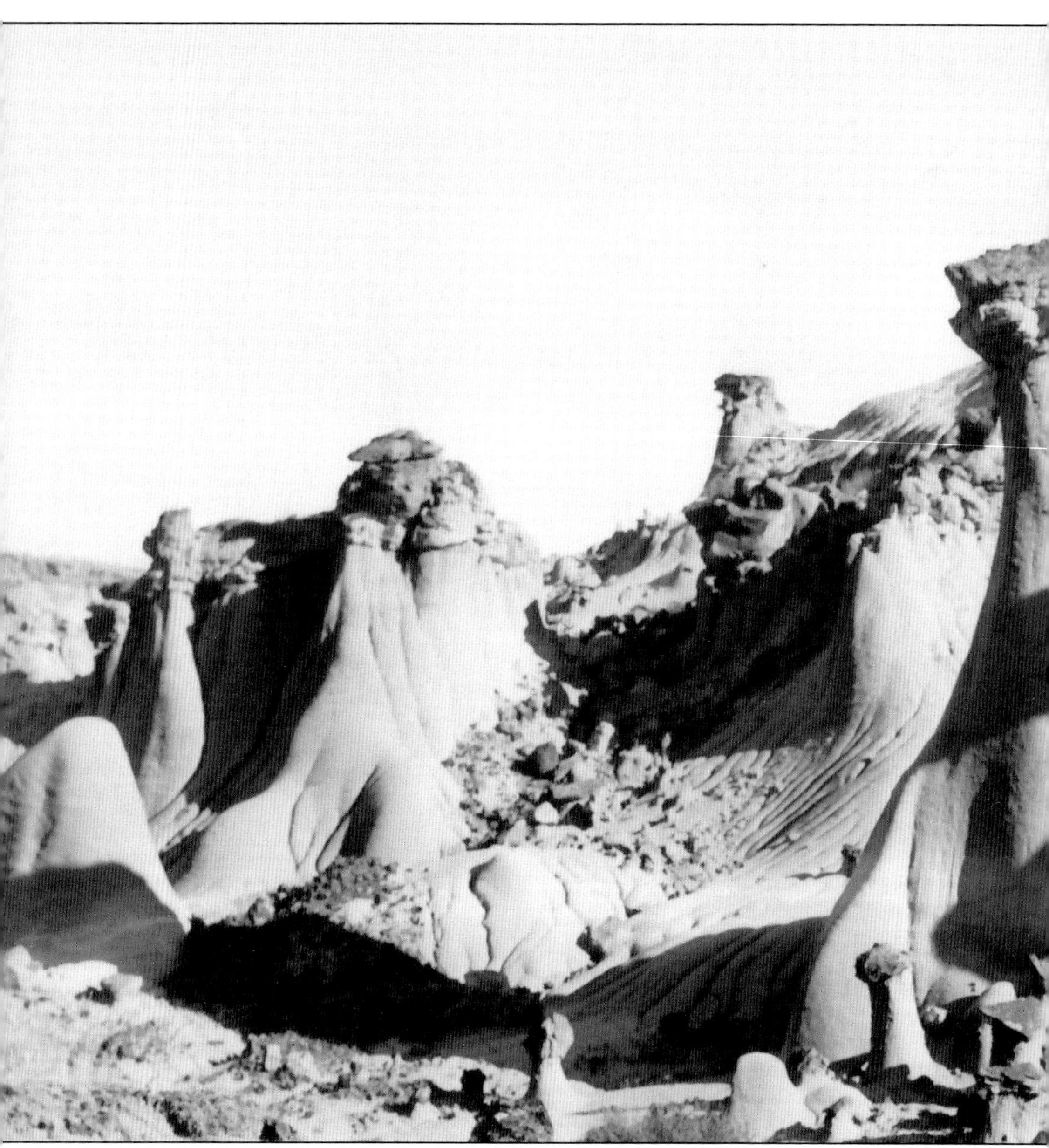

The beautifully eroded spires and hoodoos of the Makoshika Badlands have a surrealistic harmony

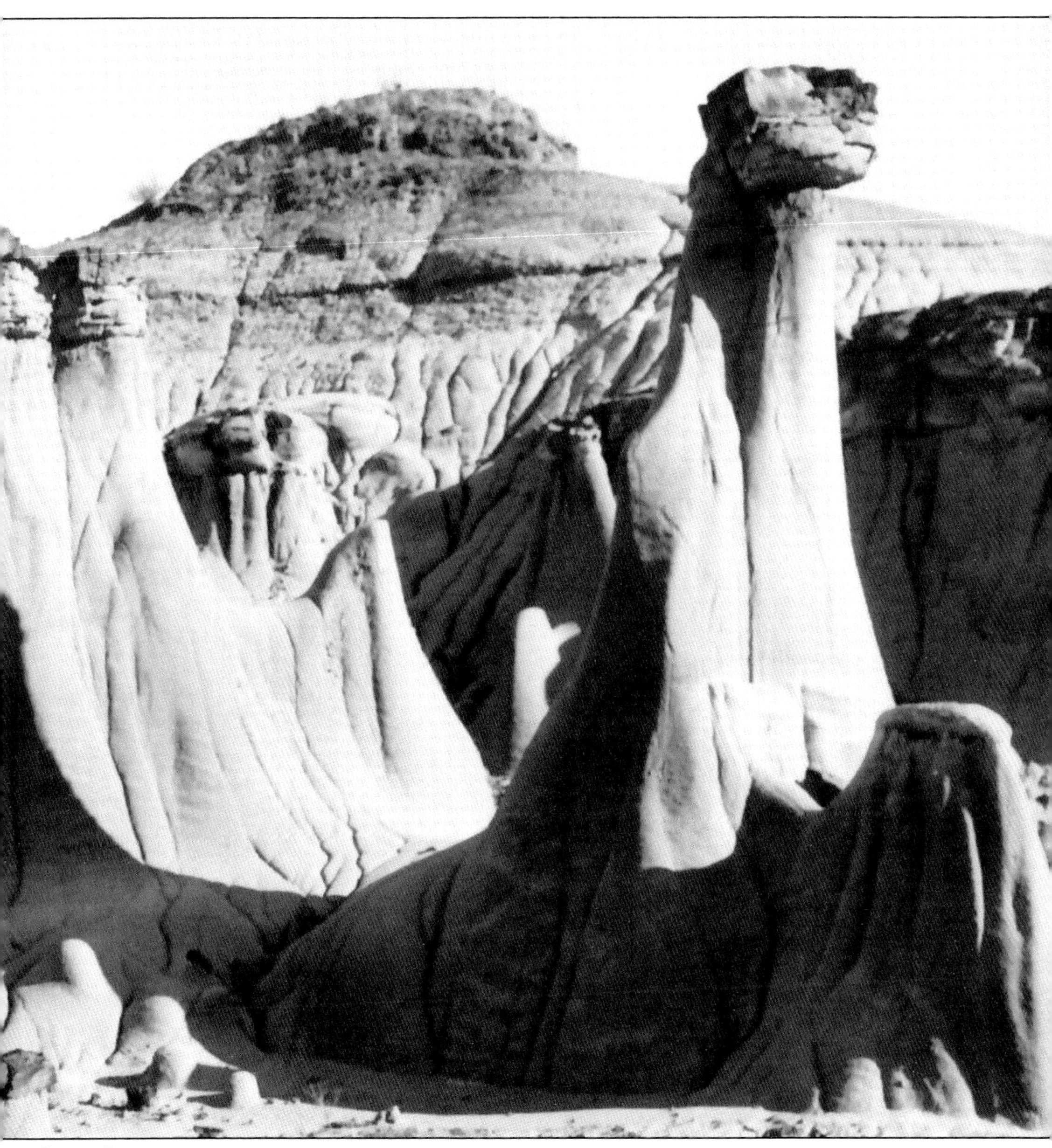

that only nature can create.

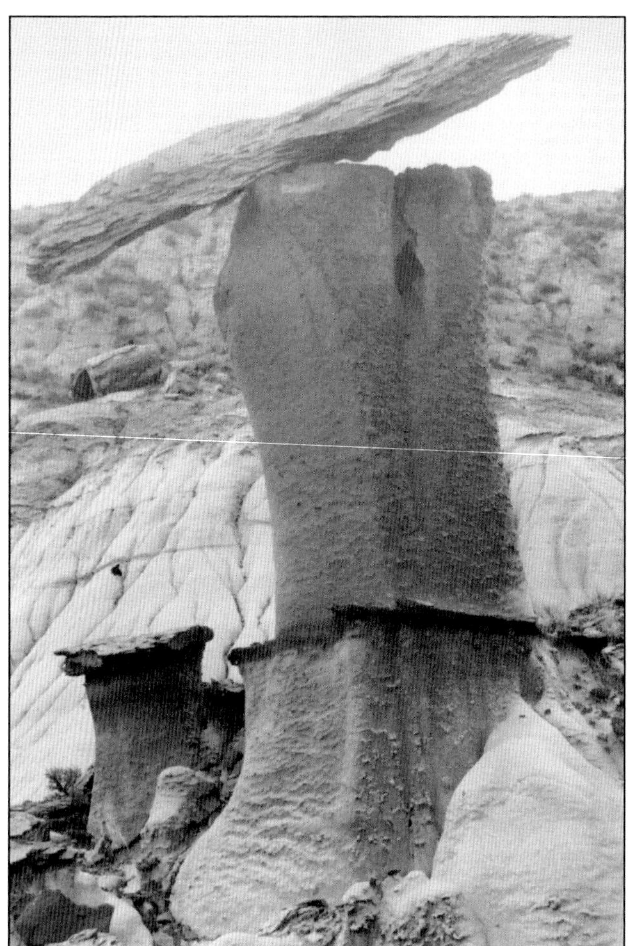

This photograph of the Balancing Rock in the Makoshika Badlands was taken by local resident J.H. Miskimen in 1916. The Balancing Rock has succumbed to erosion and no longer stands. (Miskimen Collection.)

Cain's Coulee is pictured in 1935. Now located in Makoshika State Park, the rugged, contorted scenery of this area has drawn curious visitors since the arrival of humans to the area thousands of years ago.

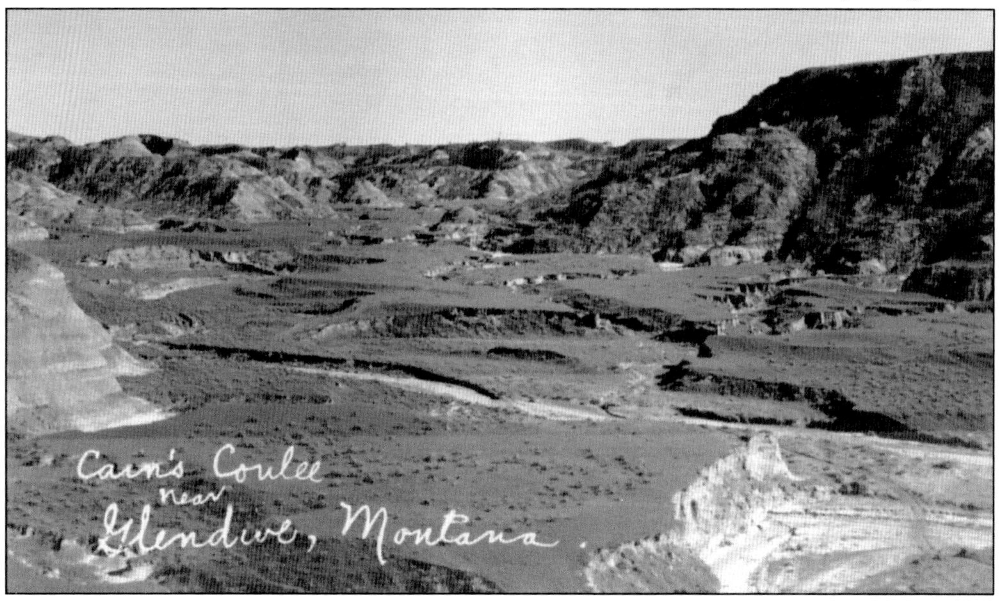

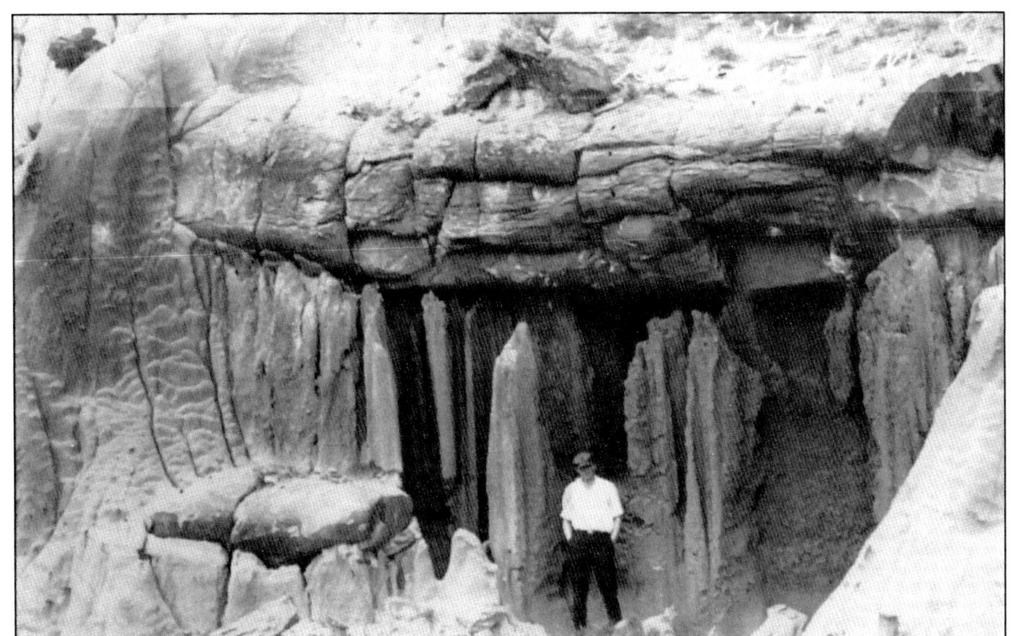

A tourist poses for a picture in the Makoshika Badlands.

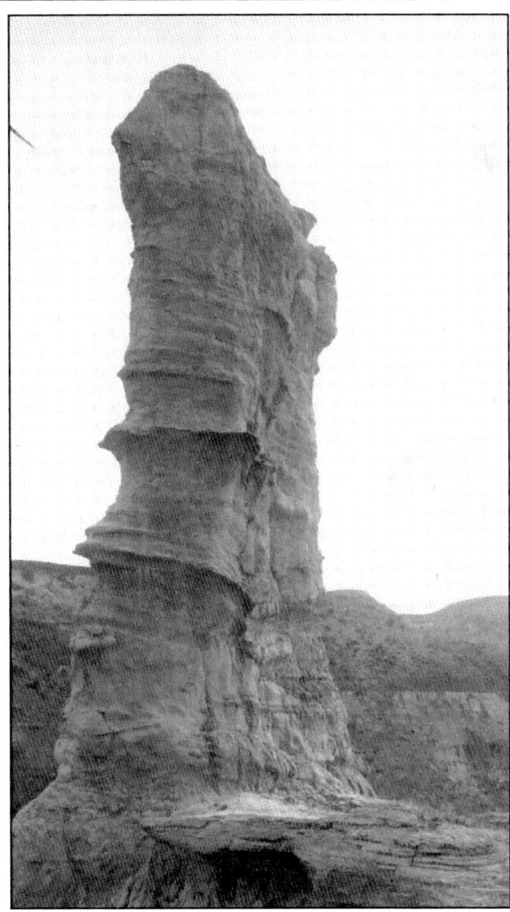

This imposing spire in the Makoshika Badlands was named Sitting Bull Tower after the Hunkpapa Sioux spiritual leader who led his people during Red Cloud's War and the Great Sioux War.

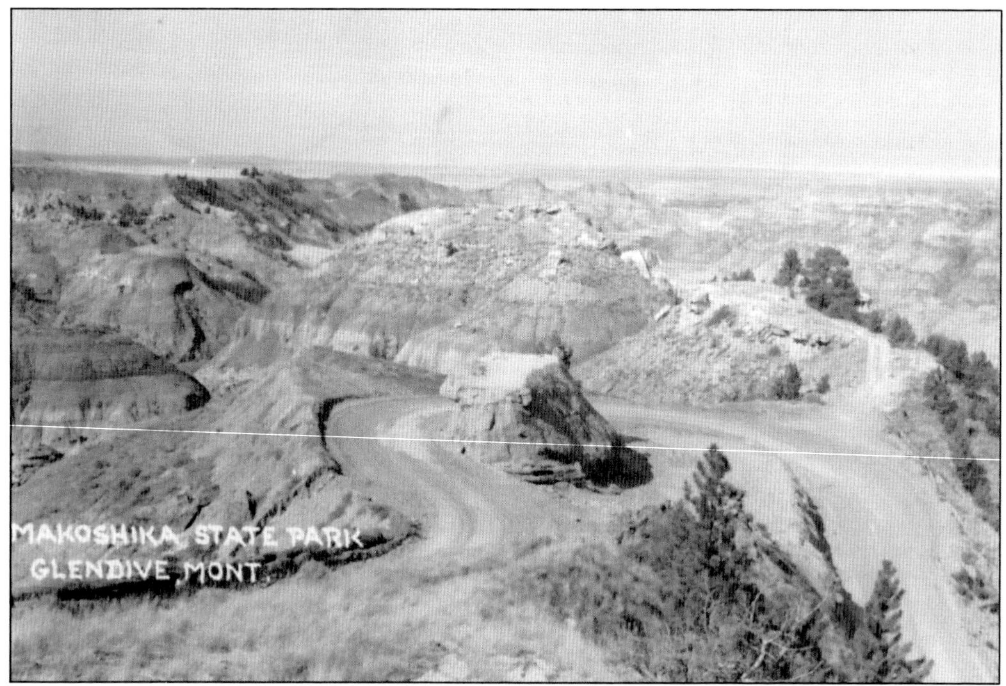

This c. 1950 photograph features a view of the road that leads to the top of the badland formations in Makoshika State Park. Because of the popularity of the badlands and the lack of infrastructure through them, the Works Progress Administration began building roads in the park in the 1930s.

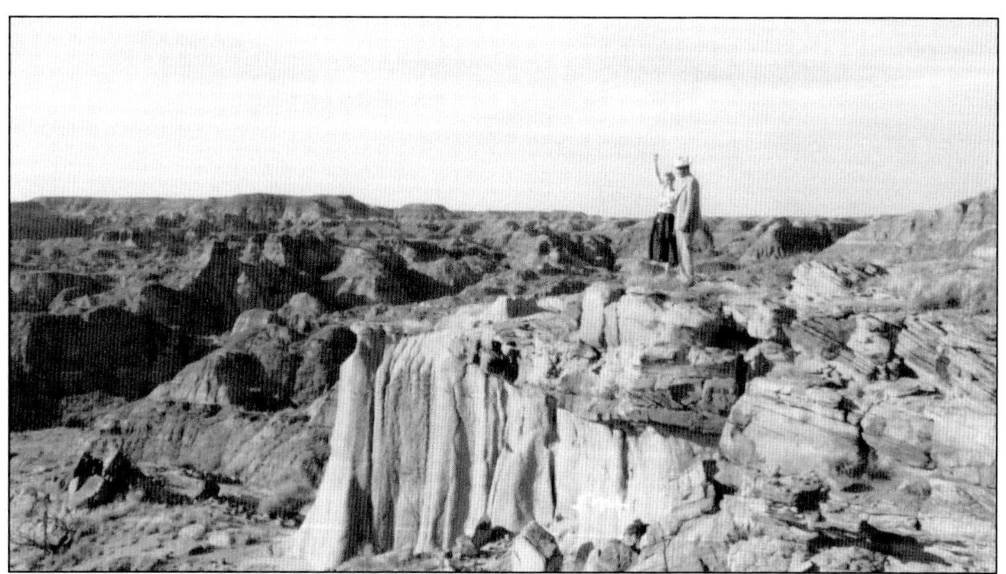

Tourists in the 1950s take in the view from the top of Makoshika State Park. From this vantage point, there are expansive views of the surrounding countryside and badland formations below.

Six

SIMPLE PLEASURES

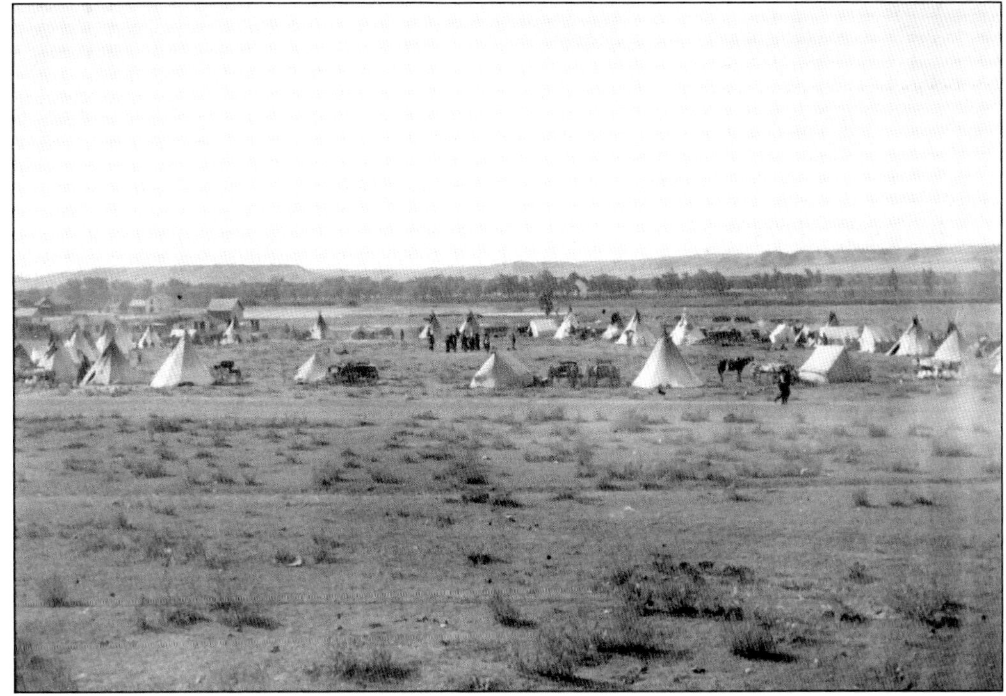

Several Indian nations came to Glendive for the county fair during the first decades of the town's development. They sold crafts and artwork and performed traditional dances for money. This photograph shows a Crow encampment at Glendive in 1882.

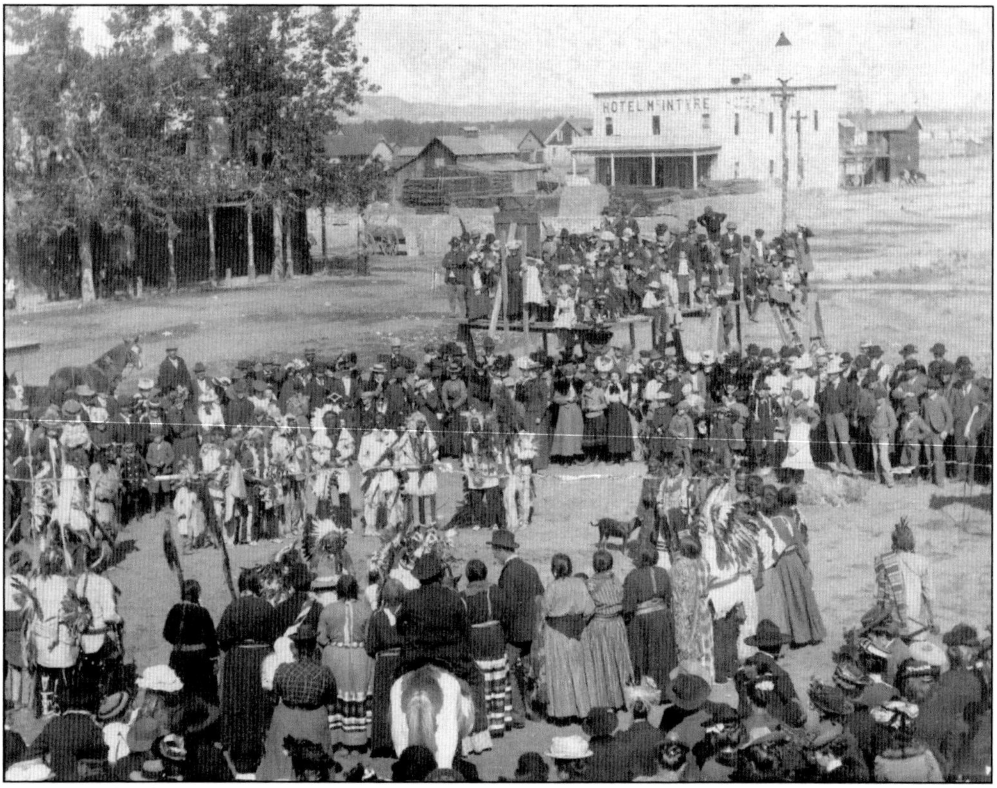

Curious Glendivians gather to watch Sioux dancers perform across the street from the newly constructed Jordan Hotel in 1900.

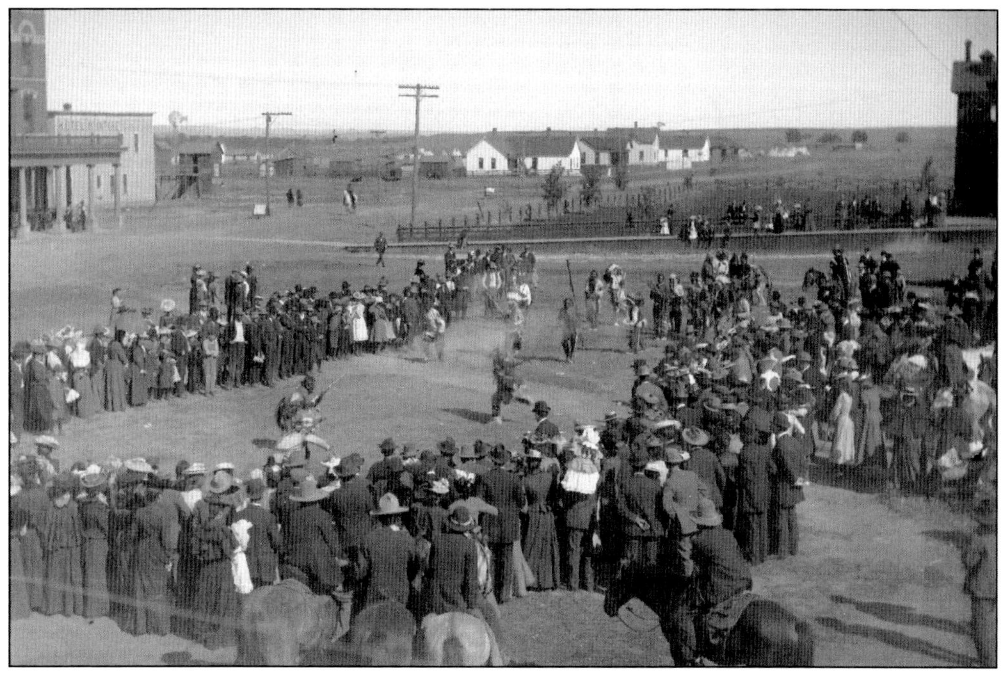

Mandan Sioux dancers perform a "war dance" during the Dawson County Fair in 1902.

Here, local Glendivians pose for a photograph with Mandan Sioux chief John Lone Dog and his wife during the Dawson County Fair in 1902.

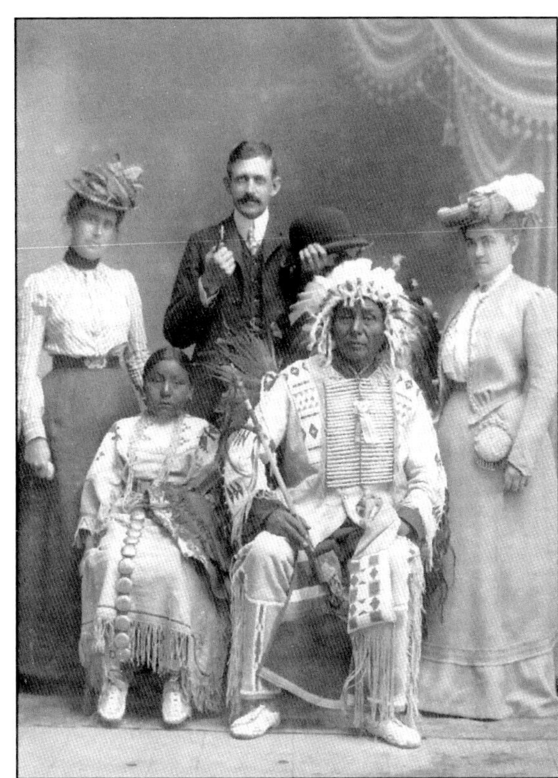

Sioux Indians march down Merrill Avenue during the Dawson County Fair around 1896. (Montana Historical Society.)

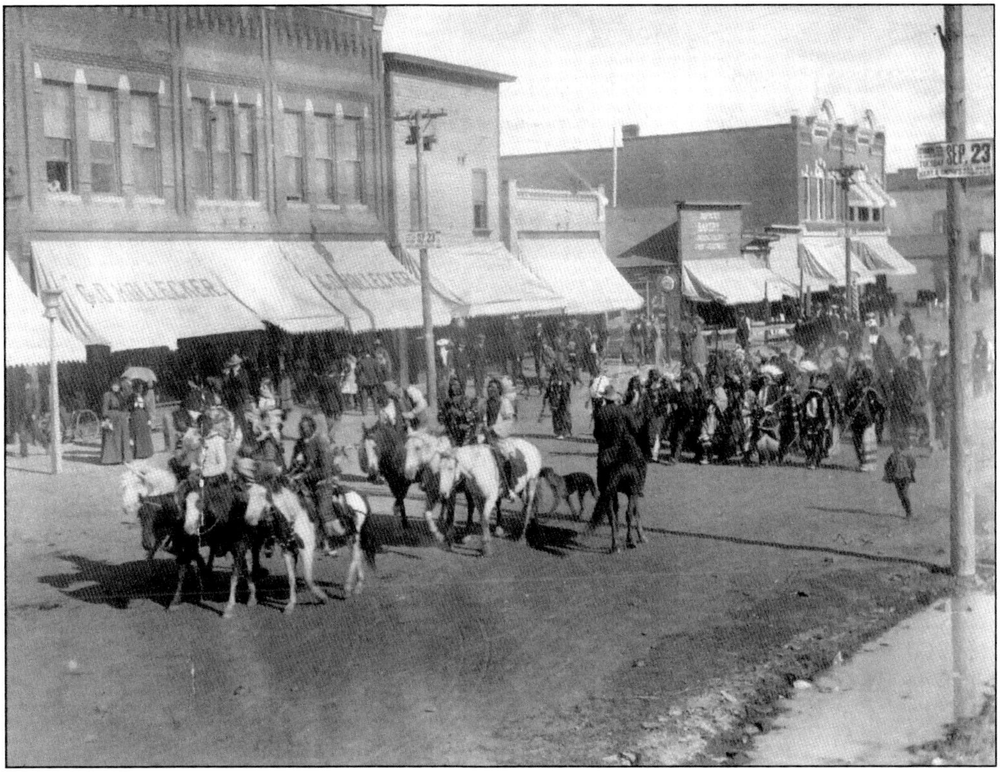

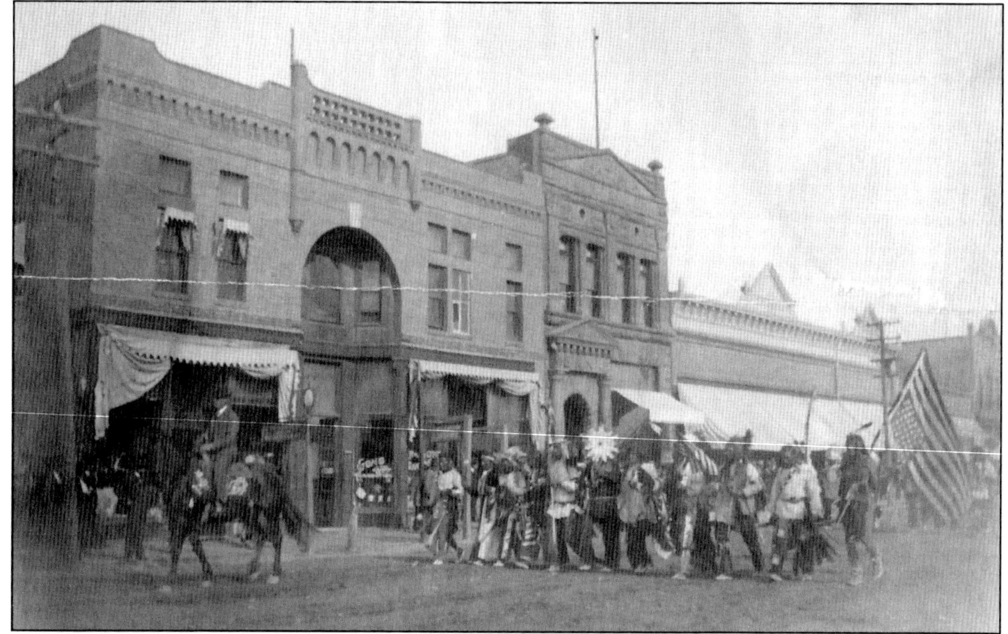

Sioux Indians march through Glendive during the Dawson County Fair in 1903. Note the upside-down American flag. By 1903, the various Siouan tribes were under the threat of cultural extinction. In Siouan and other Native American cultures, displaying an inverted American flag is a symbol of distress or mourning.

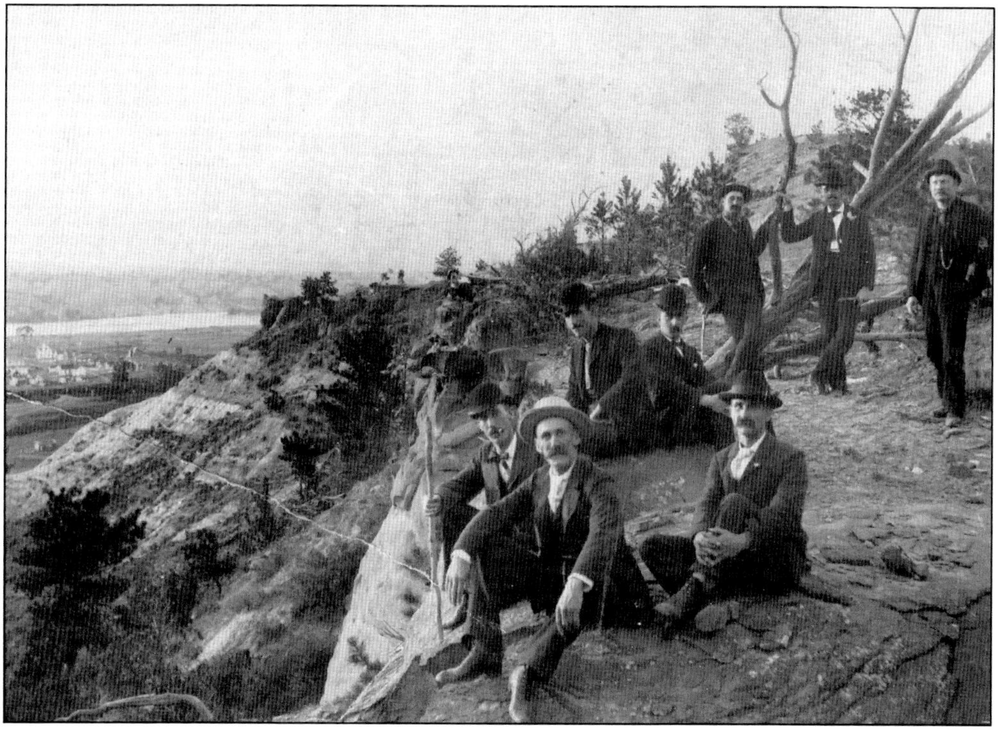

Locals pose for a photograph on Hungry Joe Hill around 1900. The town of Glendive and the Yellowstone River are in the valley below. (Andrew Foss Collection.)

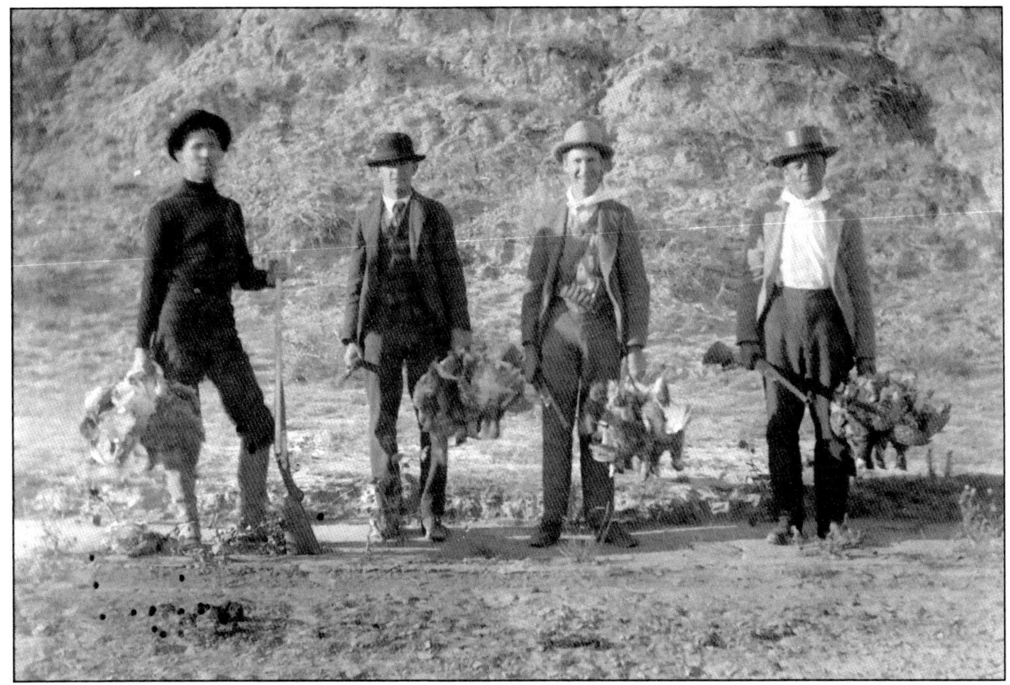

Hunting upland birds has long been a popular pastime in eastern Montana. This photograph shows men after a successful day of hunting sharp-tailed grouse in the badlands outside of Glendive around 1900. (Lowe Estate.)

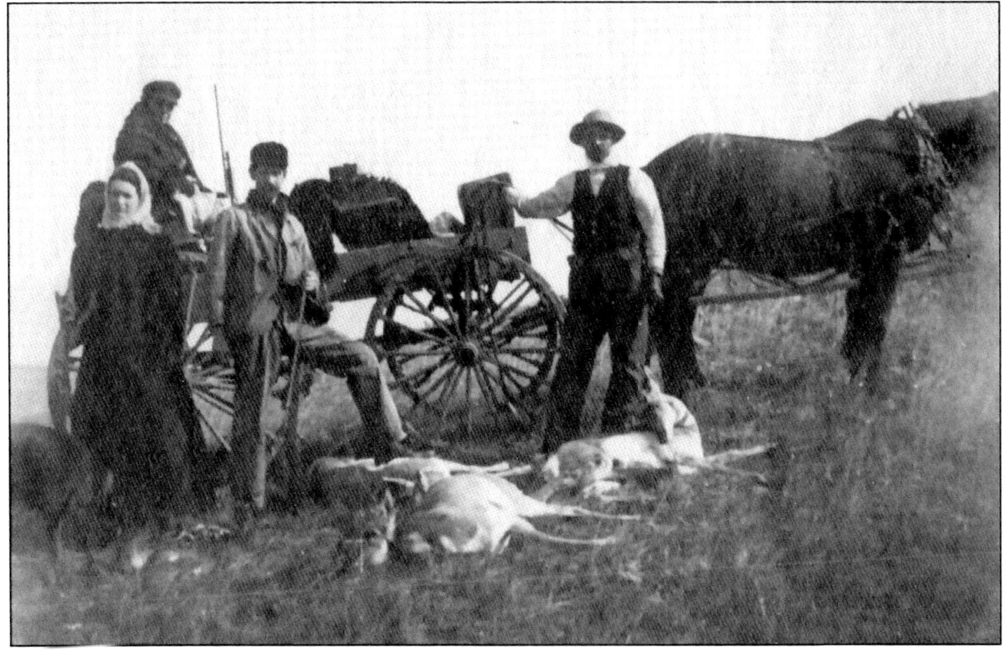

The badlands and prairies surrounding Glendive are home to an abundance of wildlife. This photograph shows the Kelly family after a successful antelope hunt near Glendive. Pictured are Harriett Kelly Banker (in wagon) and W.W. Kelly (standing on the right). (Charles and William Kelly Banker Collection.)

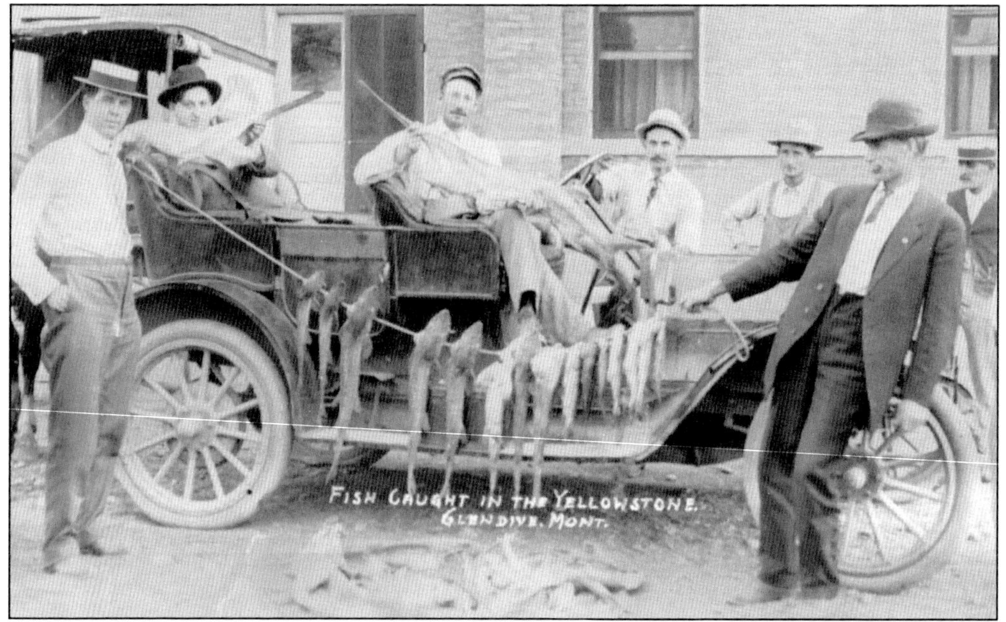

This photograph by L.A. Foster shows local men after a successful day of fishing on the Yellowstone River. The two men seated in the car hold paddlefish. Sturgeon dangle from the string in the foreground.

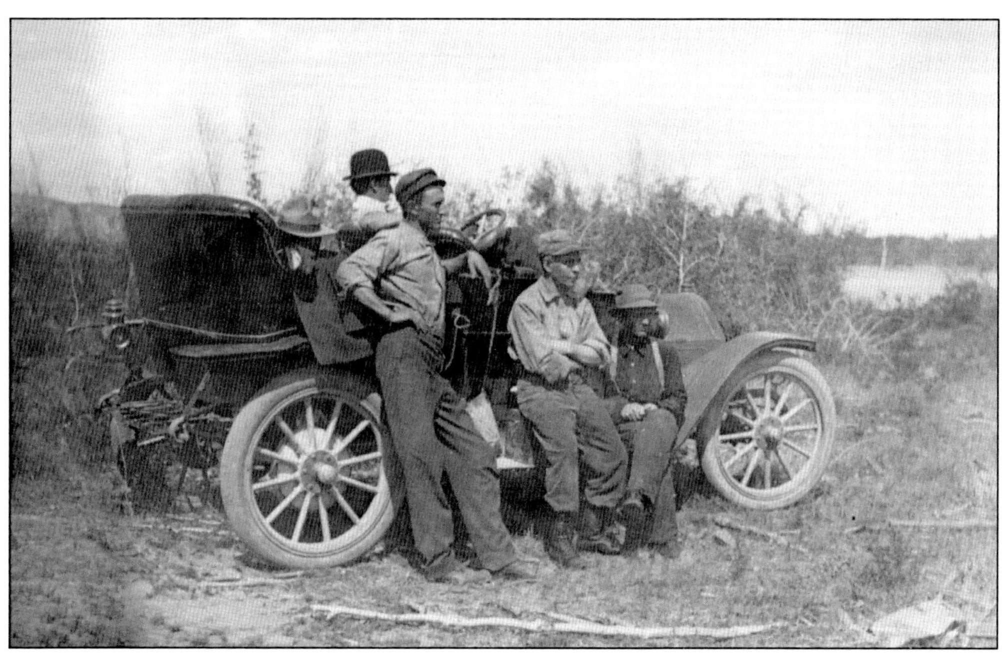

The Yellowstone River has long been a popular destination for Glendivians with leisure time. Here, five men pose by a car on the bank of the Yellowstone River.

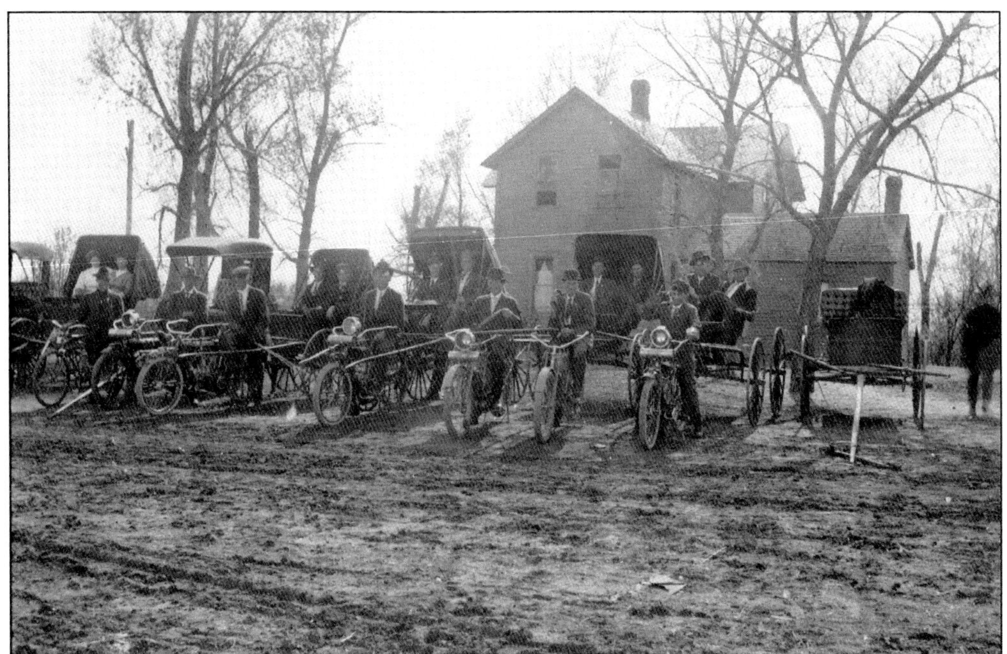

Taken in Glendive around 1905, this unusual photograph shows the juxtaposition of 19th- and 20th-century technologies in eastern Montana. A fleet of wagons is featured hooked to motorcycles.

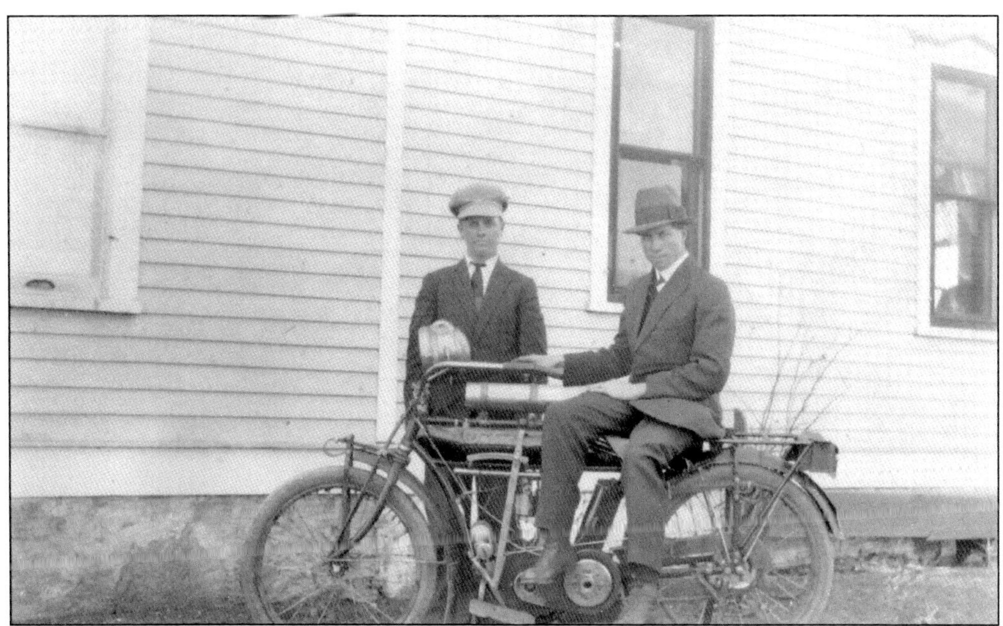

Motorcycle culture has been a part of the social fabric of Glendive since the early 1900s. This photograph shows two men posing with an early Indian motorcycle in Glendive.

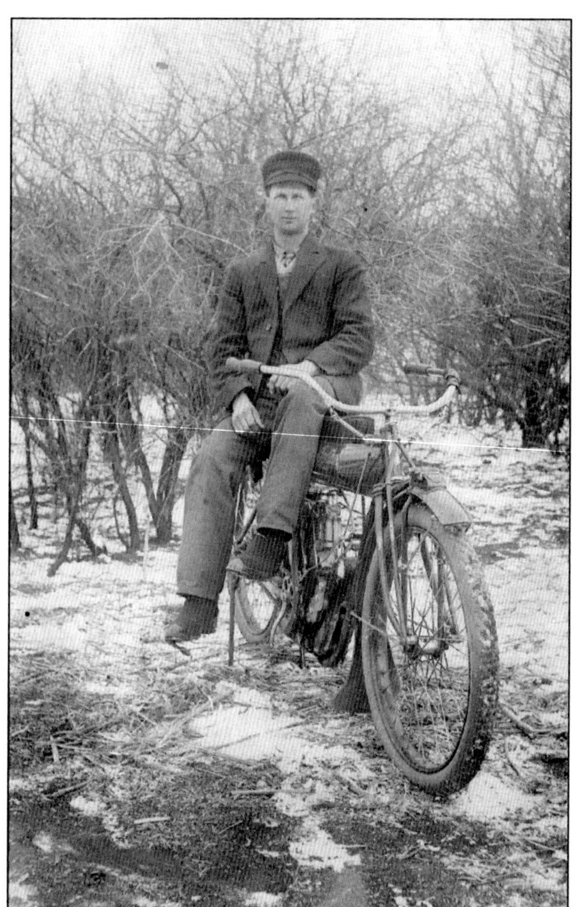

This photograph shows a local railroad worker in Glendive posing with his early-model Indian motorcycle during the winter.

One of the early signs of the end of the harsh winter season in the Glendive region is ice breakage on the Yellowstone River. When the ice breaks, gigantic sheets of ice, sometimes larger than school buses, are swept downriver and often cause ice jams. These ice jams result in devastating flooding along the banks of the untamed river. A popular activity among locals in the early spring was watching the ice go out, as these spectators are doing from the Yellowstone River Bridge around 1910. (Mary Meissner Collection.)

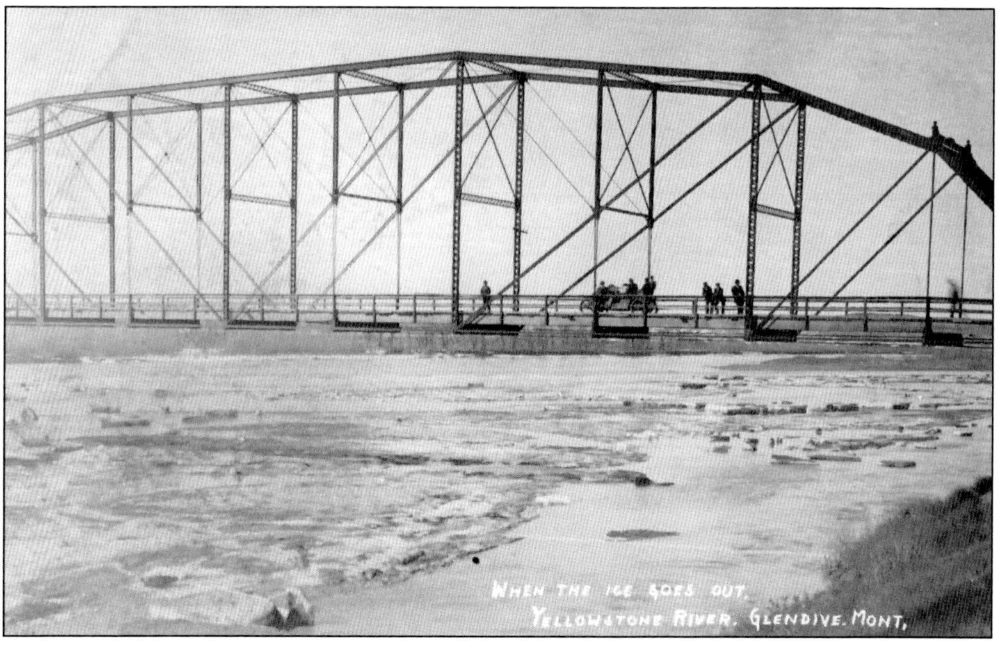

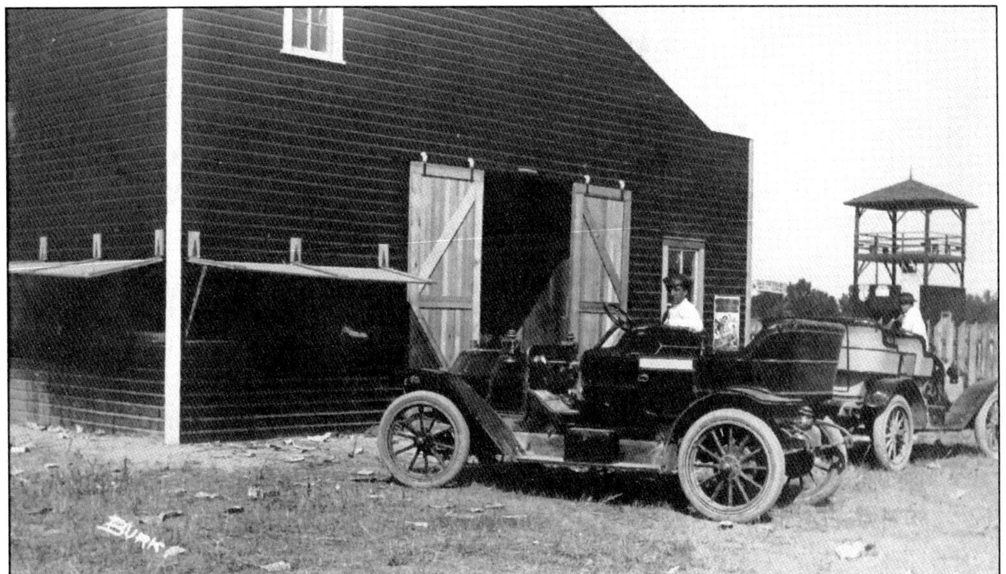

The popularity of auto racing at the Dawson County Fairgrounds in the summertime grew as cars became more commonplace in Glendive. This snapshot by L.A. Foster shows the winner of the 1909 Dawson County Fair auto race standing next to his winning Velie Model 30. The race was five miles long.

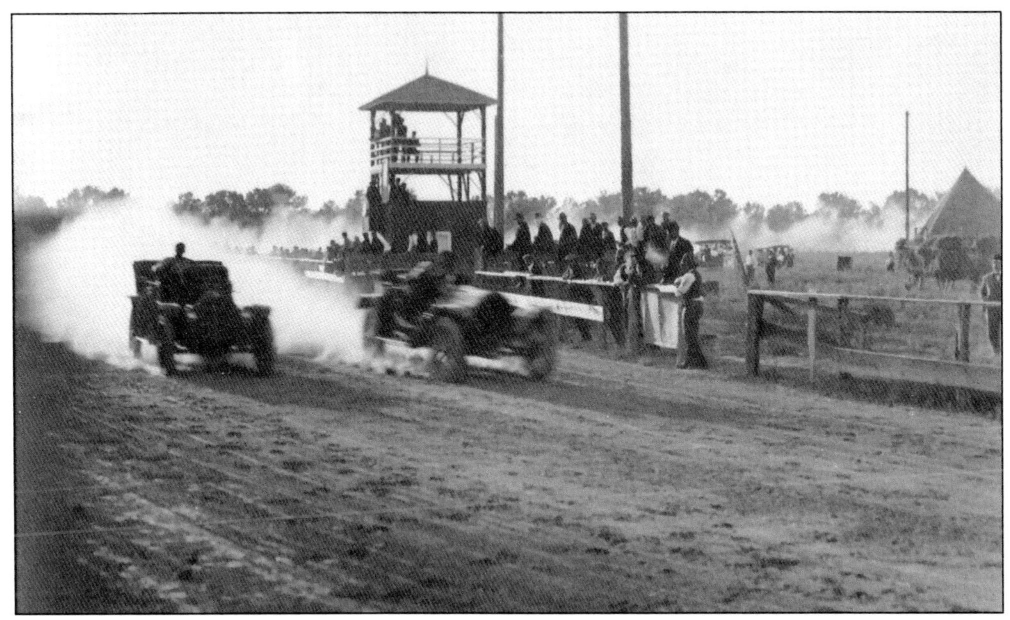

In 1912, a Cadillac narrowly beat out a Velie at the Dawson County Fair.

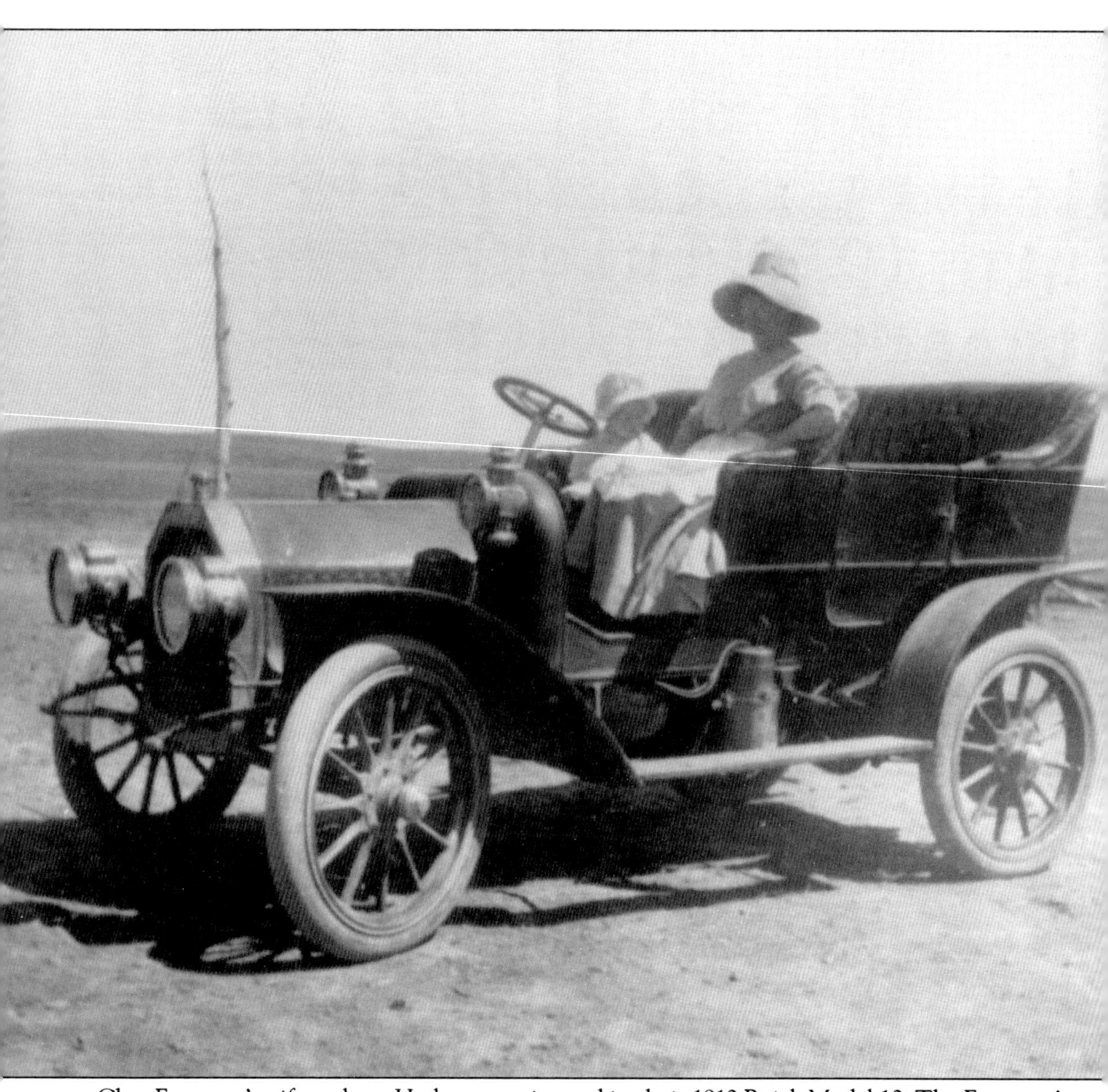

Chas Ferguson's wife and son Herbert are pictured in their 1910 Buick Model 10. The Ferguson's Buick was one of the first cars in the Clear Creek area. It was purchased for $975.

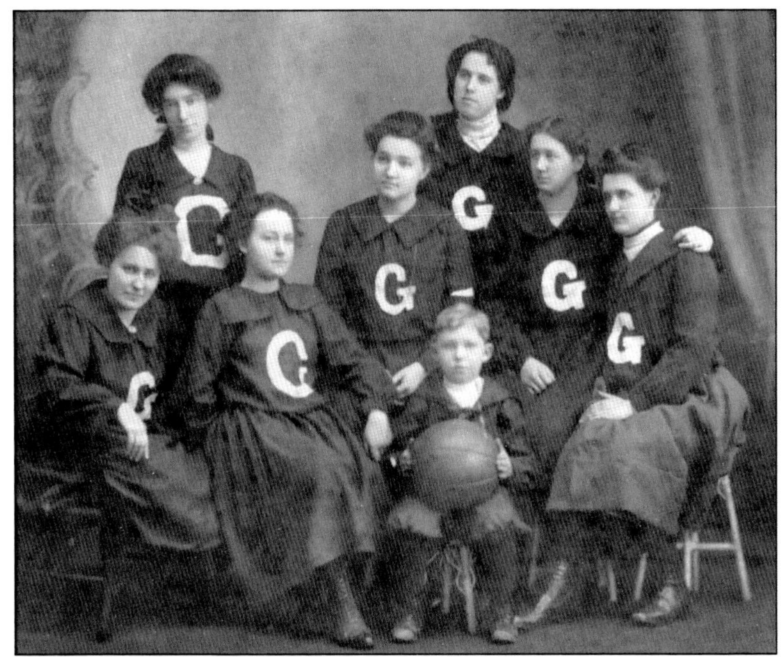

This photograph of the Glendive women's basketball club demonstrates that women's athletics has long been a feature of Glendive society.

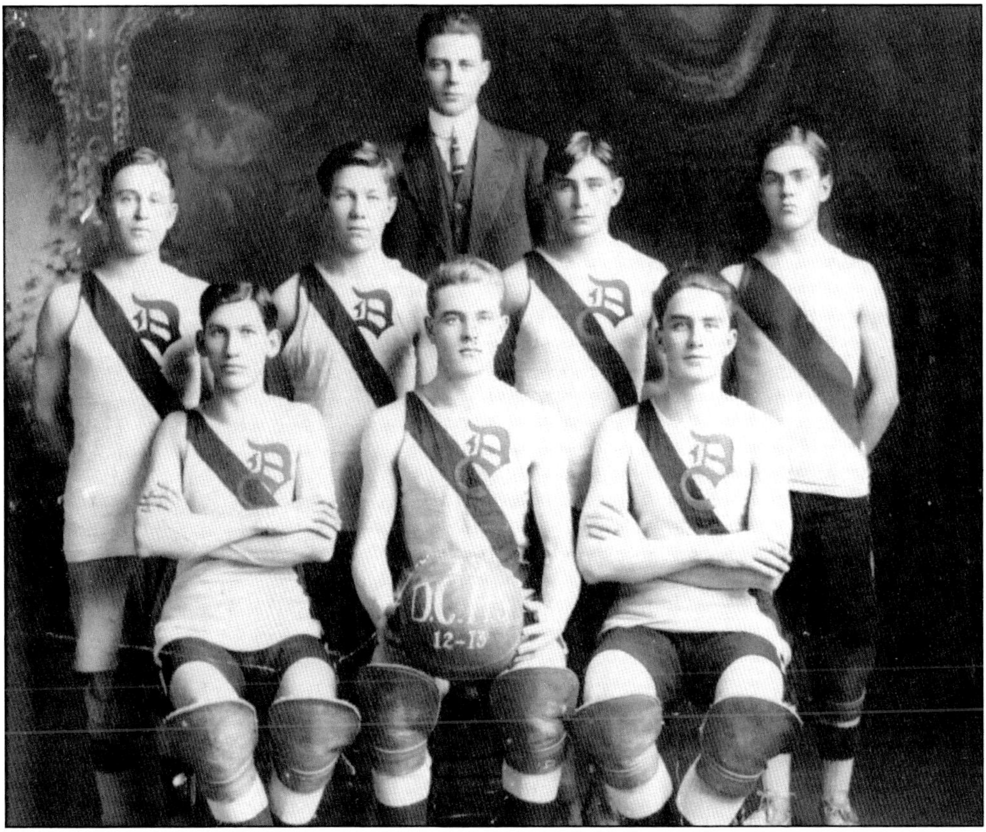

The members of the Dawson County High School men's basketball team were crowned district champions for the 1912–1913 season.

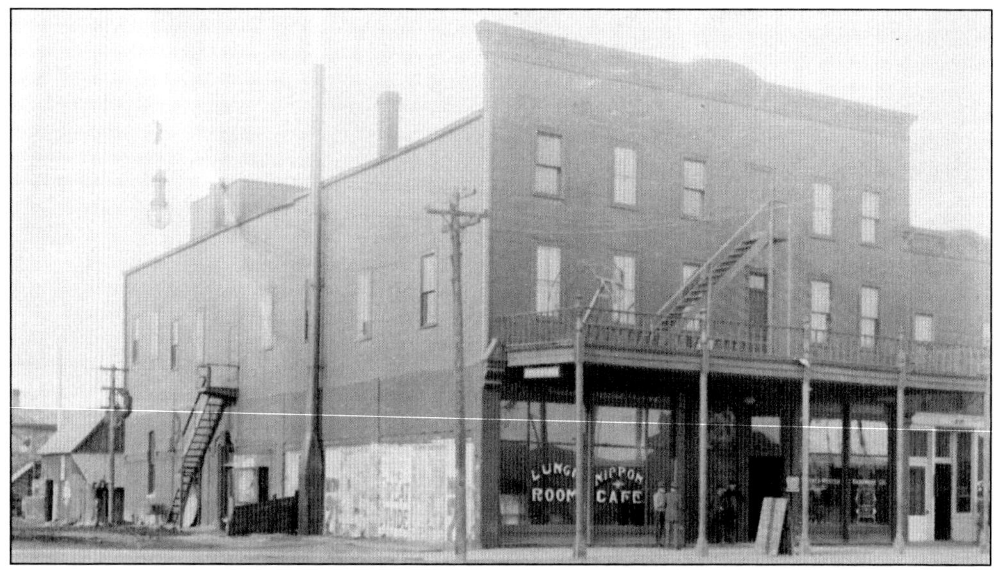

This photograph shows the Glendive Opera House (upper level) and Japanese American–owned Nippon Café and Rivenes-Wester Hardware Company (bottom) located at 120 ½ Merrill Avenue in 1907.

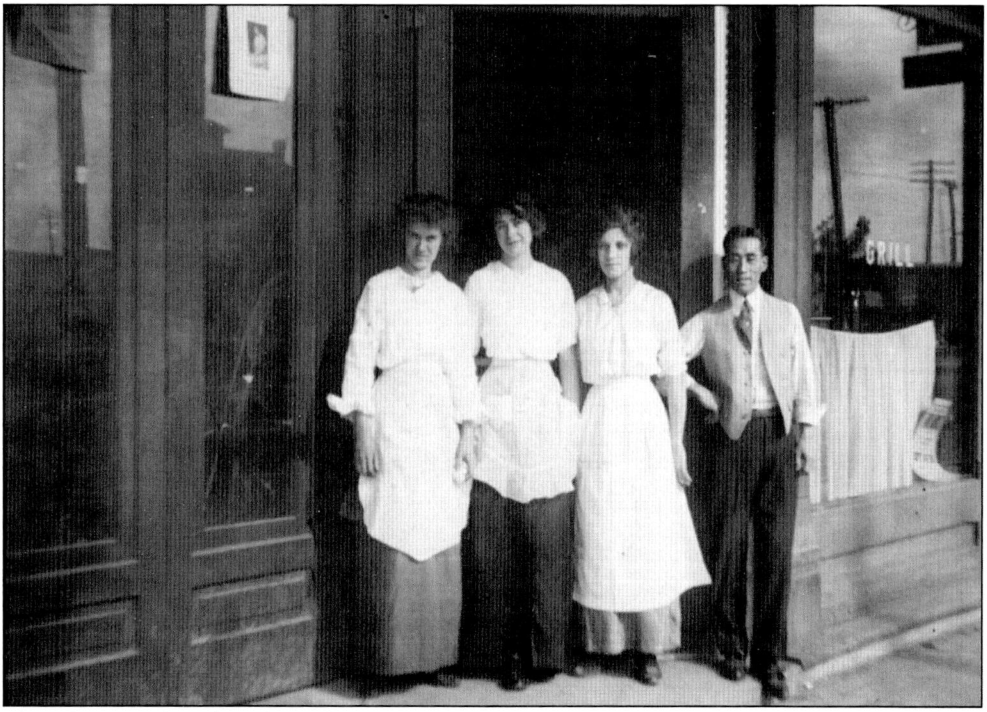

This photograph is thought to show the Japanese owner and staff of the Nippon Café. "Nippon" is a reading of kanji that means "Japan."

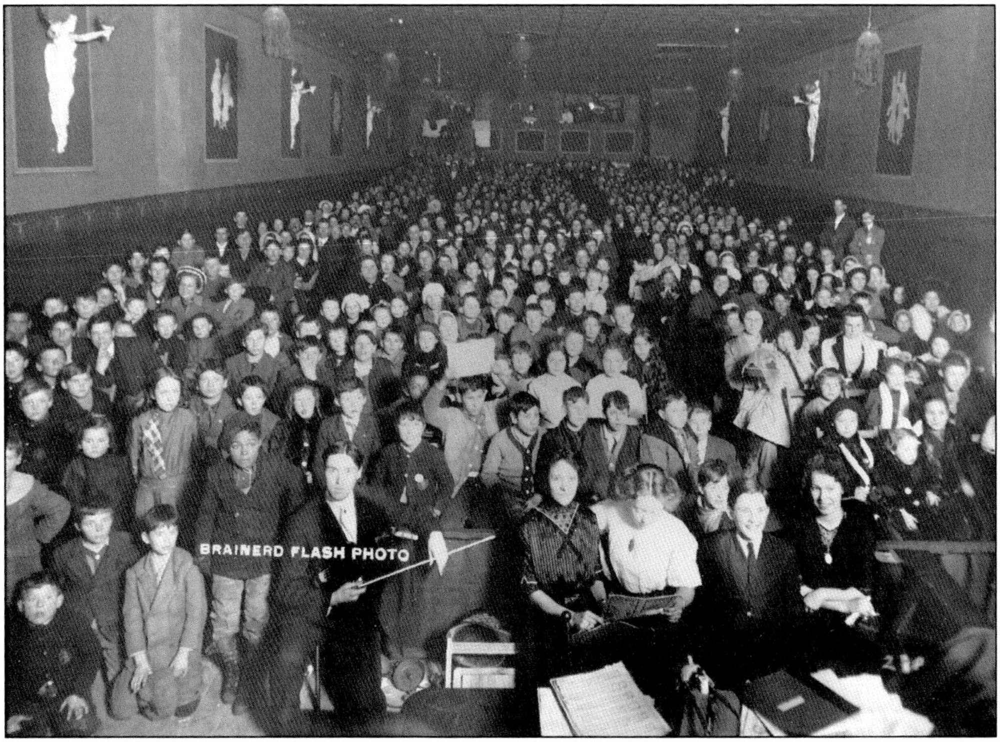

This image offers a rare glimpse inside the Glendive Opera House at the turn of the century.

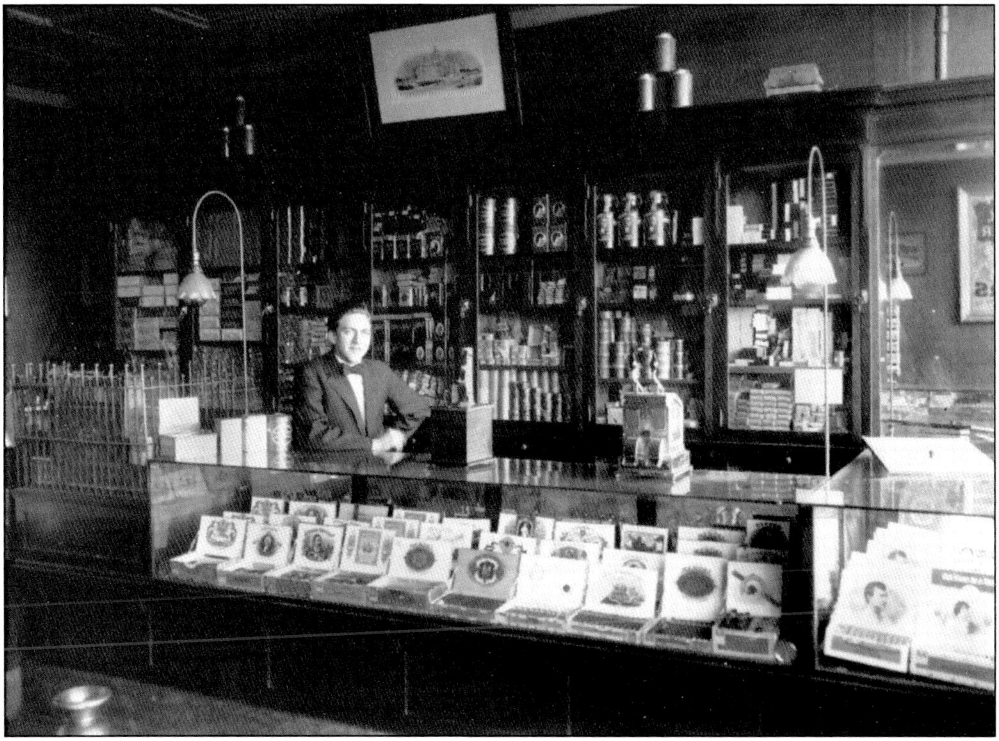

This photograph shows the interior of Healey's Cigar Store on Merrill Avenue.

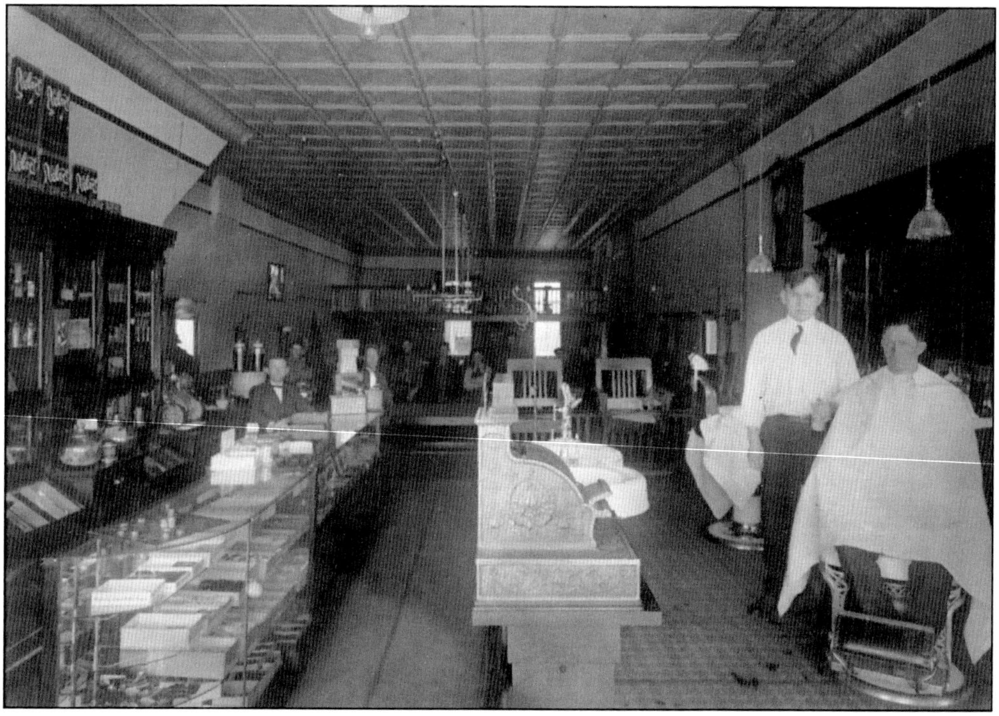

Pictured is the combined Syverson's Barbershop and M.L. Lee's Pool Hall. Patrons could enjoy a game of billiards while they waited for a haircut and shave.

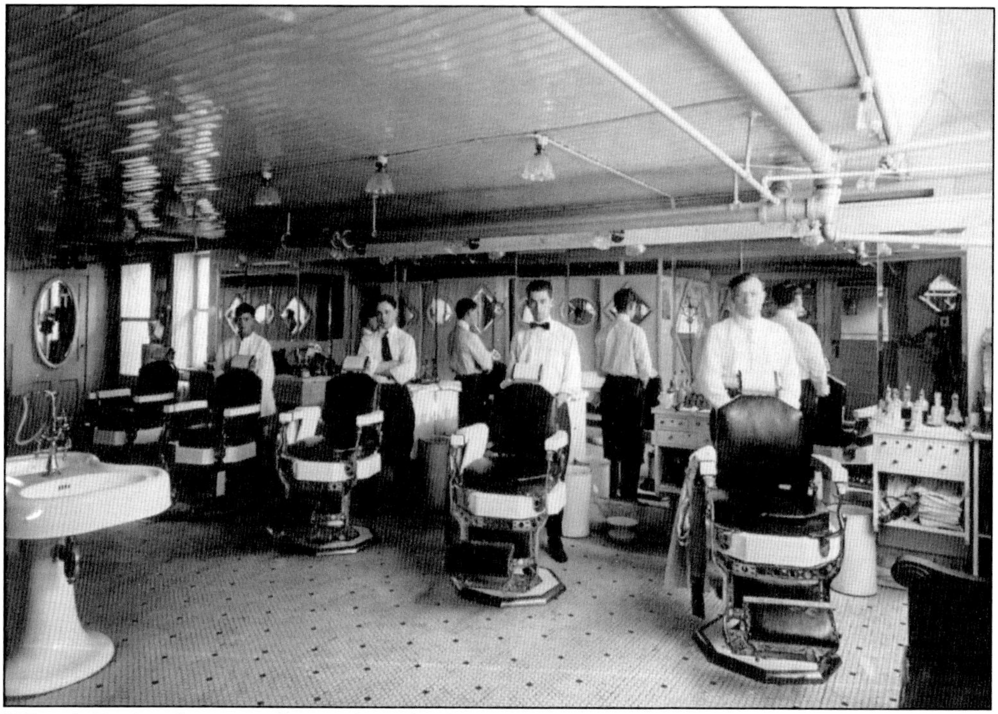

White's Barbershop was located in the basement of the Jordan Hotel and catered to an upscale clientele.

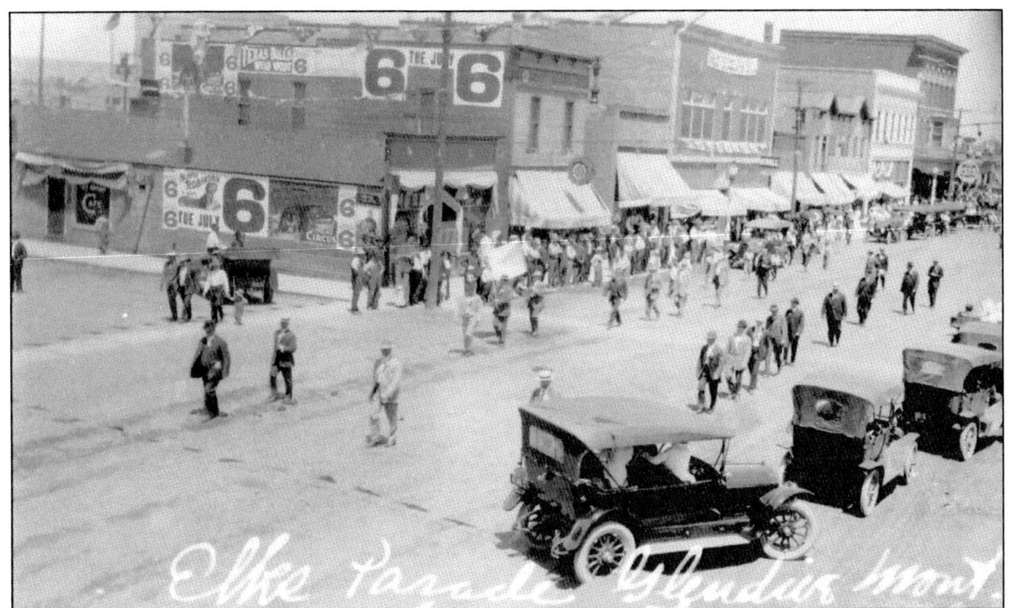

Civic organizations, like the Elk's Lodge, have long been an important part of the social fabric of Glendive. Here, members of the local Elk's Lodge march down Merrill Avenue during the annual Elk's Lodge parade in 1915. The prominent advertisements on the buildings are for the Texas Bill Wild West Show and Yankee Robinson Three-Ring Circus.

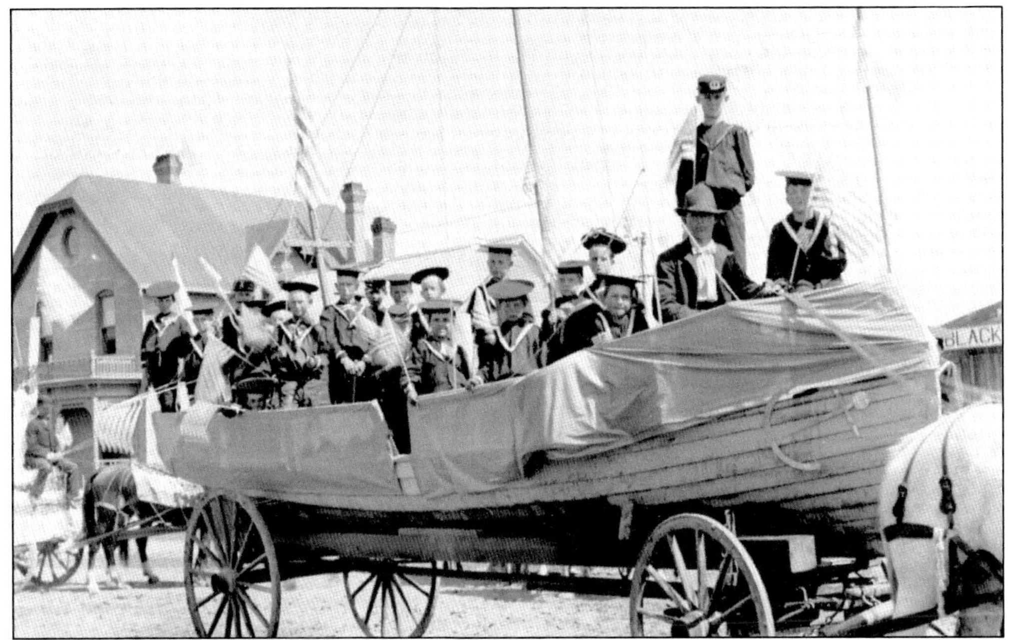

Independence Day celebrations in Glendive prior to 1945 usually encompassed three days marked by parades, rodeos, and auto races. Glendivians did not just celebrate America's independence from Britain but also the establishment of Camp Canby on July 5, 1873, and the arrival of the first Northern Pacific train on July 5, 1881. Pictured here is a float that was part of the Glendive Independence Day parade in 1898. The float, the flagship *Olympia*, was built by Professor W.S. Rowe, bandmaster of the Glendive Band.

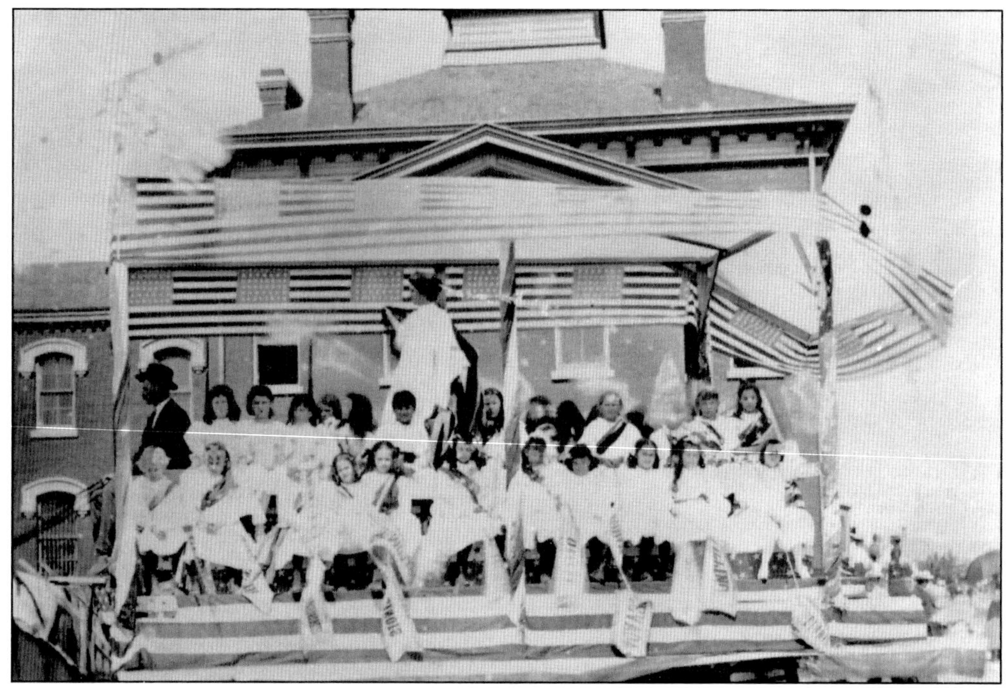

An Independence Day parade float is pictured in front of the old county courthouse in 1898. The float features 45 children representing the 45 states in the Union in 1898. Joe Hurst, who was later executed by the state for the murder of Dominic Cavanaugh in 1900, drove the float.

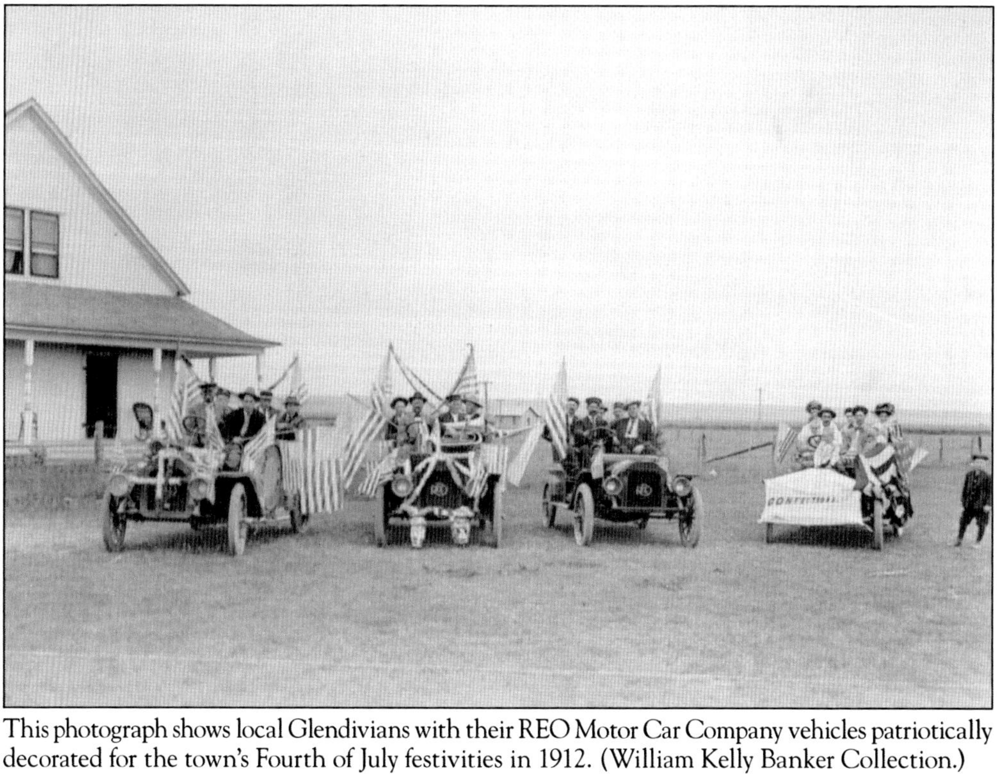

This photograph shows local Glendivians with their REO Motor Car Company vehicles patriotically decorated for the town's Fourth of July festivities in 1912. (William Kelly Banker Collection.)

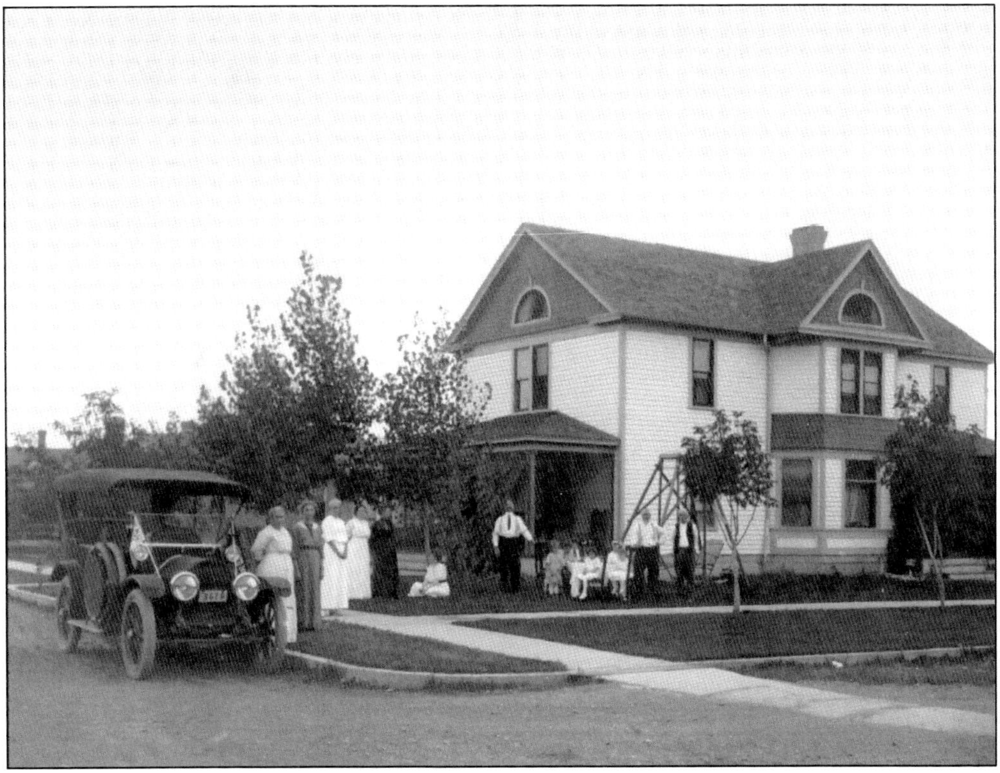

This photograph by L.A. Foster shows a simple birthday party for Llewellyn Kelly at the William W. Kelly home at 521 North Merrill Avenue in Glendive. This two-and-a-half-story middle-class frame house featured horizontal wood siding, ornamental fish scale shingles, and decorative lunette windows. (Charles and William Kelly Banker Collection.)

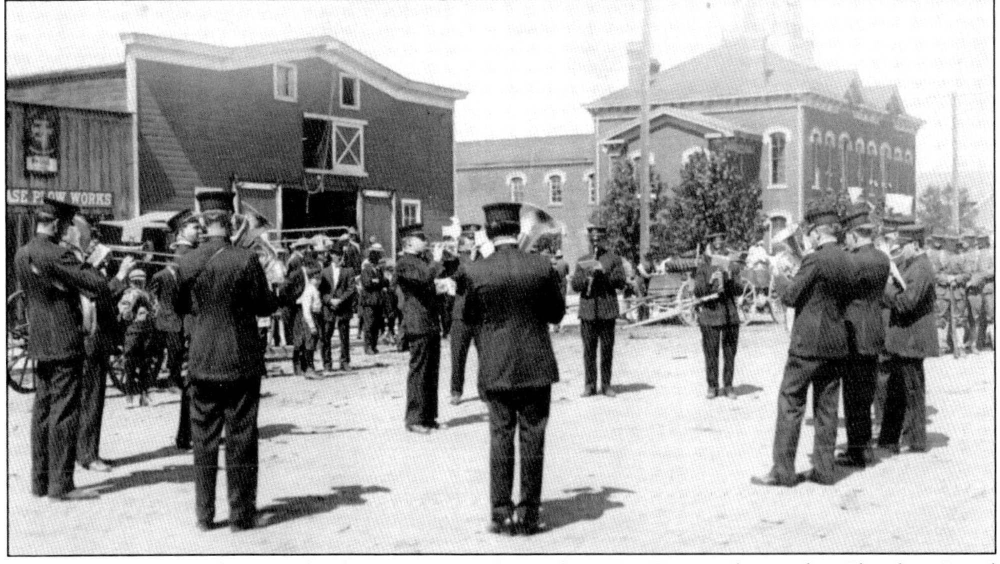

This photograph, taken in the late summer of 1917 by L.A. Foster, shows the Glendive Band playing a patriotic send-off to local soldiers shipping off to Europe to fight for the Allied cause in World War I.

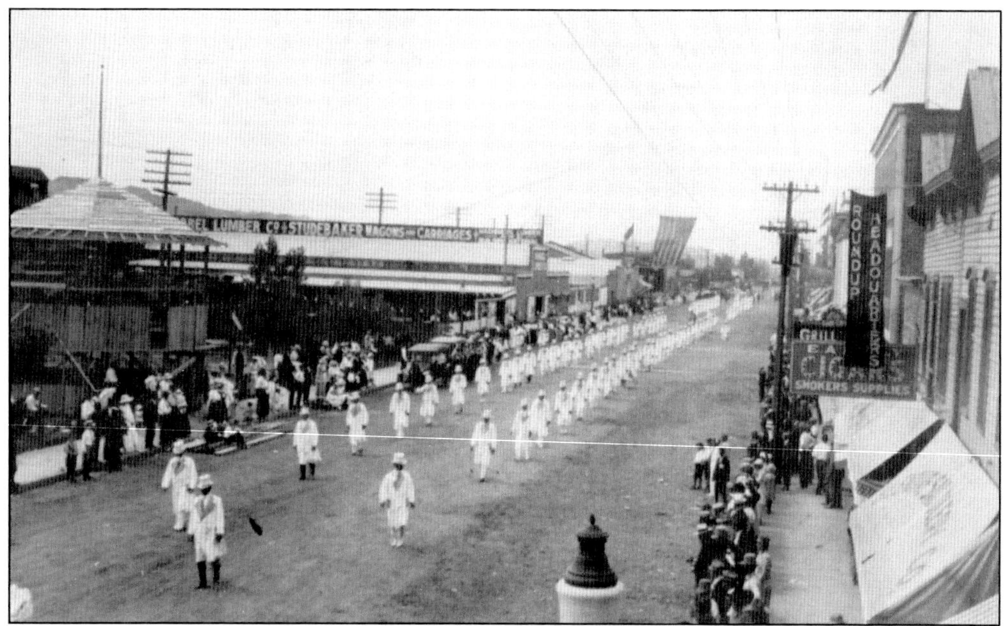

The Independence Day parade in 1919 was one of the largest parades ever held in Glendive. The focus of the parade that year was honoring the local soldiers who served in World War I.

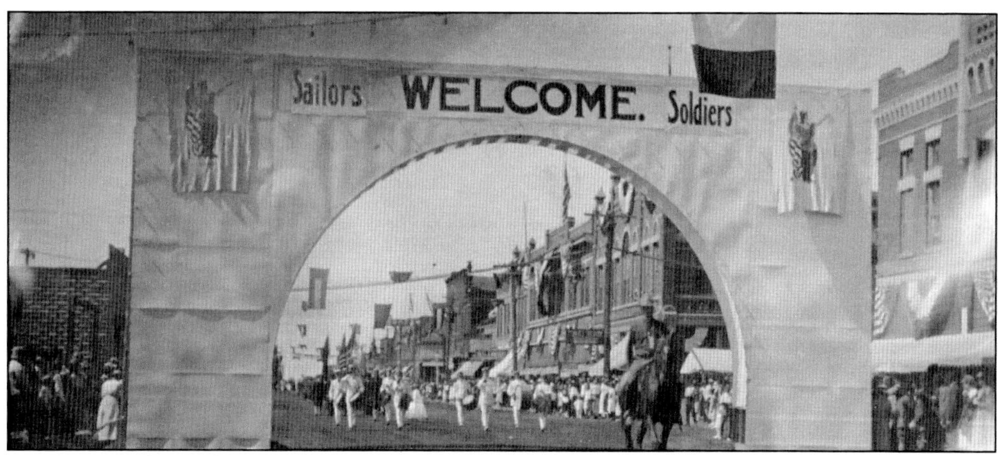

For the Fourth of July in 1919, a triumphal arch bearing the words "Welcome. Sailors, Soldiers" was erected on Merrill Avenue to honor local veterans who served in World War I.

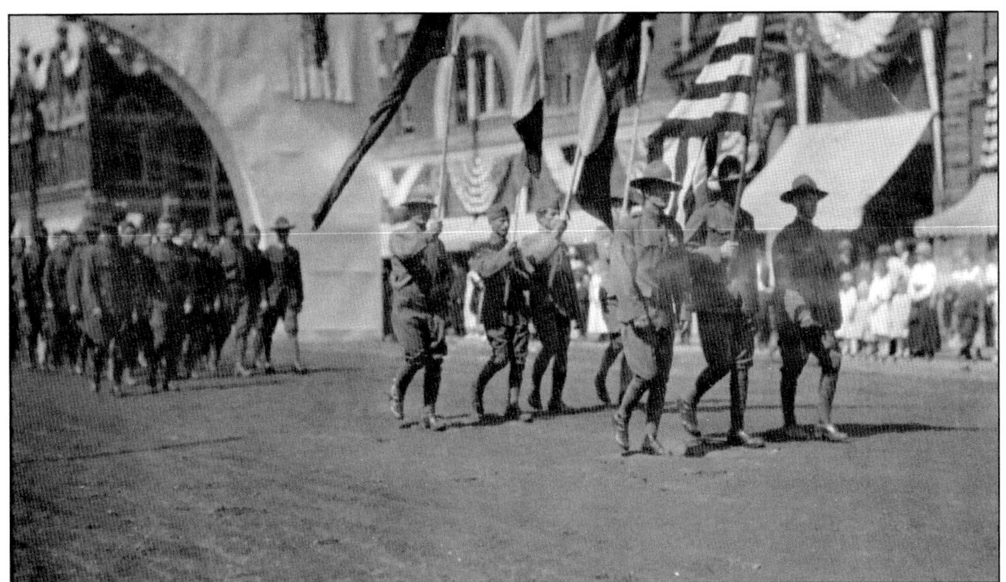

Veterans of World War I proudly march down Merrill Avenue in Glendive's Fourth of July parade in 1919.

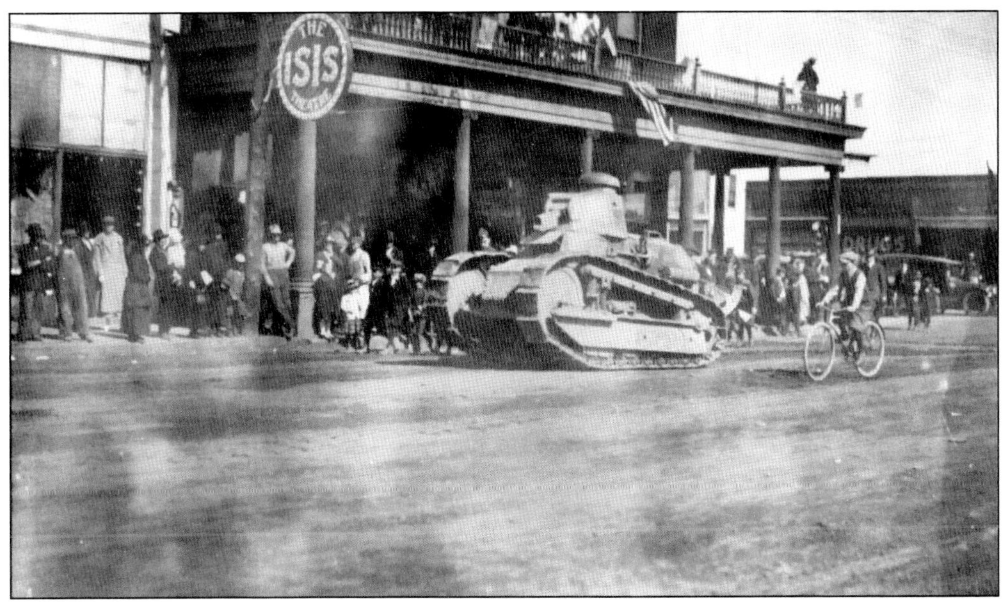

Glendive's Veterans Day parade in 1919 was almost as spectacular as its Independence Day celebration that same year. In this picture, a Renault FT-17 light tank rolls past the Jordan Hotel and Isis Theatre during the parade.

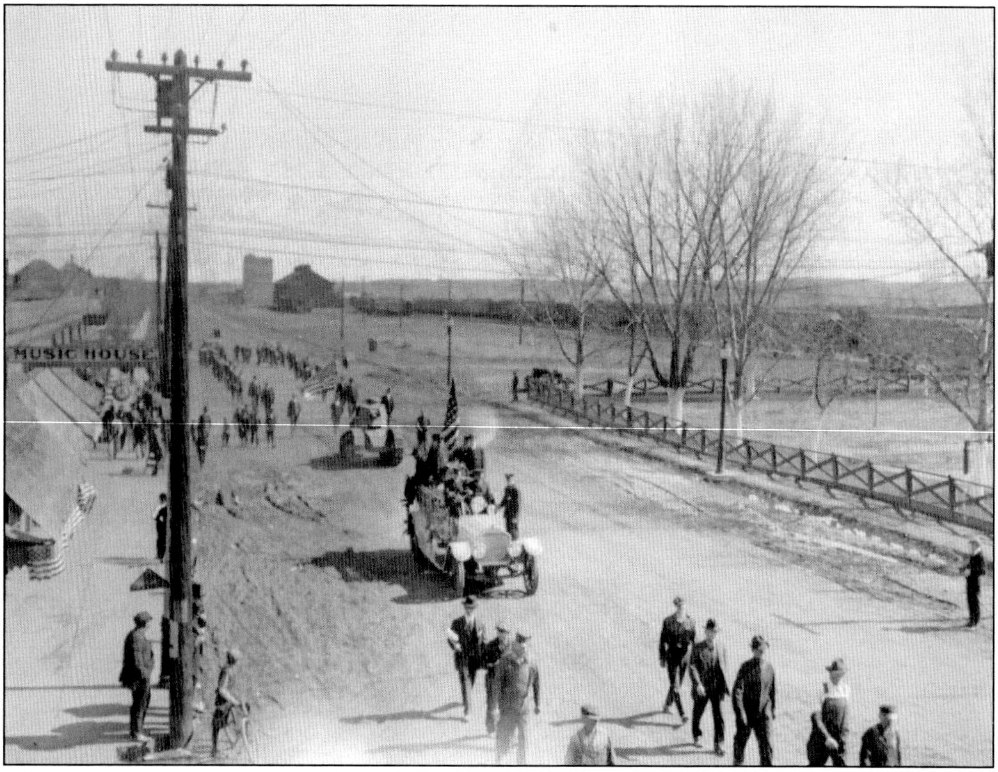

World War I veterans, escorted by a Renault FT-17 light tank, make their way down Merrill Avenue during the Veterans Day parade of 1919.

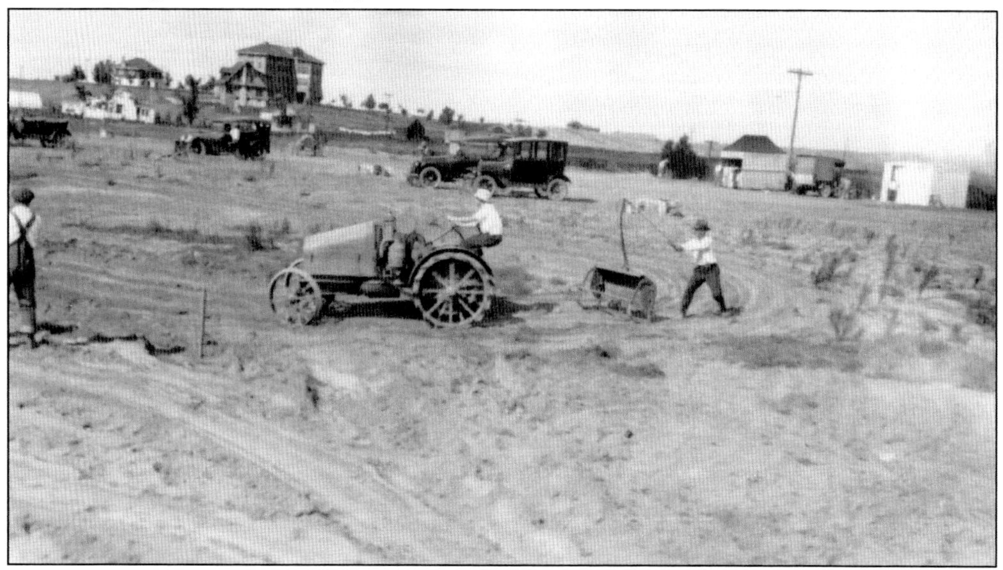

Swimming in the Lower Yellowstone River around Glendive is very dangerous and has claimed many lives over the years. Because of that fact, city leaders in the 1920s paved the way for the creation of a municipal swimming pool. This photograph shows the city preparing the land for the construction of the Glendive Tourist Park swimming pool, in what is now known as Lloyd Park, during the second decade of the 20th century.

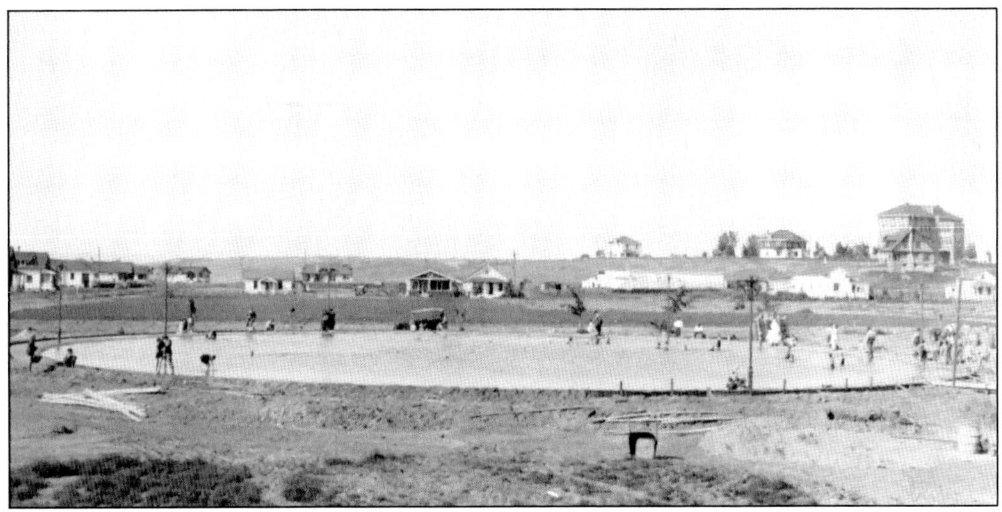

One of the most remarkable efforts at citywide cooperation was the creation of the Glendive Tourist Park swimming pool, which is pictured just after its grand opening. The Northern Pacific Hospital (large building at upper right) and Nursing Housing (smaller building behind the hospital) are located on the hill above.

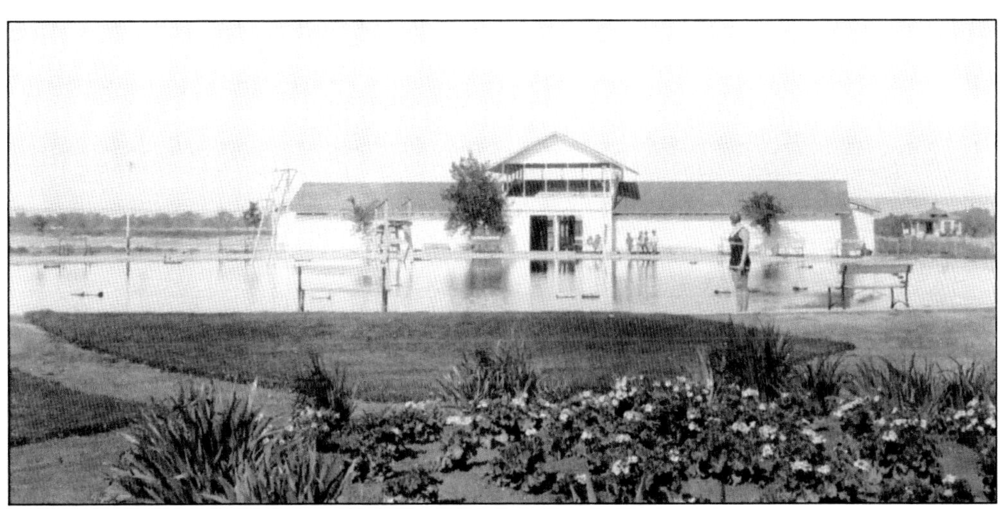

Women take a soak at the Glendive municipal bath in the 1920s.

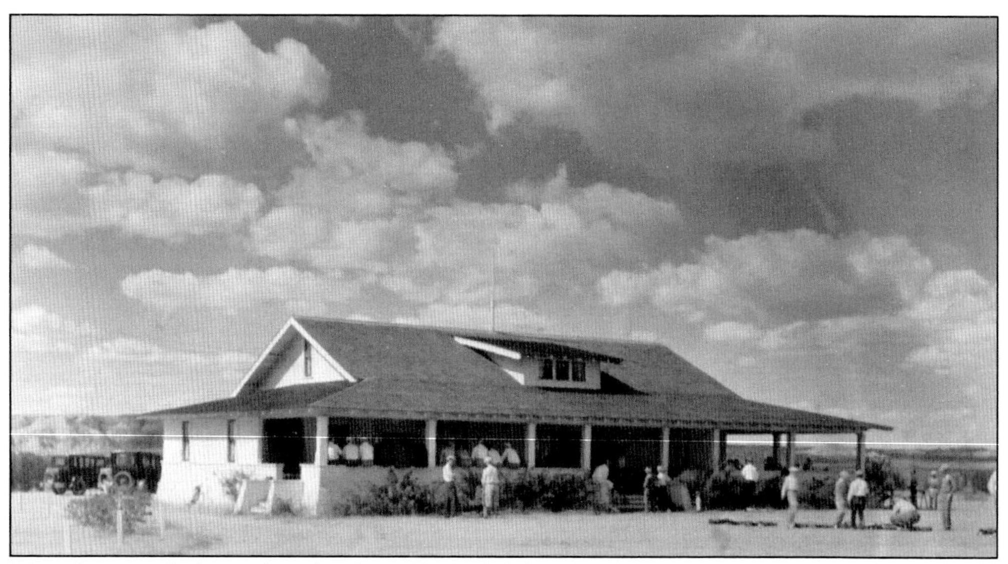

This photograph shows the Glendive Elks golf club in 1930. (Lowe Collection.)

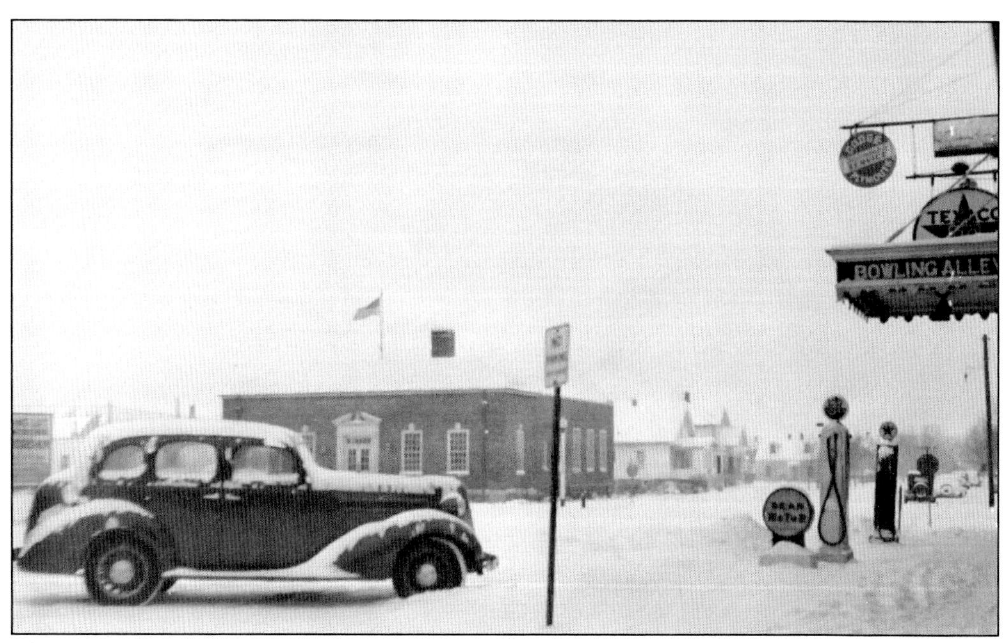

This snowy winter scene shows the Texaco station, post office, and bowling alley on Kendrick Avenue in the early 1930s.

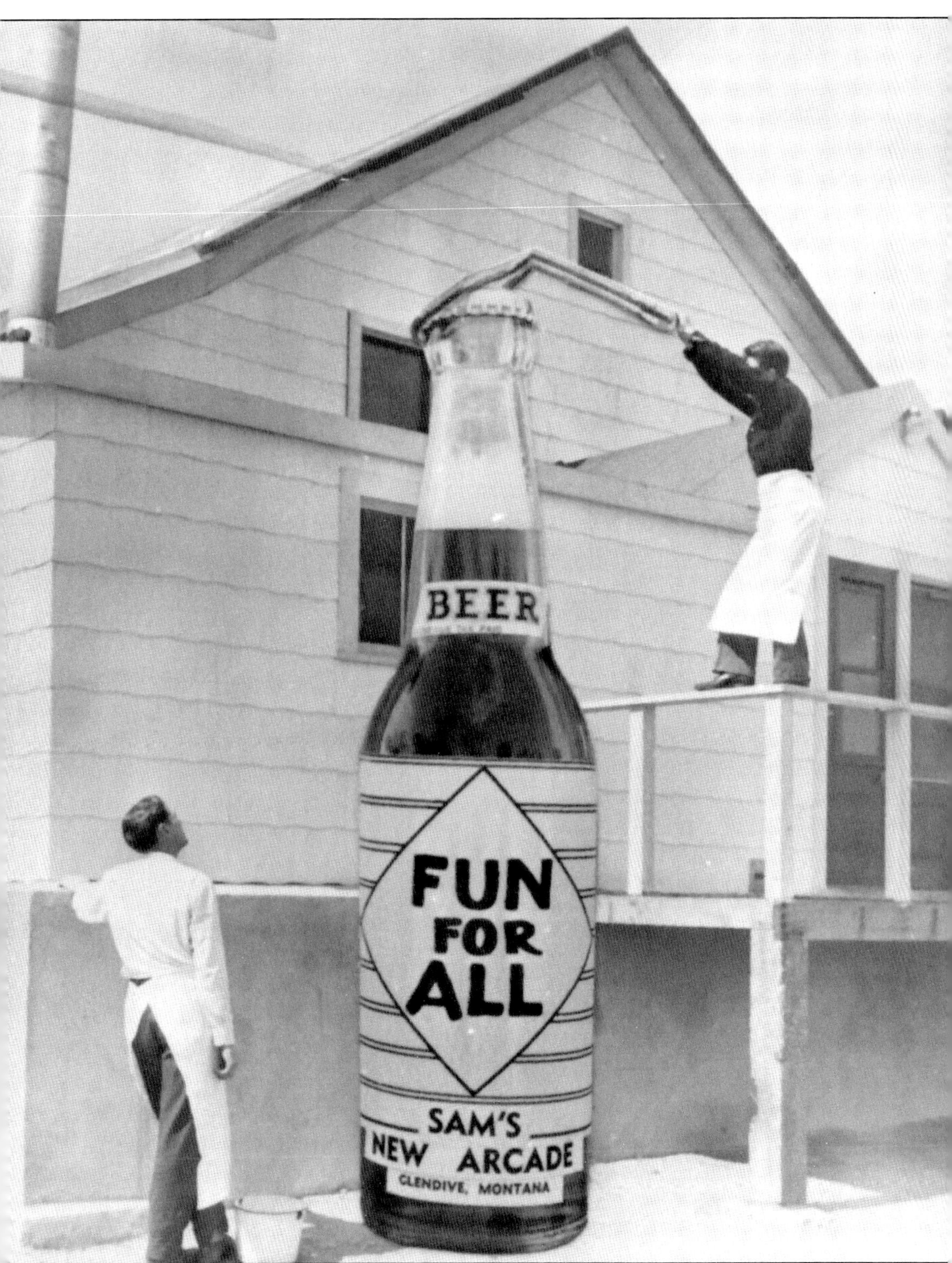

Sam's New Arcade is pictured around 1945. Sam's was a popular drinking establishment in west Glendive that hosted live music, dancing, and even roller-skating.